NORTH NOTTS

NORTH NOTTS

LIBRARY STOCK

KT-406-396

K 521
A 523

EIXAMPLE
Pages 70–83
Street Finder maps 3, 4

Eixample

0 metres   750

0 yards   750

CATALONIA

BARCELONA

0 kilometres   50

0 miles   50

NORTH NOTTS. COLLEGE

914.6

10-99

LIBRARY / LRC

EYEWITNESS TRAVEL

BARCELONA & CATALONIA

EYEWITNESS TRAVEL

BARCELONA
& CATALONIA

MAIN CONTRIBUTOR: ROGER WILLIAMS

LONDON, NEW YORK,
MELBOURNE, MUNICH AND DELHI
www.dk.com

PROJECT EDITOR Catherine Day
ART EDITORS Carolyn Hewitson, Marisa Renzullo
EDITORS Elizabeth Atherton, Felicity Crowe
DESIGNER Suzanne Metcalfe-Megginson
MAP CO-ORDINATOR David Pugh
PICTURE RESEARCH Monica Allende
DTP DESIGNERS Samantha Borland, Lee Redmond,
Pamela Shiels

MAIN CONTRIBUTOR
Roger Williams

MAPS
Jane Hanson, Phil Rose, Jennifer Skelley (Lovell Jones Ltd),
Gary Bowes, Richard Toomey (ERA-Maptec Ltd)

PHOTOGRAPHERS
Max Alexander, Mike Dunning, Heidi Grassley, Alan Keohane

ILLUSTRATORS
Stephen Conlin, Isidoro González-Adalid Cabezas
(Acanto Arquitectura y Urbanismo S.L.), Claire Littlejohn,
Maltings Partnership, John Woodcock

Reproduced by Colourscan, Singapore
Printed and bound by South China Printing Co. Ltd., China

First published in Great Britain in 1999
by Dorling Kindersley Limited
80 Strand, London WC2R 0RL
Reprinted with revisions 2000, 2001, 2002, 2003, 2004, 2005, 2006

Copyright 1999, 2006 © Dorling Kindersley Limited, London
A Penguin Company

ALL RIGHTS RESERVED. NO PART OF THIS PUBLICATION MAY BE
REPRODUCED, STORED IN A RETRIEVAL SYSTEM, OR TRANSMITTED IN ANY
FORM OR BY ANY MEANS, ELECTRONIC, MECHANICAL, PHOTOCOPYING,
RECORDING OR OTHERWISE, WITHOUT THE PRIOR WRITTEN PERMISSION
OF THE COPYRIGHT OWNER.

A CIP CATALOGUE RECORD IS AVAILABLE FROM THE BRITISH LIBRARY.

ISBN 1-4053-1093-6
ISBN 978-1405-31093-2
Front cover main image: Casa Batlló

**The information in every
DK Eyewitness Travel Guide is checked annually.**
Every effort has been made to ensure that this book is as up-to-date
as possible at the time of going to press. Some details,
however, such as telephone numbers, prices, gallery hanging
arrangements and travel information, are liable to change. The
publishers cannot accept responsibility for any consequences arising
from the use of this book, nor for any material on third-party
websites, and cannot guarantee that any website address in this
book will be a suitable source of travel information. We value the
views and suggestions of our readers highly. Please write to:
Publisher, DK Eyewitness Travel Guides,
Dorling Kindersley, 80 Strand, London WC2R 0RL.

CONTENTS

INTRODUCING BARCELONA AND CATALONIA

Jaume I, "El Conquistador",
ruler of Catalonia 1213–76

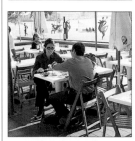

One of the many popular cafés in
Barcelona's redeveloped Old Port

BARCELONA AREA BY AREA

The small, whitewashed town of Cadaqués on the Costa Brava

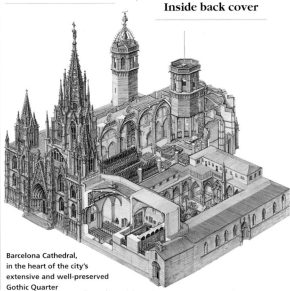

Spectacular stained-glass roof of
the Palau de la Música Catalana

CATALONIA

TRAVELLERS' NEEDS

SURVIVAL GUIDE

Pa amb tomàquet – bread rubbed
with tomato, garlic and olive oil

Barcelona Cathedral,
in the heart of the city's
extensive and well-preserved
Gothic Quarter

HOW TO USE THIS GUIDE

This guide has expert recommendations and detailed practical information to enrich any visit to Barcelona and Catalonia. *Introducing Barcelona and Catalonia* puts the area in geographical, historical and cultural context. *Barcelona and Catalonia* is a six-chapter guide to important sights: *Barcelona at a Glance* highlights the city's top attractions; *Old Town, Eixample* and *Montjuïc* explore Barcelona's central districts in more detail; *Further Afield* views sights outside the city centre; and *Catalonia* delves into the region's four provinces. *Travellers' Needs* covers hotels, restaurants and entertainment. The *Survival Guide* provides vital practical information.

BARCELONA AND CATALONIA

The region is divided into five sightseeing areas – the central districts of Barcelona, sights outside the centre, and those beyond the city. Each area chapter opens with an introduction and a list of sights covered. Central districts have a Street-by-Street map of a particularly interesting part of the area. The sights further afield have a regional map.

Sights at a Glance lists the area's key sights (great buildings, art galleries, museums and churches) by category.

Each chapter of *Barcelona and Catalonia* has a different colour-coded thumb tab.

Locator maps show where you are in relation to other parts of Barcelona or Spain.

1 Area Map of the city
Sights are numbered and located on a map, with Metro stations where helpful. The sights are also shown on the Barcelona Street Finder on pp188–97.

2 Street-by-Street map
The area shaded pink on the Area Map is shown here in greater detail with accurate drawings of all the buildings.

A suggested route for a walk covers the more interesting streets in the area.

A list of star sights recommends places no visitor should miss.

3 Detailed information on each sight
The sights listed at the start of the section are described individually and follow the numbering on the Area Map. A key to symbols summarizing practical information is shown on the back flap.

Introduction to Catalonia

4 *The chapter on Catalonia has its own introduction, providing an overview of the history and character of the region. The area covered is highlighted on the map of Spain shown on page 109. The chapter explores Catalonia's rich historical, cultural and natural heritage, from the monasteries of Montserrat and Poblet to Tarragona's* casteller *festivals, from the sandy beaches of the Costa Daurada to the snowy peaks of the Pyrenees.*

Pictorial Map

5 *This gives an illustrated overview of the whole region. All the sights covered in this chapter are numbered, and the network of major roads is marked. There are also useful tips on getting around the region by bus and train.*

6 Detailed information on each sight

All the important cities, towns and other places to visit are described individually. They are listed in order following the numbering given on the Pictorial Map. Within each town or city there is detailed information on important buildings and other sights.

Stars indicate the best features and works of art.

The Visitors' Checklist
provides a summary of the practical information you will need to plan your visit.

7 The top sights

These are given two or more full pages. Historic buildings are dissected to reveal their interiors. For larger historic sites, all the important buildings are labelled to help you locate those that most interest you.

INTRODUCING
BARCELONA
AND CATALONIA

FOUR GREAT DAYS IN BARCELONA

Days are long in Barcelona. The morning extends until well after midday, with lunch often starting around 2pm, and the late opening hours mean that afternoon merges into evening. With so much time at your disposal you'll want to make

Sagrada Familia

the most of your visit with a bit of planning. Each of these four itineraries follows a theme and sights are reachable using public transport. Prices include travel, food and admission. Family prices are for two adults and two children.

La Rambla, an exciting avenue for a stroll at any time

HISTORIC TREASURES

- **A stroll round the Gothic quarter and museums**
- **A Modernista concert hall**
- **Non-stop life on Spain's most famous street**

TWO ADULTS allow at least 40€

Morning
Barcelona's preserved medieval centre is the **Barri Gotic** *(see pp54–5)*, a warren of streets where it is easy to get lost. You can happily spend the morning here without walking great distances. The focal point is the **Cathedral** *(see pp58–9)*. Next to it is the **Palau Reial** (Royal Palace), part of which is now the **Museu d'Historia** *(see pp56–7)*, where you can take a fascinating subterranean stroll over the excavated ruins. The palace also houses what is perhaps Barcelona's most fascinating museum, the eclectic **Museu Frederic Marès** *(see p56)*. There are plenty of places for a budget lunch in this area – try a restaurant on Carrer de Call.

Afternoon
Take a guided tour of the **Palau de la Musica Catalana** *(see pp62–3)* and its dazzling Modernista interior (you need to book this in advance). After that, plunge into the atmospheric **Born district** *(see pp102–3)*, with its trendy shops. Take a look in the **Museu Picasso** *(see pp64–5)*, then wander to **La Rambla**, a busy street where there is always plenty of activity.

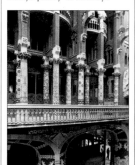

Richly ornamental interior of Palau de la Musica Catalana

GAUDÍ GREATS

- **Casa Batlló's organic forms**
- **Gaudí's extraordinary church, Sagrada Familia**
- **An evening's shopping in style in Passeig de Gràcia**

TWO ADULTS allow at least 40€

Morning
For many visitors, Barcelona is synonymous with the unique architecture of Antoni Gaudí. He created many great buildings, all of which are worth visiting, but here are two places to make a start. Begin your day with a visit to Gaudí's most colourful and eccentric house, **Casa Batlló** *(see pp76–7)*. Discover its fantastic organic forms and pay the extra fee to extend your tour to see the roof with its remarkable chimneys and "dragon's back". A little further up the road is the equally renowned **Casa Milà** *(see p79)*. This can also be visited, but if you're short of time its remarkable façade can be admired from the outside. For lunch, you'll find there are several budget-priced restaurants in the streets near and parallel to Passeig de Gràcia.

Afternoon/Evening
Visit Gaudí's greatest, unfinished work, the **Sagrada Família** *(see pp80–3)*. Allow plenty of time to make sense of the dense detail on the two façades of this extraordinary church – the Passion façade and the Nativity façade – and to go up and down the vertigo-inducing fantasy

Casa Batllo, a house in an alternative architectural universe

towers (by lift or stairs – it's your choice). Coming back down to reality, return to the **Passeig de Gràcia** and browse in its stylish shops. Look out for **Vinçon** *(see p155)*, which is housed in a Modernista building.

Museu d'Art Contemporani façade

ART FOR ART'S SAKE

- **Romanesque marvels on Montjuïc hill**
- **Contemporary works of art**
- **Collection of Old Masters**

TWO ADULTS allow at least 50€

Morning
The number of great galleries you can cram into a day depends on your appetite and stamina but here are four to give you a taster. Start at 10 am when the **Museu National d'Art de Catalunya** *(see p88)* opens on Montjuïc hill (also take time to enjoy the great view). Here, you'll see what is arguably the best collection of Romanesque art in any museum. Close by is the city's latest contemporary art gallery, **CaixaForum** *(see p98)*, situated in a Modernista factory. Lunch in a local café.

Afternoon
For a change of pace, make your way to the **Monestir de Pedralbes** *(see p95)*, a lovely monastery with part of the Thyssen-Bornemisza collection of Old Masters. Back in the city centre, visit the **Museu d'Art Contemporani** *(see pp62–3)*, where you can be sure of something surprising.

FAMILY FUN

- **A trip to the funfair**
- **A harbour cruise**
- **Sharks at the aquarium**
- **IMAX cinema experience**

FAMILY OF 4 allow at least 100€

Morning
Tibidabo Amusement Park *(see pp98–9)*, on the highest hill behind Barcelona, is a family day out in itself, with getting there by tram and funicular half the fun. But if you don't want to go that far, stroll down Las Ramblas and take the lift up the **Monument a Colom** *(see pp68–9)* for a good view of this part of the city. From the nearby quayside, board a **Golondrina** *(see pp68–9)* for a cruise round the harbour. Then cross the wavy footbridge for the Maremagnum shopping centre, also the best place to grab a bite to eat.

Afternoon/evening
Attractions that are specifically for children can, if you want to extend the day, be saved until after dark. The **Aquarium** *(see pp68–9)* offers several activities for kids, as well as tanks full of sharks and other fascinating creatures. Next to it, watch the hugely realistic (and stomach-churning) show at the **IMAX Cinema** *(see p164)*. A short walk away is the relaxing, child-friendly **Museu d'Historia de Catalunya** *(see pp68–9)* with exhibits on daily life in earlier times.

Barcelona's Aquarium, a wonderful experience for children

Putting Barcelona and Catalonia on the Map

Catalonia lies in the northeastern corner of the Iberian
Peninsula and occupies six per cent of Spain. Barcelona,
its capital, lies almost exactly halfway along its
coastline, which in turn stretches a quarter of the way
down Spain's Mediterranean seaboard. Barcelona is
the main bridging point to
the Catalan-speaking
Balearic Islands.

Satellite image showing Catalonia

KEY

✈	International airport
⛴	Ferry service
▬	Motorway (highway)
▬	Major road
═	Minor road
—	Main railway (railroad)
⊷	AVE high-speed rail link

◁ *Paral.lel any 1930*, a portrait of one of Barcelona's main avenues in 1930 by Emili Bosch Roger (1894–1980)

The Canary Islands
This chain of seven islands in the Atlantic is 1,150 km (700 miles) southwest of Cádiz and 150 km (70 miles) off Morocco

THE CANARY ISLANDS

Cádiz

Cádiz

Arrecife

Santa Cruz de la Palma

Puerto de la Cruz

Santa Cruz de Tenerife

Puerto del Rosario

San Sebastián de la Gomera

Las Palmas de Gran Canaria

Valverde

Maspalomas

Biarritz

Bilbo (Bilbao)

Donostia (San Sebastián)

F R A N C E

Iruña (Pamplona)

N804

N1 (E5)

N111

N240

A15

ANDORRA

Perpignan

A9 (E15)

AP7 (E15)

N230

Girona

C17

N11

A68 AP68 (E804)

Huesca

N240

N320

Genoa

Ebro

A23 (E7)

N111

Soria

N122

A Z A R A G O Z A

Lleida

NII A2

A2 AP2 (E90)

Barcelona

N234

A2 AP2 (E90)

Tarragona

C32

See next page

I N

N232

M e d i t e r r a n e a n   S e a

N320

Cuenca

N330

N234

Maó

NIII (E901)

A3 (E901)

N301

Valencia

Palma de Mallorca

Albacete

Júcar

N430 A31

N322

N330 A31

A7 AP7 (E15)

N340

Alacant (Alicante)

Eivissa (Ibiza)

0 kilometres   100

0 miles   50

Segura

N340 A7 (E15)

Murcia

N301

Oran

N332

Almería

(15)

Metilia

EUROPE AND NORTH AFRICA

NORWAY

FINLAND

SWEDEN

ESTONIA

RUSSIAN FED.

LATVIA

DENMARK

LITHUANIA

RUSSIAN FED.

BELARUS

IRELAND

UNITED KINGDOM

NETHERLANDS

GERMANY

POLAND

BELGIUM

LUXEMBOURG

CZECH REPUBLIC

UKRAINE

SLOVAKIA

FRANCE

SWITZERLAND

AUSTRIA

HUNGARY

SLOVENIA

ROMANIA

ITALY

CROATIA

BOSNIA AND HERZEGOVINA

SERBIA AND MONTENEGRO

BULGARIA

ALBANIA

GREECE

Barcelona

PORTUGAL

SPAIN

MOROCCO

TUNISIA

ALGERIA

LIBYA

Catalonia's Frontiers
Catalonia's northern border with France runs along the crest of the Pyrenees and is punctuated by Catalan-speaking Andorra. Its western and southern borders adjoin the Spanish regions of Aragón and Valencia.

Barcelona City Centre

Set between the mountains and the sea, which still play an integral part in city life, Barcelona is a rare city, a patchwork of distinctive districts telling the story of its growth from a medieval core to the 19th-century expansion and today's ultra-modern showpieces. The three main sightseeing areas described in this guide illustrate this startling diversity. The hill of Montjuïc, abutting the sea, forms the southwestern end of an arc of steep hills that almost completely encloses the city. It is a district of monumental buildings and open spaces. The Old Town has a superb Gothic heart with a myriad of narrow streets twisting among ancient houses. The densely populated Eixample, in contrast, is a district of immensely long, straight streets and superb Modernista architecture.

Montjuïc

There are wonderful views from the top of this large hill. Several of Barcelona's best museums are here, including the Archaeological Museum (see p88) which displays this Roman mosaic excavated in the city.

0 kilometres   1

0 miles   0.5

KEY

▢	Major sight
◈	Metro station
▣	Train station
▦	Bus stop
▥	Cable car
▧	Funicular
▨	Tramway stop
▦	Police station
▮	Tourist information
✚	Church

Eixample
This area covers the most interesting part of the city's 19th-century expansion. Walks along its streets will reveal countless details of the Modernista style, such as this ornate doorway of Casa Comalat (see p27) in Avinguda Diagonal.

Old Town
This area includes all the oldest districts of Barcelona and its port, the 18th-century fishing "village" of Barceloneta and the new waterside developments. This new swing bridge is in the Old Port (see p66).

Catalonia
Much of Catalonia is mountainous, with Barcelona sited on a narrow coastal plain. Sant Pere de Galligants (see p23) is one of many Romanesque churches.

KEY

▢	Barcelona and environs
▬	Motorways (highways)
▬	Other major roads

0 kilometres 50

0 miles 50

A PORTRAIT OF CATALONIA

B*arcelona is one of the great Mediterranean cities. Few places are so redolent with history, few so boldly modern. Animated and inspired, it is a city that sparkles as much at night-time as in the full light of day. It is famous for its main avenue, La Rambla, for its bars, its museums and its enthusiasm for life.*

Barcelona is the capital of the autonomous region of Catalonia, the most northeasterly corner of Spain, bordering France. The region is divided into four provinces, named after their provincial capitals: Barcelona, Girona, Lleida and Tarragona.

The city of Barcelona lies between two rivers, the Llobregat and the Besòs, and is backed by the Collserola hills which rise to a 512-m (1,680-ft) peak at the Tibidabo amusement park. The city grew up as the industrial sweatshop of Spain, though the shunting yards and seaside warehouses have now gone. Around four million people live in Barcelona and its suburbs – about half the population of Catalonia. It is Spain's second city after its old rival, Madrid.

La dama del paraigua

POLITICS AND SOCIETY

Catalonia is governed by the Generalitat, housed in the Palau de la Generalitat in the heart of the Old Town and on the site of the Roman forum. The region's parliament is located in the Parc de la Ciutadella.

The city of Barcelona has a separate administration, and its town hall, the Casa de la Ciutat, faces the Generalitat across the Plaça de Sant Jaume. Catalonia is developing its own police force, which has now taken over from Spain's national police in most of Catalonia.

Catalans are conservative and, as in many other countries, people in rural areas are more conservative than those in the cities. For the 23 years since Franco's death, the Generalitat was

Strollers and shoppers on La Rambla enjoying Barcelona's plentiful winter sunshine

◁ Stunning floral mosaic pillars at the Palau de la Música Catalana in Barcelona

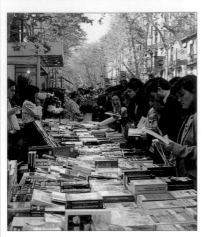

St George's Day in April – the day for giving books

Catalans are not burdened with self doubt. The vigour with which they have rebuilt parts of their capital since the early 1980s shows flair and a firm hand. Places of great sentimental value, such as Barceloneta's beach-side restaurant shacks, were torn down. Stunning new buildings such as the Museu d'Art Contemporani were put up in the Old Town, and old buildings such as the Cafè Zurich, a famous rendezvous for writers, artists and intellectuals on La Rambla, were restored without hesitation.

run by the conservative Convergència i Unió under the presidency of Jordi Pujol, while the city council was run by a socialist party. In 2003, however, Catalans elected a socialist Generalitat to power under Pascual Maragall.

Catalans, who have no taste for bull-fighting and whose sedate national dance, the *sardana*, is unruffled by passion, are a serious, hardworking people. Some would rather be associated with northern Europeans than with other Spaniards, whom they regard as indolent. Part of their complaint against Madrid has been that, as one of the richest regions of Spain, they put more into the national coffers than they take out.

Two emotions are said to guide Catalans: *seny*, which means solid common sense, and *rauxa*, a creative chaos. A bourgeois, conservative element of Barcelona society can be seen at concerts and in pastry shops, but a certain surreal air is often evident, on La Rambla, for instance, where some-times it seems that anything goes. The two elements are mixed in each per-son, and even the most staid may have the occasional *cop de rauxa*, or moment of chaotic ecstasy. Such outbursts are used to explain the more incendiary moments of Catalonia's history.

LANGUAGE AND CULTURE

A Romance language similar to the old Langue d'Oc, or Provençal, once used in France, Catalan is Catalonia's official language, spoken by some eight million people. It has always been a living language and it continued to be spoken in the home even when it was banned by Franco. Catalans do not think it rude to talk to each other in Catalan in front of

Street performer on La Rambla

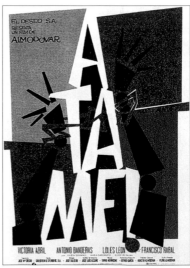

Poster for a Pedro Almodóvar film

Beach at Tossa de Mar on the Costa Brava

Catalans read more books than other Spaniards. New Catalan writing has burgeoned since the 1970s and there are many literary prizes, but few Catalan writers of any era have been translated into English.

WORK AND LEISURE

Catalans stay true to their traditions and their families. Sunday lunch is a time to get together, although even during the week, most people who can do so return home for lunch. This creates a rush hour four times a day, with a lull in the early afternoon. Shops close around 8pm, and between 6pm and 8pm the streets are crowded. Dinner or entertainment starts around 10pm, but there is increasing pressure for business hours to conform with the rest of Europe.

Allegiance to the local football team, Barça, is a matter of national pride for its supporters. Meals out, concerts and the cinema are popular activities. The week begins quietly but, as the weekend approaches, streets fill and visitors leaving La Rambla at midnight to go to bed may feel they are leaving a good party too soon.

someone who speaks only Spanish. All public signs and official documents in Catalonia are in Spanish and Catalan.

If *rauxa* is responsible for the creative spirit as claimed, then Catalonia has been blessed with an abundance. Modernisme, led by Antoni Gaudí, is the region's gift to world architecture. Painters Joan Miró, Salvador Dalí and Antoni Tàpies were born here, while Pablo Picasso spent his formative years in Barcelona. Designs by Javier Mariscal, creator of the 1992 Olympic motifs and Cobi, the mascot, furniture by Oscar Tusquets and fashion by Toni Miró help make Barcelona a city of great style. Bigas Luna, locally-born director of *Jamón Jamón*, and Pedro Almodóvar, whose film *All About My Mother* was shot in Barcelona have raised the area's profile in the cinema.

Montserrat Caballé

Over the last 150 years, some outstanding musicians have emerged from Catalonia. The composers Isaac Albéniz (1860–1909), Enric Granados (1867–1916) and Frederic Mompou (1893–1987) brought music imbued with a true Iberian idiom into the classical mainstream. Pau Casals (1876–1973) was considered one of the greatest of all cellists, and Montserrat Caballé and Josep Carreras can fill opera houses anywhere in the world.

Demonstration for Catalan independence

Flowers of the Matollar

Yellow bee orchid

The Matollar is the distinctive landscape of Spain's eastern Mediterranean coast. This scrubland rich in wild flowers is the result of centuries of woodland clearance, during which the native holm oak was felled for timber and to provide land for grazing and cultivation. Many colourful plants have adapted to the extremes of climate here. Most flower in spring, when hillsides are daubed with yellow broom and pink and white cistuses, and the air is perfumed by aromatic herbs such as rosemary, lavender and thyme. Buzzing insects feed on the abundance of nectar and pollen.

Spanish broom *is a small bush with yellow flowers on slender branches. The black seed pods split when dry, scattering the seeds on the ground.*

The century plant's flower stalk can reach 10 m (32 ft).

Aleppo pine

Rosemary

Jerusalem sage, *an attractive shrub which is often grown in gardens, has tall stems surrounded by bunches of showy yellow flowers. Its leaves are greyish-white and woolly.*

Rose garlic *has round clusters of violet or pink flowers at the end of a single stalk. It survives the summer as the bulb familiar to all cooks.*

Common thyme *is a low-growing aromatic herb which is widely cultivated for use in the kitchen.*

FOREIGN INVADERS

Several plants from the New World have managed to colonize the bare ground of the *matollar*. The prickly pear, thought to have been brought back by Christopher Columbus, produces a delicious fruit which can be picked only with thickly gloved hands. The rapidly growing century plant, a native of Mexico which has tough, spiny leaves, sends up a tall flower shoot only when it is 10–15 years old, after which it dies.

Prickly pear in bloom

Flowering shoots of the century plant

The mirror orchid, *a small plant which grows on grassy sites, is easily distinguished from other orchids by the brilliant metallic blue patch inside the lip, fringed by brown hairs.*

CLIMATE CHART

Temp (°C) / Rainfall (mm)

— Temperature   ▢ Rainfall

Most plants found in the *matollar* come into bloom in the warm, moist spring. The plants protect themselves from losing water during the dry summer heat with thick leaves or waxy secretions, or by storing moisture in bulbs or tubers.

WILDLIFE OF THE MATOLLAR

The animals which live in the *matollar* are most often seen early in the morning, before the temperature is high. Countless insects fly from flower to flower, providing a source of food for birds. Smaller mammals, such as mice and voles, are active only at night when it is cooler and there are few predators around.

Holm oaks *are very common in eastern Spain. The leaves are tough and rubbery to prevent water loss.*

The strawberry tree *is an evergreen shrub with glossy serrated leaves. Its inedible strawberry-like fruit turns red when ripe.*

Tree heather

Ladder snakes *feed on small mammals, birds and insects. The young are identified by a black pattern like the rungs of a ladder, but adults are marked with two simple stripes.*

Scorpions *hide under rocks or wood by day. When disturbed, the tail is curled quickly over the body in a threatening gesture. The sting, lethal to small animals, can cause some irritation to humans.*

Grey-leaved cistus, *growing on sunny sites, has crumpled petals and bright yellow anthers.*

Narrow-leaved cistus *exudes a sticky aromatic gum used in perfumes.*

The Dartford warbler, *a skulking bird which has a dark plumage and a cocked tail, sings melodiously during its mating display. Males are more vividly coloured than females.*

The swallow-tail butterfly *is one of the most conspicuous of the great many insects living in the* matollar. *Bees, ants and grasshoppers are also extremely common.*

Star clover *is a low-growing annual whose fruit develops into a star-shaped seed head. Its flowers are often pale pink.*

Romanesque Art and Architecture

Catalonia has an exceptional collection of medieval buildings constructed between the 11th and 13th centuries in a distinctive local Romanesque style. There are more than 2,000 examples, most of them churches. Those in the Pyrenees, which have largely escaped both attack and modernization, have survived particularly well. Churches had lofty bell towers, barrel-vaulted naves, rounded arches and imaginative sculpture, as well as remarkable wall paintings. Some frescoes and furniture have come to rest in the Museu Nacional d'Art de Catalunya (see p88) in Barcelona, which has the largest Romanesque collection in the world.

Sant Jaume de Frontanyà (see p114) *is a former Augustinian canonry with typical 11th-century features, such as the Lombard bands below the roofs of the three apses. The large octagonal central lantern is, however, unusual.*

Vielha

Pont de Suert

Sort

Andorra la Vella

Puigcerdà

La Seu d'Urgell

Berga

Sant Climent de Taüll, *an exemplary church in the Vall de Boí (see p113), was consecrated in 1123. Its frescoes, including a* Christ in Majesty *(see p88), are replicas, but the originals, which are now in Barcelona, are among the best in Catalonia.*

0 kilometres   30

0 miles   15

MONESTIR DE SANTA MARIA DE RIPOLL

The saints

The story of Solomon

The Old Testament

David and his musicians

The story of Moses

Christ with historical figures

The visions of Daniel

Plinth with patterns

The portal of the church of the former Benedictine monastery at Ripoll is known as "The Ripoll Bible" for its allegorical carvings. Although the church was founded in 879 and rebuilt under Abbot Oliva in 1032, the portal was added only in the late 12th century. In this fine piece of Romanesque decoration Christ sits above the doorway amid the beasts symbolizing the Apostles, and the monthly agricultural occupations are represented on the doorway pillars. There are seven biblical friezes running the length of the wall. The top frieze *(see p114)* over the tympanum represents the old men of the Apocalypse; the others are described in the captions above.

Sant Pere de Camprodon (see p115), *consecrated in 1169, is a monastery church in mature Romanesque style with five square apses. The slightly pointed barrel vault over the nave hints at the Gothic style to come.*

AREA OF MAJOR ROMANESQUE INTEREST

Sant Cristòfol de Beget (see p115) *is a beautiful church in a picturesque hamlet hidden deep in a valley. It has a uniquely preserved interior which includes a Romanesque baptismal font and this famous 12th-century crucifix – the* Majestat.

Sant Pere de Rodes, *situated at 600 m (1,968 ft) above sea level, was a Benedictine monastery. In its church's nave are the pillars of a Roman temple once on this site. Restoration work is in progress.*

Figueres

Roses

Ripoll

Olot

Girona

Vic

Sant Feliu de Guíxols

Sant Pere de Besalú (see p115) *is the 12th-century church of an earlier Benedictine monastery. Stone lions guard this window over the portal. Inside, the ambulatory has finely carved capitals.*

Sant Pere de Galligants (see p116), *a former Benedictine abbey, captures the very essence of Romanesque style. It has an 11th-century portal with a rose window, three naves and an octagonal bell tower. The cloister capitals are carved with biblical scenes. It now houses Girona's archaeology museum.*

The Museu Episcopal de Vic (see p124) *adjacent to the cathedral has an exquisite collection of Romanesque art. It includes this richly coloured and moving portrayal of the Visitation which was originally an altar decoration in Lluçà monastery.*

Gaudí and Modernisme

Chimney, Casa Vicens

Towards the end of the 19th century a new style of art and architecture, Modernisme, a variant of Art Nouveau, was born in Barcelona. It became a means of expression for Catalan nationalism and counted Josep Puig i Cadafalch, Lluís Domènech i Montaner and, above all, Antoni Gaudí i Cornet *(see p78)* among its major exponents. Barcelona's Eixample district *(see pp70–83)* is full of the highly original buildings that they created for their wealthy clients.

All aspects of decoration *in a Modernista building, even interior design, were planned by the architect. This door and its tiled surround are in Gaudí's 1906 Casa Batlló* (see p78).

A dramatic cupola *covers the central salon, which rises through three floors. It is pierced by small round holes, inspired by Islamic architecture, giving the illusion of stars.*

Upper galleries are richly decorated with carved wood and cofferwork.

The spiral carriage ramp *is an early sign of Gaudí's predilection for curved lines. He would later exploit this to the full in the wavy façade of his masterpiece, the Casa Milà* (see p79).

THE EVOLUTION OF MODERNISME

1859 Civil engineer Ildefons Cerdà i Sunyer submits proposals for expansion of Barcelona

1878 Gaudí graduates as an architect

1900 Josep Puig i Cadafalch builds Casa Amatller *(see p78)*

1903 Lluís Domènech i Montaner builds Hospital de la Santa Creu i de Sant Pau *(see p79)*

Hospital detail

1850	1865	1880	1895	1910	1925

1883 Gaudí takes over design of Neo-Gothic Sagrada Família *(see pp80–1)*

Detail of Sagrada Família

1888 Barcelona Universal Exhibition gives impetus to Modernisme

1910 Casa Milà completed

1905 Domènech i Montaner builds Casa Lleó Morera *(see p78)*. Puig i Cadafalch builds Casa Terrades *(see p79)*

1926 Gaudí dies

Bizarrely decorated chimneys
*became one of the trademarks
of Gaudí's later work. They
reach a fantastic
extreme on the
gleaming, hump-
backed roof of the
Casa Batlló.*

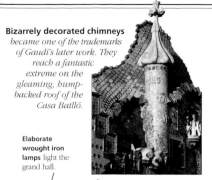

**Elaborate
wrought iron
lamps** light the
grand hall.

Ceramic tiles decorate
the chimneys.

GAUDÍ'S MATERIALS

Gaudí designed, or collaborated on designs, for almost every known media. He combined bare, undecorated materials – wood, rough-hewn stone, rubble and brickwork – with meticulous craftwork in wrought iron and stained glass. Mosaics of ceramic tiles were used to cover his fluid, uneven forms.

**Stained-glass window
in the Sagrada Família**

**Mosaic of ceramic tiles,
Parc Güell** (see p98)

**Detail of iron gate, Casa
Vicens** (see pp26-7)

**Tiles on El Capricho in
Comillas, Cantabria**

Parabolic arches,
*used extensively by
Gaudí, beginning in
the Palau Güell, show
his interest in Gothic
architecture. These
arches form a corridor
in his 1890 Col·legi
de les Teresianes, a
convent school in the
west of Barcelona.*

Escutcheon alludes to
the Catalan coat of arms.

PALAU GUELL

Gaudí's first major building in the centre of the city, on La Rambla (see p60), established his international reputation for outstanding, original architecture. Built in 1889 for his life-long patron, the industrialist Eusebi Güell, the mansion stands on a small plot of land in a narrow street, making the façade difficult to see. Inside, Gaudí creates a sense of space by using carved screens, recesses and galleries.

Organic forms *inspired the wrought iron around the
gates to the palace. Gaudí's later work teems with wildlife,
such as this dragon, covered with brightly coloured tiles,
which guards the steps in the Parc Güell.*

La Ruta del Modernisme

The examples of Modernista architecture in Barcelona, mapped here, lie along a route designed by the city's tourist office. A *Multi-ticket*, available from Casa Amatller *(see p78)*, allows entry into a total of three museums and affords you the freedom to plan your own itinerary. The Casa Lleó Morera, Palau Güell and Palau de la Música Catalana all have guided tours, and entry is half price at the selected museums. Many of the other premises are shops, cafés and hotels in private hands, and often, tantalizingly, the interiors are not open to the public. The best-known sites are described in detail elsewhere in this book.

Casa Vicens

This bright, angular, turreted building by Antoni Gaudí, with ceramic mosaics and patterned brickwork, shows Moorish influence. The iron gate and fencing are hallmarks of his work ㊽

Palau Baró de Quadras

Built in 1906, this handsome house is by Josep Puig i Cadafalch. The intricate, sculptured frieze above the first floor windows has close affinities to Spanish early Renaissance Plateresque style ㊶

Casa Lleó Morera

The first-floor dining room of this house is one of Barcelona's most stunning interiors. The stained-glass windows are by Lluís Rigalt and the eight ceramic mosaic wall panels, depicting idyllic country scenes, are by Gaspar Homar ⑲

Antiga Casa Figueres

The mosaic, stainedglass and wrought iron decoration of this, the most famous of the city's Modernista stores, was carried out in 1902 by Antoni Ros i Güell. It is today the elegant Pastisseria Escribà ⑦

KEY

- - - Walking route

— — Bus route

—— Metro route

| 0 metres | 500 |
| 0 yards | 500 |

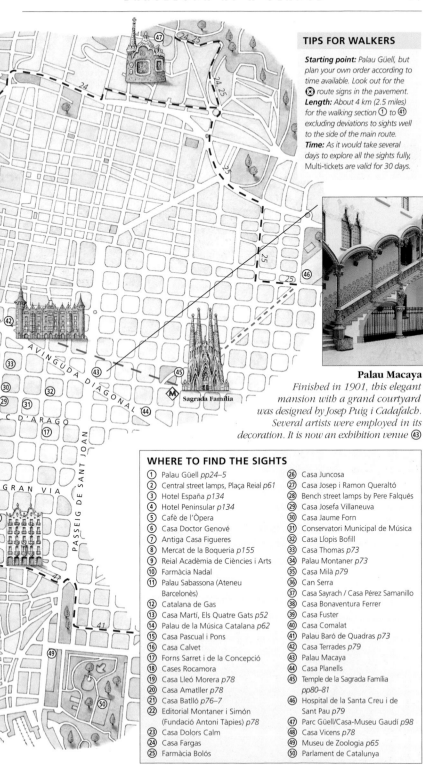

TIPS FOR WALKERS

Starting point: Palau Güell, but plan your own order according to time available. Look out for the ⊙ route signs in the pavement.
Length: About 4 km (2.5 miles) for the walking section ① to ㊶ excluding deviations to sights well to the side of the main route.
Time: As it would take several days to explore all the sights fully, Multi-tickets are valid for 30 days.

Palau Macaya
Finished in 1901, this elegant mansion with a grand courtyard was designed by Josep Puig i Cadafalch. Several artists were employed in its decoration. It is now an exhibition venue ㊸

WHERE TO FIND THE SIGHTS

① Palau Güell pp24–5
② Central street lamps, Plaça Reial p61
③ Hotel España p134
④ Hotel Peninsular p134
⑤ Cafè de l'Òpera
⑥ Casa Doctor Genové
⑦ Antiga Casa Figueres
⑧ Mercat de la Boqueria p155
⑨ Reial Acadèmia de Ciències i Arts
⑩ Farmàcia Nadal
⑪ Palau Sabassona (Ateneu Barcelonès)
⑫ Catalana de Gas
⑬ Casa Martí, Els Quatre Gats p52
⑭ Palau de la Música Catalana p62
⑮ Casa Pascual i Pons
⑯ Casa Calvet
⑰ Forns Sarret i de la Concepció
⑱ Cases Rocamora
⑲ Casa Lleó Morera p78
⑳ Casa Amatller p78
㉑ Casa Batlló p76–7
㉒ Editorial Montaner i Simón (Fundació Antoni Tàpies) p78
㉓ Casa Dolors Calm
㉔ Casa Fargas
㉕ Farmàcia Bolós

㉖ Casa Juncosa
㉗ Casa Josep i Ramon Queraltó
㉘ Bench street lamps by Pere Falqués
㉙ Casa Josefa Villanueva
㉚ Casa Jaume Forn
㉛ Conservatori Municipal de Música
㉜ Casa Llopis Bofill
㉝ Casa Thomas p73
㉞ Palau Montaner p73
㉟ Casa Milà p79
㊱ Can Serra
㊲ Casa Sayrach / Casa Pérez Samanillo
㊳ Casa Bonaventura Ferrer
㊴ Casa Fuster
㊵ Casa Comalat
㊶ Palau Baró de Quadras p73
㊷ Casa Terrades p79
㊸ Palau Macaya
㊹ Casa Planells
㊺ Temple de la Sagrada Família pp80–81
㊻ Hospital de la Santa Creu i de Sant Pau p79
㊼ Parc Güell/Casa-Museu Gaudí p98
㊽ Casa Vicens p78
㊾ Museu de Zoologia p65
㊿ Parlament de Catalunya

Catalan Painting

Catalonia has a fine, if uneven, painterly tradition. It began where Spanish medieval painting was born – in the Pyrenees, where Romanesque churches were brightened by bold frescoes full of imagination *(see pp22-3)*. The subsequent Gothic period, which represented Catalonia at the height of its powers, was followed by a long period of lesser artistic achievement until the wealth of the 19th century revived the creative spirit. This fostered some of Europe's great 20th-century painters, all of whom, as Catalans, felt a close affinity to the spirit of Catalonia's incomparable Romanesque art.

St George and the Princess (late 15th century) by Jaume Huguet

GOTHIC

One of the first-named artists in Catalonia was Ferrer Bassa (1285–1348), court painter to Jaume II. Bassa's exquisite decoration in the chapel of the Monastery of Pedralbes *(see p95)* constitutes the first-known example of oil-painted murals, a style undoubtedly influenced by contemporary Italian painting.

In sculpture, Catalan Gothic begins with the work of Mestre Bartomeu (1250–1300), whose extraordinary, Oriental-looking *Calvary* is in the fine Gothic collection of Girona's Museu d'Art *(see p117)*.

There are also Gothic collections in Vic and Solsona *(see p124)* and particularly Barcelona, where the Museu Nacional d'Art de Catalunya *(see p88)* has the most impressive. Important works include those by Lluís Borrassà (1365–

1425), who painted Tarragona cathedral's altarpiece, and Lluís Dalmau (d. 1463), who visited Bruges and studied under Jan van Eyck. A feature of Catalan Gothic is *esgrafiat*, a process of gilding haloes, garments and backgrounds, which was favoured by one of the greatest Catalan Gothic artists, Jaume Huguet (1415–92). His *St George and the Princess* seems to capture the full majesty of a cultured and prosperous nation.

RENAISSANCE TO NEO-CLASSICAL

Artistically, Catalonia languished from the 16th to the 18th century, a period dominated by great masters from elsewhere in Spain: El Greco in Toledo, Murillo and Zurbarán in Seville, Ribera in Valencia, and Velázquez and later Goya in Madrid. A few

of their works can be seen at the Museu Nacional d'Art de Catalunya alongside Catalonia's only two distinguished artists of the period – Francesc Pla and Antoni Viladomat.

Procession outside Santa Maria del Mar (c.1898) by Ramon Casas

THE 19TH CENTURY

Barcelona's art school opened above La Llotja *(see p62)* in 1849 and new patrons of the arts appeared with wealth generated by the industrial revolution. Industry had, however, already begun to train its own artists. In 1783 a school was founded in Olot *(see p115)* to train designers for local textile firms. An Olot School of artists developed; its main figures were Josep Berga i Boix (1837–1914) and Joaquim Vayreda i Vila (1843–94), who also founded the Art Cristià (Christian Art) workshops which today still produce church statuary.

The greens and browns of the Olot landscape artists were countered by the pale

The Gardens at Aranjuez (1907) by Santiago Rusiñol

Waiting for Soup (1899) by Isidre Nonell

blues and pinks of the Sitges Luminists – Arcadi Mas i Fontdevila (1852–1943) and Joan Roig i Soler (1852–1909). They were influenced by Marià Fortuny, who was born in Reus in 1838 and had lived in Rome and Paris. He was commissioned by Barcelona's city council to paint a vast canvas of the Spanish victory at Tetuán, Spanish Morocco, in which 500 Catalan volunteers had taken part. It is now in the Museu d'Art Modern.

In 1892, 18 years after the first Impressionist exhibition in Paris, Mas i Fontdevila staged an exhibition in Sitges bringing together the Olot School and the Luminists. It was seen as the first Modernista event and featured two other artists: Santiago Rusiñol (1861–1931) and Ramon Casas (1866–1932), the towering figures of Modernista painting. Rusiñol, the son of a textile magnate, bought a house in Sitges, Cau Ferrat (*see p128*), which became a Modernista haunt. Casas, the first man in Barcelona to own a car, drew all the famous people of the day and also painted large, powerful canvases such as *The Charge* and *Vile Garroting*. Rusiñol and Casas were founding members of Els Quatre Gats café, modelled on Le Chat Noir in Paris.

The Cathedral of the Poor (1897) by Joaquim Mir

THE 20TH CENTURY

Although Pablo Ruiz Picasso (1881–1973) lived in Barcelona for only eight years (*see p63*), they were extremely formative. His early work was strongly influenced by the city and its surroundings, as can be seen in the Museu Picasso (*see p63*), as well as by the leading Catalan artists – landscape painter Isidre Nonell (1873–1911), Joaquim Mir (1873–1940), and Rusiñol and Casas. He shared their view that Paris was essential to an artistic life and soon joined its Catalan fraternity. Despite a self-imposed exile during the Franco years, he kept in touch with Catalonia all his life.

Joan Miró (1893–1983) also attended the art school. Thrown out for poor draughtsmanship, he went on to become one of the 20th-century's most original talents, remarkable for his playful abstracts.

A sense of play was also never far from Salvador Dalí (*see p117*), whom Miró encouraged in the way that he himself had been encouraged by Picasso. Dalí joined them in Paris, where Miró introduced him to the Surrealists. Unlike his mentors, Dalí remained in Catalonia after the Civil War, and his house in Port Lligat (*see p120*) is in many ways his finest creation.

Also to remain was Josep-Maria Sert (1876–1945). He was a more traditional painter, best remembered for vast murals in Barcelona's Casa de la Ciutat (*see p57*), and in Rockefeller Center and the dining room of the Waldorf Astoria in New York. His startling work in Vic cathedral (*see p124*) was burnt out in the Civil War, but he was able to repaint it before he died.

Today, Catalonia's best-known living painter is Antoni Tàpies. A modest, uncompromising man, he is, like many before him, deeply rooted in his own culture. Though an abstract painter, he often uses the colours of the Catalan flag and admits to an influence of Romanesque art. Like Picasso and Miró, he has his own museum (*see p78*). Other living Catalan artists' work can be seen at Barcelona's Museu d'Art Contemporani (*see p60*).

Lithograph (1948) in Catalan flag colours by Antoni Tàpies

The Flavours of Catalonia

Food is central to the Catalan soul, and it's no accident that Barcelona's most famous literary creation, detective Pepe Carvalho, is a discerning gourmet. Reflecting Barcelona's status as the undisputed style capital of the Mediterranean, the culinary scene in Catalonia is now one of the most exciting in Europe, with innovative chefs like Ferran Adrià, of the legendary El Bullí restaurant *(see p151)*, taking Catalonia's venerable gastronomic traditions and transforming them with spectacular flair. But the old ways survive in small, family-run restaurants, authentic, sawdust-strewn tapas bars, and particularly in the superb local markets.

Ceps (bolets)

Barcelona café serving traditional pastries and desserts

Visit any one of Barcelona's excellent markets to see the spectacular variety of fresh produce that is available in Catalonia: stalls are heaped high with glistening fish from the Mediterranean; superb-quality meat and game from the mountains; and a quite dazzling array of fruit and vegetables from the plains. Catalan cuisine, even at its most experimental, is essentially simple, and relies on the superb quality and range of the local produce. It is also very much a seasonal cuisine, and each time of the year has its specialities, from the onion-like *calçots* which appear in the spring, and the luscious plethora of summer fruit, to the wild mushrooms, roasted meats and hearty, warming stews of the autumn and winter.

MEAT AND GAME

Catalan cured meats are justly famous throughout Spain, particularly the pungent cured sausage *fuet*. Pork finds its way onto almost every menu, with *peus de porc* (pigs' trotters) an old-fashioned favourite. Its mountain cousin, wild boar *(porc sanglar)* is popular in late autumn, along with game, especially

Xoriço picant · Fuet · Llonganissa · Xoriço · Pernil salat · Xoriço curat

Selection of Catalan cured meats, known as embutits

LOCAL DISHES AND SPECIALITIES

Pa amb tomaquet

Some things are hallowed in Catalan cuisine, and none more so than the quartet of classic sauces which underpin almost everything. King of them all is *sofregit* (mentioned in the first Catalan cookbook of 1324), a reduction of caramelized onions, fresh tomatoes and herbs. *Samfaina* is made like *sofregit* but with the addition of roast aubergines (eggplant), courgettes (zucchini) and peppers. *Picada* is spicier, and ingredients vary but normally include breadcrumbs, garlic, almonds, saffron and pine nuts. *All i oli* is a garlicky, mayonnaise-like (but eggless) sauce, usually served with grilled meat and vegetables. But the classic Catalan dish is *pa amb tomàquet* – crusty bread rubbed with fresh tomatoes and garlic, then drizzled with olive oil. Simple, but utterly delicious.

Escalivada *is a salad of marinated onions, peppers and aubergines (eggplant) that have been roasted until sweet.*

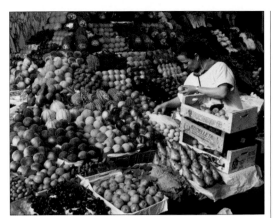

Summer fruits and vegetables lovingly displayed at La Boquería market

FRUIT AND VEGETABLES

Spring is heralded by *calçots*, a cross between leeks and onions, tiny broad (fava) beans and delicate asparagus spears. In summer, market stalls blaze with the colours of cherries, strawberries, figs, peaches and melons, gleaming aubergines (eggplants), courgettes (zucchini), tomatoes and artichokes. In autumn, Catalans head for the hills to seek out wild mushrooms *(bolets)*, and classic Catalan bean dishes appear on menus as winter approaches.

BEST FOOD SHOPPING

La Boquería *(see p155).*

Xocoa Carrer d'en Bot (93 318 8991) Excellent chocolate in slick designer packaging.

Casa del Bacalao Carrer Comtal 8 (93 301 6539) Traditional temple to *bacallà*.

La Pineda Carrer del Pi (93 302 43 93) Delightful old grocer's, specializing in hams.

Tot Formatge, Passeig del Born 13, (93 319 5375). Superb cheeses from Catalonia, Spain and elsewhere.

Botifarrería de Santa María, Carrer Santa María 4 (93 319 9123) Cured meats of all kinds.

Origens 99.9% Carrer Vidreria 6–8 (93 310 7581) Catalan products, organic where possible, including cheeses, hams, oils and conserves.

partridge *(perdiu)*. Rabbit *(conill)* and snails *(cargols)*, come into their own in hearty winter dishes. Meat and fish are sometimes combined in dishes known as *mar i muntanya* (sea and mountain).

FISH

Barcelona excels at seafood. Tapas bars commonly serve mouthwatering sardines, and rosy prawns grilled or tossed in garlic. Restaurants and markets offer a dizzying array of fresh fish, including monkfish, bass, hake, sole, squid, octopus, and every possible variety of shellfish. Fish is often served simply grilled *(a la brasa)*, or perhaps with a simple sauce. It's especially good cooked paella-style in *fideuà*, or in a stew such as

suquet de peix. But humble dried, salted cod *(bacallà)*, still reigns supreme in Catalan cuisine, and is at its most delicious when baked with tomatoes, garlic and wine *(a la llauna)*.

Locally caught sardines being grilled over charcoal

Conill amb cargols *is a hearty country stew of rabbit and snails with tomatoes, spices and a splash of wine.*

Suquet de peix, *a rich stew of firm-fleshed fish (often hake), with tomatoes, garlic and toasted almonds.*

Crema Catalana, *the Catalan version of crème brûlée, is a rich, eggy custard with a caramelized sugar topping.*

Cava Country

Cordoníu's world-famous *cava* label

Cava is one of Catalonia's most appreciated exports. This relatively inexpensive sparkling wine is made in the same way as French champagne, undergoing a second fermentation in the bottle in which it is sold. It was made commercially from the mid-19th century and, in 1872, full-scale production was begun by Josep Raventós, head of Codorníu. This famous winery is still run by his descendants in Sant Sadurní d'Anoia, *cava* capital of the Penedès wine-producing region. Today *cava* continues to be made using local grape varieties – Macabeo, Xarel·lo and Parellada – and some pleasant pink *cava* is also produced. The literal meaning of *cava* is simply "cellar".

Codorníu, *the first wine to be made using the* méthode champenoise, *brought cava international renown as one of the great sparkling wines.*

Freixenet *was established by the Sala family in 1914 and is now one of the leading* cava *brands. Their estate is in Sant Sadurní d'Anoia, heart of* cava *country, and Freixenet's distinctive black bottle is recognized throughout the world.*

Raïmat, *developed by the Raventós family using the Chardonnay grape, is considered by many to be the ultimate* cava. *Wrested from wasteland, the 3,000-hectare (7,410-acre) Raïmat estate, 14 km (9 miles) west of Lleida, has its own railway station and workers' village and has been declared a "model agricultural estate" by the Spanish government.*

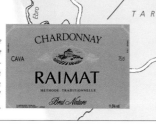

THE OTHER WINES OF CATALONIA

Wine *(vi)* in Catalonia is *negre* (red), *rosat* (pink) or *blanc* (white). *Garnatxa* is a dessert wine named after the grape it comes from; *ranci* is a matured white wine. A tradition, now only practised at local *festes* or old-style bars, is to pour wine into the mouth from a *porró* (long-spouted wine jug). There are seven official DO *(Denominació de Origen)* regions:

Empordà-Costa Brava: light wines from the northeast. They include *vi de l'any*, drunk in the year it is produced. *Cava* is made in Peralada.
Alella: a tiny region, just north of Barcelona, with good light whites.
Penedès: great reds as well as some whites, with names such as Torres and Codorníu. Visit the wine museum in Vilafranca del Penedès *(see p125)*.
Conca de Barberà: small quantities of both reds and whites.
Costers del Segre: includes the delicious reds from the Raïmat estate.
Priorat: characterful reds and good whites (Falset) from a pretty region of small villages west of Tarragona.
Tarragona and Terra Alta: traditionally hefty wines, but getting lighter.

A porró for drinking wine

The Art Nouveau *winery in Sant Sadurní d'Anoia is Codorníu's Modernista showpiece, designed by Josep Puig i Cadafalch in 1906. There are 26 km (16 miles) of cellars on five floors and visitors are taken round on a small train.*

SPAIN

Madrid

Gold medals were awarded to Codorníu for its *cava* as early as 1888. By 1897 it was being served at state functions instead of champagne.

KEY

☐ Main cava districts

0 kilometres 20

0 miles 20

E D È S

Manresa

Igualada

Masquefa ⑥

Terrassa

Sabadell

Àrrega NII A2

② ①
③ Sant Sadurní
d'Anoia

BARCELONA

T E R S   D E L
E G R E

Montblanc ④
Vilafranca del Penedès

Valls

Castelldefels

El Vendrell
Vilanova
i la Geltrú

eus Tarragona

BEST PRODUCERS

Codorníu
  Sant Sadurní d'Anoia ①
Freixenet
  Sant Sadurní d'Anoia ②
Gramona
  Sant Sadurní d'Anoia ③
Mascaró
  Vilafranca del Penedès ④
Raïmat
  Costers del Segre ⑤
Raventós Rosell
  Masquefa ⑥

CAVA TIPS

What to buy
As with champagne, the drier the wine, the higher the price. The driest *cavas* are *brut de brut* and *brut nature*. *Brut* and *sec* are slightly less dry. Sweet *semiseco* and *dulce* are best with desserts. Although inexpensive compared with the French equivalent, costs do vary, with small, specialist producers commanding high prices.

Visiting a winery
The main *cava* producers are open to the public during office hours (but many close in August). Sant Sadurní d'Anoia is 45 minutes by train from Barcelona's Sants station and the most impressive cellars to visit here are Freixenet's and Codorníu's. Vilafranca del Penedès tourist office (*see p125*) has details of all *cava* winery visits.

A rewarding tour *can be had by visiting the Freixenet cellars. The company sells more bottles of cava each year than the French sell champagne.*

CATALONIA THROUGH THE YEAR

Each *barri* (district) in Barcelona and every town and village in Catalonia has a saint's day to be celebrated in an annual *festa major*. The *sardana (see p129)* is danced and, on the Costa Brava, *havaneres* (habaneras) are sung. Food is central to any event, and open-air feasts and special pastries and cakes feature strongly. Many towns, including Barcelona,

Men give women a red rose on Sant Jordi's Day

have parades of giants *(gegants)*, bigheads *(capgrosses)* and dwarfs *(nans)* – papier-mâché caricatures of people once linked with local trade guilds. Demons and dragons provide drama. Catalans love pyrotechnics, and the fires at the midsummer *Revetlla de Sant Joan* are a lavish incendiary event. Many celebrations often start on the eve of the feast day proper.

Book stalls set up in Barcelona on Sant Jordi's Day, *el dia del llibre*

SPRING

Almond blossom gives way to cherry and apple as the earth warms and the melting snows swell the rivers. The fishing season for trout and other freshwater fish starts in late March. At Easter, families get together, often going out of town to visit relatives, or to picnic and search for wild asparagus. May is the best month in which to see wild flowers, which are particularly spectacular in the Pyrenees.

MARCH

Sant Medir *(3 Mar).* In Barcelona processions distribute sweets in the district of Gràcia, and in Sants a week later.
Sant Josep *(19 Mar).* Many Catalans are called Josep (often shortened to Pep). This is a holiday in Spain, although not in Catalonia. People celebrate their "name day" – the day of the saint they are named after – more than they

celebrate their birthday.
Terrassa Jazz Festival *(whole of Mar).* Concerts by musicians from all over the world.
Setmana Santa (Holy Week) is the week before Easter and is filled with events.

APRIL

Diumenge de Rams (Palm Sunday). Palm leaves are blessed in church, notably at the Sagrada Família in Barcelona. Processions of Roman soldiers turn out in Girona, and *via crucis* (passion plays) are put on in several places, notably the spa town of Sant Hilari Sacalm, Girona province.
Dijous Sant (Maundy Thursday), Verges, Girona province. Men dressed as skeletons perform a death dance *(dansa de la mort)* thought to date back to times of plague in the 1300s.
Pasqua (Easter). On Good Friday *(Divendres Sant)* crucifixes are carried through the streets following the Stations of the Cross. On Easter Monday

(Dilluns de Pasqua) godparents buy their godchildren *mona* (egg cake), and bakers compete to make the most elaborate confections.
Sant Jordi *(23 Apr).* Feast of St George, patron saint of Catalonia, and a day devoted to the memory of Cervantes *(see p43),* who died on this day in 1616. Men and boys give single red roses to their mothers, wives and girlfriends, who give them books in return. The festival is also known as *el dia del llibre* (book day).

MAY

Fira de Sant Ponç *(11 May).* Ancient celebration around the Carrer de l'Hospital in Barcelona, once the site of the city hospital. Aromatic and medicinal herbs and honey are sold.
Corpus Christi *(May/Jun).* Flowers are laid in the streets of Sitges, and in Berga, Barcelona province, a monster dragon (la Patum) dances through the town's streets.

The feast of Corpus Christi, when carpets of flowers cover the streets

AVERAGE DAILY HOURS OF SUNSHINE

Hours

Jan Feb Mar Apr May Jun Jul Aug Sep Oct Nov Dec

Sunshine Chart
Barcelona is a sunny city, enjoying clear blue skies for a large part of the year and often up to ten hours' sunshine a day in summer. In winter, even though it can be cold in the shade, the sun is high enough to give it warming power and it can be pleasant to sit outdoors on a sheltered, sunny terrace or patio.

SUMMER

The majority of Barcelona's inhabitants live in apartments, so they like to head out of town at weekends, either to the coast or the mountains. Motorways (highways) on Friday afternoons and Sunday evenings are best avoided. School holidays are long, starting at the end of June when the sea is warm enough for swimming. Crowds throng the marinas, the aroma of barbecued sardines fills the air, and a plethora of summer entertainment provides limitless options. Many businesses in Barcelona close in August.

JUNE

Festival del Grec *(Jun–Jul)*. In this summer arts festival, there are national and international performances throughout Barcelona; the main venues are the Teatre Grec, Mercat de les Flors and Poble Espanyol.
Revetlla de Sant Joan *(24 Jun)*. St John's (Midsummer's) Eve is celebrated with fireworks, especially on Montjuïc in Barcelona. Bonfires are lit throughout Catalonia and lighted torches are brought down from the top of Mont Canigó, just over the border in France. *Cava* – a sparkling white wine *(see pp32–3)* – is drunk with a special *coca* (cake) sprinkled with pine nuts and crystallized fruit *(see p31)*.
Castellers *(24 Jun)*. In Valls, Tarragona, a province famous for its *casteller* festivals, teams of men stand on each other's shoulders hoping to take the prize for building the highest human tower *(see p125)*.

Holidaymakers at Platja d'Aro, a popular Costa Brava resort

Concert season *(Jun/Jul)*. Classical music concerts, held at different parks in Barcelona, are organized by the Institut Municipal de Parcs i Jardins.

JULY

Cantada d'havaneres *(first Sun in Jul)*. Drinking *cremat* (coffee and rum), musicians and singers belt out *havaneres* in towns along the coast, most famously at Calella de Palafrugell on the Costa Brava.

A team of *castellers* in action

Virgen del Carmen *(16 Jul)*. A maritime festival that takes place around Barcelona's port. As well as processions, there are bands playing *havaneres*.
Santa Cristina *(24 Jul)*. The biggest festival of Lloret de Mar, Costa Brava, when a statue of the Virgin is brought ashore by a decorated flotilla.

AUGUST

Festa major de Gràcia *(one week beginning around 15 Aug)*. Each district of Barcelona hosts its own *festa* in which streets try to outdo each other in the inventiveness of their decorations. The *festa* in the old district of Gràcia is the biggest and most spectacular and incorporates concerts, balls, music, competitions and street games.
Festa major de Sants *(around 24 Aug)*. The big annual *festa* in the Sants district of Barcelona.
Festa major de Vilafranca del Penedès *(mid-Aug)*. This town's annual festival is one of the best places to see *casteller* (human tower) competitions *(see p125)*.

AVERAGE MONTHLY RAINFALL (BARCELONA)

Rainfall Chart
Barcelona experiences modest rainfall year round – just sufficient to maintain the city's green spaces. However, rain tends to fall in sudden, but short-lived, torrential downpours and heavy thunder storms are a feature of the summer months. Grey, drizzly weather lasting for days on end is very rare.

AUTUMN

The grape harvest *(verema)* is a highlight of the autumn, just before the vines turn red and gold. It is the season for seeking out mushrooms which swell the market stalls. From October hunters set off to bag red-legged partridge, migrating ducks and wild boar. Hardier people can be seen swimming in the sea right up until November.

SEPTEMBER

Diada de Catalunya *(11 Sep).* Catalonia's national day marks Barcelona's fall to Felipe V in 1714 *(see p44)* when the region lost its autonomy. Political demonstrations convey strong separatist sentiment. *Sardana (see p129)* bands and people singing *Els segadors (see p44)* can be heard and Catalan flags are everywhere.
La Mercè *(24 Sep).* This annual festival in Barcelona honours *Nostra Senyora de la Mercè* (Our Lady of Mercy) in a week of concerts, masses and dances. Look out for the

Cattle descending from the Pyrenees at the end of the summer

carrefoc – a parade of fire-breathing dragons, giants and monsters; and the *piro musical* – fireworks set to music.
Sant Miquel *(29 Sep).* Celebrations for Barceloneta's patron saint recall Napoleon's occupation of Spain *(see p45).* Bum Bum, a Napoleonic general, parades through the streets to salvoes of gunfire. There is dancing on the beach.

OCTOBER

Festes de Sarrià i de Les Corts *(first Sun in Oct).* Each of these Barcelona districts has a festival for its patron saint.
Dia de la Hispanitat *(12 Oct)* National holiday to mark the discovery of America in 1492 *(see p44),* but most Catalans do not celebrate this anniversary.

NOVEMBER

Tots Sants (All Saints' Day) *(1 Nov).* Roast chestnuts and sweet potatoes are eaten and the next day – *Dia dels difunts* (All Souls' Day) – people visit the graves of their relatives.

Harvesting grapes in autumn with high hopes for a successful crop

PUBLIC HOLIDAYS

Any Nou *(New Year's Day)* 1 Jan
Reis Mags *(Epiphany)* 6 Jan
Divendres Sant *(Good Friday)* Mar/Apr
Dilluns de Pasqua *(Easter Monday)* Mar/Apr
Festa del Treball *(Labour Day)* 1 May
Sant Joan *(Saint John's Day)* 24 Jun
Assumpció *(Assumption Day)* 15 Aug
Diada de Catalunya *(National Day)* 11 Sep
La Mercè 24 Sep
Dia de la Hispanitat *(Day of the Spanish-speaking nations)* 12 Oct
Tots Sants *(All Saints' Day)* 1 Nov
Dia de la Constitució *(Constitution Day)* 6 Dec
Immaculada Concepció *(Immaculate Conception)* 8 Dec
Nadal *(Christmas)* 25 Dec
Sant Esteve 26 Dec

AVERAGE DAILY TEMPERATURE (BARCELONA)

Temperature Chart
This chart shows the average minimum and maximum daily temperatures recorded in Barcelona. The sunshine in winter can be deceptive, as daytime temperatures can occasionally dip to near freezing. Summer days are consistently hot. Hats and a high-factor sun screen are essential.

WINTER

Ski resorts in the Pyrenees are a popular destination at weekends. Though days can be sunny and lunches still taken alfresco, the weather is unpredictable and the nights can be chilly. Christmas is a particularly delightful time to be in Barcelona, when the city vibrates with the spirit of celebration and sharing. Crafts and decorations are on sale in the Feria de Santa Llúcia in front of the Cathedral.

A ski resort in the Pyrenees, a popular destination for weekenders

DECEMBER

Nadal and **Sant Esteve** *(25 & 26 Dec)*. Christmas is a time for people to come together. Traditional Christmas lunch consists of an *escudella* (meat stew) followed by turkey stuffed with apples, apricots, prunes, pine nuts and raisins.
Revellón *(31 Dec)*. All over Spain on New Year's Eve it has become a custom for people to eat a grape between

each chime of the midnight bell. To manage the feat brings good luck all year.

JANUARY

Reis Mags *(6 Jan)*. On the eve of the Epiphany the three kings arrive in various guises throughout Catalonia giving sweets to children. The main cavalcade in Barcelona is down by the port.
Santa Eulàlia *(12 Jan)*. The feast of the ancient patron saint of Barcelona is celebrated in the old town. There is

dancing and many people dress up as giants.
Els Tres Tombs *(17 Jan)*. Horsemen in top hats and tails ride three times through the city to honour St Anthony, patron saint of animals.
Pelegrí de Tossa *(20 & 21 Jan)*, Tossa de Mar. A 40-km (25-mile) pilgrimage marking the end of the plague; this town's biggest annual event.

FEBRUARY

Carnestoltes (Carnival) *(Feb/Mar)*. King Carnival presides over the pre-Lent celebrations, children wear fancy dress and every *barri* (district) in Barcelona puts on a party. Sausage omelettes are eaten on Shrove Tuesday *(Dijous gras)*, and on Ash Wednesday *(Dimecres de cendra)* a sardine is ceremoniously buried *(Enterrament de la sardina)*. There are big celebrations in Platja d'Aro on the Costa Brava and Vilanova on the Costa Daurada. Sitges is the place to go to see the full transvestite indulgence of the feast.
Rally Internacional de Cotxes d'Època *(around first Sun in Lent)*. A veteran car rally from Barcelona to Sitges.

The winter festival of Els Tres Tombs in Vilanova i la Geltrú

Procession of *gegants* (giants) during the September festival of La Mercé in Barcelona ▷

THE HISTORY OF CATALONIA

he Catalans have always been great seafarers, merchants and industrialists. Since they were united under the House of Barcelona, their nationhood has been threatened by marriages, alliances and conflicts with Madrid, and the road to their present status as a semi-autonomous region within Spain has been marked by times of power and wealth and troughs of weakness and despair.

Barcelona was not a natural site for human settlement. Its port was negligible and its heights, Montjuïc, had no water. The oldest evidence of man in Catalonia comes rather from other sites scattered across the region, notably the dolmens of the Alt (high) Empordà and passage graves of the Baix (low) Empordà and Alt Urgell.

In the first millennium BC the lands around Barcelona were settled by the agrarian Laeitani, while other parts of Catalonia were simultaneously colonized by the Iberians. The latter were great builders in stone and remains of one of their settlements are still visible at Ullastret on the Costa Brava. Greek traders arrived on the coast around 550 BC, founding their first trading post at Empúries (Emporion, *see p120*) near Ullastret. It was the Carthaginians from New Carthage in southern Spain who put Barcelona on the map. They named the city after Hamil Barca, father of Hannibal who led his army of elephants from Catalonia over the Pyrenees and Alps to attack Rome.

Roman mosaic floor excavated in Barcelona depicting the Three Graces

In reprisal, the Romans arrived at Empúries and began the subjugation of the whole Iberian peninsula. They wiped out the Carthaginians as well as the Laeitani and established Tarraco (Tarragona, *see p128*) in the south of Catalonia as the imperial capital of Tarraconensis, one of the three administrative regions of the peninsula.

Roman Barcelona can be seen in the city gate beside the cathedral, while the 3rd-century walls that once encircled the town lie by the medieval Royal Palace *(see p56)*. Foundations of the Roman city have been excavated in the basement of the Museu d'Història de la Ciutat *(see p56-7)*, and pillars from the Temple of Augustus can be glimpsed inside the Centre Excursionista de Catalunya *(see p55)* behind the cathedral.

When the Roman empire collapsed, Visigoths based in Toulouse moved in to fill the vacuum. They had been vassals of Rome, practised Roman law, spoke a similar language and in 587 their Aryan king, Reccared, converted to the Christianity of Rome.

TIMELINE

	500–200 BC Fortified Iberian settlements at Ullastret. Cyclopean walls of Tarragona	**550 BC** Greeks establish trading settlement at Empúries
1000–500 BC Indo-Europeans invade Ter and Llobregat valleys; Iberians settle Montjuïc		*Visigothic Cross*

2500 BC	1500 BC	500 BC	AD 500
2000–1500 BC Megalithic monuments built throughout Catalonia	*Hannibal*	**230 BC** Barcelona founded by Hamil Barca, father of Hannibal	**218 BC** Romans arrive at Empúries to subjugate Spain

AD 531 Visigoths established in Barcelona after fall of Rome

AD 258 Barcelona city walls built after a Frankish invasion

◁ Troops fraternizing with local militia in the Baixada de la Llibreteria, Barcelona, during the 1833–9 Carlist War

THE MOORS AND CHARLEMAGNE

The Visigoths established their capital at Toledo, just south of modern Madrid. When King Wirtzia died in 710, his son, Akhila, is said to have called on the Saracens from north Africa for help in claiming the throne. In 711, with astonishing speed, Muslim and Berber tribes began to drive up through the Iberian peninsula, reaching Barcelona in 717, then Poitiers in France in 732, where they were finally stopped by the Frankish leader, Charles Martel.

Page from a 15th-century manuscript of the *Llibre del Consolat de Mar*

The Muslims made their capital in Córdoba in southern Spain, while the Visigothic nobles found hiding places in the Pyrenees, from which they conducted sorties against the invaders. They were aided by Charles Martel's grandson, Charles the Great (Charlemagne). In 801 Barcelona was retaken by the Franks, only to be lost and taken again. The shortness of the Muslim occupation left Catalonia, unlike the rest of Spain, unmarked by the culture and language of Islam.

Ramon Berenguer I of Barcelona (1035–76)

THE COUNTS OF BARCELONA

Charlemagne created the Hispanic Marc, a buffer state along the Pyrenees, which he entrusted to local lords. The most powerful figure in the east was Guifré el Pelós (Wilfred the Hairy), who consolidated the counties of Barcelona, Cerdanya, Conflent, Osona Urgell and Girona and founded the monastery of Ripoll *(see p114)* – *el bressol de Catalunya* (the cradle of Catalonia). Guifré died in battle against the Moors in 897, but he had started a dynasty of Counts of Barcelona which was to last, unbroken, for 500 years.

Before the end of the 11th century, under Ramon Berenguer I, Catalonia had established the first constitutional government in Europe with a bill of rights, the *Usatges*. By the early 12th century, under Ramon Berenguer III, Catalonia's boundaries had pushed south past Tarragona. Catalan influence also spread north and east when he married Dolça of Provence, linking the two regions and, more lastingly, the principality of Barcelona was united with its neighbour Aragon in 1137 by the marriage of Ramon Berenguer IV and Petronila of Aragon. In 1196 the great monastery of Poblet *(see pp126–7)* in Tarragona province took the place of Ripoll as the pantheon of Catalan royalty.

TIMELINE

	717 Catalonia occupied by Muslims	**801** Moors ejected. Charlemagne sets up buffer state	*Charlemagne (742–814)*	**1060** Constitution, *Usatges*, is drawn up around the time that the word Catalan is first recorded
AD 700		**800**	**900**	**1000**
711 North African Muslims invade Spanish mainland	*Moorish sword*	**778** Charlemagne, leader of the Franks, begins campaign to drive Moors from Spain	**878** Guifré el Pelós (Wilfred the Hairy), Count of Cerdanya-Urgell, consolidates eastern Pyrenees and gains virtual autonomy. He starts 500-year dynasty of Counts of Barcelona	**1008–46** Abbot Oliva builds church at Ripoll and oversees Benedictine buildings including Vic and Monserrat

MARITIME EXPANISION

Under Jaume I the Conqueror (1213–76), Catalonia began a period of prosperity and expansion. By the end of the 13th century the Balearic islands and Sicily had been conquered; many of the ships used in the enterprise were built at the vast Drassanes shipyards in Barcelona (*see p 67*). Catalonia now ruled the seas and the *Llibre del Consolat de Mar* was a code of trading practice that held sway throughout the Mediterranean. Swashbuckling admirals included Roger de Llúria, who won a definitive victory over the French fleet in the Bay of Roses in 1285, and Roger de Flor, leader of a bunch of fierce Catalan and Aragonese mercenaries, the Almogàvers. These won battles for both the King of Sicily and the Byzantine emperor before Roger de Flor was murdered in 1305.

During Jaume I's long reign the *Corts* (parliament) was established, the city walls were rebuilt to enclose an area ten times larger than that enclosed by the old Roman walls, and noble houses arose down the new Carrer Montcada

Ex voto in the form of a 15th-century ship

(*see pp 64*). La Llotja (the stock exchange) was sited by what was then the main port, and the church of Santa Maria del Mar (*see p63*) was built by grateful merchants. Under Pere IV (1336–87) two great halls were built: the Royal Palace's Saló del Tinell and the Casa de la Ciutat's Saló de Cent (*see pp 56– 7*).

Prosperity brought a flowering of Catalan literature. Jaume I wrote his own *Llibre dels Feits (Book of Deeds)*, and Pere el Gran's conquest of Sicily in 1282 was described in glowing terms in a chronicle of Catalan history written by Bernat Desclot around 1285. The great Catalan poet Ramon Lull (1232–1315), born in Mallorca, was the first to use a vernacular language in religious writing. From 1395 an annual poetry competition, the Jocs Florals, was held in the city, attracting the region's troubadours. In 1450, Joanot Martorell began writing his Catalan chivalric epic narrative *Tirant lo Blanc*, though he died in 1468, 22 years before it was published. Miguel de Cervantes, author of *Don Quijote*, described it as simply "the best book in the world".

Wall painting showing Jaume I during his campaign to conquer Mallorca

1137 Barcelona united to neighbouring Aragon by royal marriage	1258–72 *Consolat de Mar*, a code of trading practice, holds sway throughout the Mediterranean	1282 Pere el Gran takes Sicily. His exploits are recorded in Desclot's *Chronicles*	1347–8 Black death kills a quarter of the population	
			1359 Generalitat founded	1423 Conquest of Naples

1100	1200	1300	1400

1148 Frontier with Moors pushed back to Riu Ebre	1213–35 Jaume I (The Conqueror) takes Mallorca, Ibiza and Formentera		1324 Sardinia captured
			1302–5 Catalan mercenaries under Admiral Roger de Flor aid Byzantium against the Turks
	Jaume I (1213–76)		1287 Conquest of Mallorca under Alfons III

FERNANDO AND ISABEL OF CASTILE

Catholic Spain was united in 1479 when Fernando II of Catalonia-Aragon married Isabel of Castile, a region which by then had absorbed the rest of northern Spain. In 1492 they drove the last of the Moors from the peninsula, then, in a fever of righteousness, also drove out the Jews, who

Baptizing Jews during the era of the Catholic Monarchs

had large and commercially important populations in Barcelona (*see p56*) and Girona. This was the same year that Columbus had set foot in America, returning in triumph to Barcelona with six Carib Indians (*see p58*). However, the city lost out when the monopoly on New World trade was given to Seville and Cádiz. Though it still had great moments, such as its involvement in the victory over the Turks at Lepanto in 1571 (*see p67*), Barcelona went into a period of decline.

REVOLTS AND SIEGES

During the Thirty Years War with France (1618–59), Felipe IV forced Barcelona's *Corts* to raise an army to fight the French, towards whom the Catalans bore no grudge. A viceroy was imposed on the city and unruly Spanish troops were billeted throughout the region. In June 1640 the population arose, and harvesters (*segadors*) murdered the viceroy. The *Song of the Harvesters* is still sung at Catalan gatherings (*see p36*). Barcelona then allied itself with France, but was besieged and defeated by Felipe. The peace of 1659 ceded Catalan lands north of the Pyrenees to France.

Wall tile for a Catalan trade guild

A second confrontation with Madrid arose during the War of the Spanish Succession when Europe's two dominant royal houses, the Habsburgs and Bourbons, both laid claim to the throne. Barcelona, with England as an ally, found itself on the losing side, supporting the Habsburgs. As a result, it was heavily

The great siege of Barcelona in 1714 during the War of the Spanish Succession

TIMELINE

AD 1450	AD 1500	AD 1550	AD 1600	AD 1650

1492 Columbus discovers Americas. Barcelona barred from trade with the New World. Jews expelled

1494 Supreme Council of Aragon brings Catalonia under Castilian control

The Spanish Inquisition, active from 1478

1619 Spanish capital established in Madrid

1659 Treaty of the Pyrenees at end of Thirty Years War draws new border with France; Roussillon ceded to France

1479 Fernando II of Catalonia-Aragon marries Isabel of Castile, uniting all the houses of Spain

1490 *Tirant lo Blanc*, epic tale of chivalry by Martorell (*see p43*), published in Catalan

1571 Vast fleet sets sail from Barcelona to defeat the Ottomans at sea at Lepanto

1640 Revolt of the harvesters (*segadors*) against Spanish exploitation of Catalan resources during Thirty Years War with France

Women joining in the defence of Girona against the Napoleonic French in 1809

(see pp122–3) were sacked and pillaged. They suffered further in 1835 under a republican government when many were seen as too rich and powerful and were dissolved. This was a politically vigorous time, when a minority of largely rural reactionaries fought a rearguard action against the liberal spirit of the century in the Carlist Wars.

THE CATALAN RENAIXENÇA

Barcelona was the first city in Spain to industrialize, mainly around cotton manufacture, from imported raw material from the Americas. It brought immigrant workers and a burgeoning population, and in 1854 the city burst out of its medieval walls (see p71). Inland, industrial centres such as Terrassa and Sabadell flourished and *colònies industrials* (industrial workhouses) grew up along the rivers where mills were powered by water.

Just as the wealth of the 14th century inspired Catalonia's first flowering, so the wealth from industry inspired the *Renaixença*, a renaissance of Catalan culture. Its literary rallying points were Bonaventura Aribau's *Oda a la patria* and the poems of a young monk, Jacint Verdaguer, who won poetry prizes in the revived Jocs Florals (see p43).

besieged by troops of the incoming Bourbon king, Felipe V. The city fell on 11 September 1714, today celebrated as National Day (see p36). Felipe then proceeded to annul all of Catalonia's privileges. Its language was banned, its universities closed and Lleida's Gothic cathedral became a barracks. Felipe tore down the Ribera district of Barcelona and, in what is now Ciutadella Park (see p64-5), built a citadel to keep an eye on the population.

With the lifting of trade restrictions with the Americas, Catalonia began to recover economically. Progress, however, was interrupted by the 1793–95 war with France and then by the 1808–14 Peninsular War (known in Spain as the War of Independence) when Napoleon put his brother Joseph on the Spanish throne. Barcelona fell in early 1808, but Girona withstood a seven-month siege. Monasteries, including Montserrat

Well-to-do barcelonins *selecting from a wide range of locally produced calico in the early 19th century*

Felipe V (1700–24)

AD 1700	AD 1750	AD 1800	AD 1850

1808–14 Peninsular War (War of Independence): Girona besieged, Barcelona occupied, Monastery of Montserrat sacked

1823–6 French occupy Catalonia

1835 Monasteries dissolved

1833–9 First Carlist War

1859 Revival of Jocs Florals poetry competition feeds Renaissance of Catalan culture.

1714 Barcelona sacked by Felipe V, first Bourbon king. Catalan universities closed. Catalan language banned

1778 Catalonia allowed to trade with the Americas, bringing new wealth

1849 Spain's first railway built to link Barcelona and Mataró

1833 Aribau's *Oda a la patria* published

Poet Bonaventura Carles Aribau i Farriols

A hall of Spanish goods at the 1888 Universal Exhibition

CATALANISM AND MODERNISME

The *Renaixença* produced a new pride in Catalonia, and "Catalanism" was at the heart of the region's accelerating move towards autonomy, a move echoed in Galicia and the Basque Country. Interruptions by the Carlist Wars came to an end in 1876 and resulted in the restoration of the Bourbon monarchy.

The first home-rule party, the *Lliga de Catalunya*, was founded in 1887, and disputes with the central government continued. It was blamed for the loss of the American colonies, and therefore lucrative transatlantic trade, and for involving Spain in unnecessary conflict in Morocco. *La setmana tràgica* (tragic week) of 1909 saw the worst of the violent protests: 116 people died and 300 were injured.

Meanwhile, on a more cultural and artistic level and to show off its increasing wealth, Barcelona held in 1888 a

Poster for 1929 Exhibition

Universal Exhibition in the Parc de la Ciutadella where Felipe V's citadel had recently been torn down. The urban expansion *(eixample)* inland was carefully ordered under a plan by Ildefons Cerdà *(see p71)* and industrial barons employed imaginative architects to show off their wealth, most successfully Eusebi Güell and Antoni Gaudí *(see pp24–5)*. The destruction of the monasteries had left spaces for sumptuous buildings such as the Palau de la Música Catalana *(see p62)*, the Liceu opera house and La Boqueria market *(see p155)*.

Spain's non-involvement in World War I meant that Catalonia's Modernista architecture was unscathed. Barcelona's place as a showcase city was confirmed with the 1929 International Exhibition on Montjuïc, many of whose buildings still remain.

Antoni Gaudí, Modernisme's most creative architect

CIVIL WAR

The *Mancomunitat*, a local council established in 1914, disappeared on the arrival in 1923 of the dictator Primo de Rivera, Barcelona's military governor. In 1931 Francesc Macià declared himself President of the Catalan Republic, which lasted three days. Three years later Lluís Companys was arrested and sentenced to 30 years' imprisonment for attempting to do the same.

TIMELINE

1872–6 Third and last Carlist War	**1888** Universal Exhibition held in Parc de la Ciutadella, showing off the new Modernista style	*Primo de Rivera (1870–1930)*	
		1909 *Setmana tràgica:* violent protest against Moroccan Wars	
AD 1875		**AD 1900**	**AD 192**
	1893 Anarchist bombs in Liceu opera house kill 14	**1901** *Lliga Regionalista*, new Catalan party, wins elections	**1929** International Exhibition on Montjuïc
Carlist soldiers			**1931** Francesc Macià declares independence for Catalonia

Refugees on the march in 1939, fleeing towards the Pyrenees to seek asylum in France

Finally, on 16 July 1936, General Francisco Franco led an army revolt against the Republican government and the fledgling autonomous states. The government fled Madrid to Valencia, then Barcelona. City and coast were bombed by German aircraft, and shelled by Italian warships. When Barcelona fell three years later, thousands escaped to camps in France and thousands, including Companys, were executed in Franco's reprisals. Catalonia lost all it had gained, and its language was outlawed once more.

The *noche negra*, the dark night that followed Franco's victory, left Barcelona short of resources and largely neglected by Madrid. The 1960s, however, brought new economic opportunities, and between 1960 and 1975 two million Spaniards came to work in the city. The arrival of the first tourists to the coast during that time, to the Costa Brava and Costa Daurada, changed the face of Spain for ever.

LIFE AFTER FRANCO
Champagne flowed freely in Barcelona's streets on the news of Franco's death in 1975. Democracy

and the monarchy, under the Bourbon Juan Carlos, were restored and Jordi Pujol of the conservative *Convergència i Unió* party was elected leader of the Generalitat, Catalonia's regional government. Catalonia has since won a large degree of autonomy, including tax-raising powers.

Pasqual Maragall, Barcelona's mayor until 1997 and the current president of Catalonia, steered through the radical shake-up of the city for the 1992 Olympic Games. In less than a decade Barcelona changed dramatically, with a bold new waterfront, inspired urban spaces, new access roads, and state-of-the-art museums and galleries.

Opening ceremony, 1992 Barcelona Olympic Games

1939 50,000 go into exile in France. Catalan President Companys executed		**1975** Franco dies. King Juan Carlos restores Bourbon line	
	1947 Spain declared a monarchy with Franco as regent	**1979** Partial autonomy granted to Catalonia	**1992** Olympic Games held in Barcelona
AD 1950		**AD 1975**	**AD 2000**
1953 US bases welcomed	**1960s** Costa Brava leads package holiday boom	**1985** Medes Islands become Spain's first marine nature reserve	
1936–9 Spanish Civil War. Republican government retreats from Madrid to Valencia, then Barcelona		**1986** Spain enters European Union	

Cobi, the Olympic mascot

BARCELONA AND CATALONIA

Introducing Barcelona

Barcelona, one of the Mediterranean's busiest ports,is more than the capital of Catalonia. In culture, commerce and sports it not only rivals Madrid, but also considers itself on a par with the greatest European cities. The success of the 1992 Olympic Games, staged in the Parc de Montjuïc, confirmed this to the world. Although there are plenty of historical monuments in the Ciutat Vella (Old Town), Barcelona is best known for the scores of buildings in the Eixample left by the artistic explosion of Modernisme *(see pp24–5)* in the decades around 1900. Always open to outside influences because of its location on the coast, not too far from the French border, Barcelona continues to sizzle with creativity: its bars and the public parks speak more of bold contemporary design than of tradition.

Casa Milà (see p79) *is the most avant-garde of all the works of Antoni Gaudí (see p78). Barcelona has more Art Nouveau buildings than any other city in the world.*

Palau Nacional (see p88), *on the hill of Montjuïc, dominates the monumental halls and the fountain-filled avenue built for the 1929 International Exhibition. It now houses the Museu Nacional d'Art de Catalunya, with an exceptional collection of medieval art, rich in Romanesque frescoes.*

MONTJUÏC
(see pp84–91)

Montjuïc Castle (see p89) *is a massive fortification dating from the 17th century. Sited on the crest of the hill of Montjuïc, it offers panoramic views of the city and port, and forms a sharp contrast to the ultra-modern sports halls built nearby for the 1992 Olympic Games.*

Christopher Columbus *surveys the waterfront from the top of a 60-m (200-ft) column (see p67) in the heart of the Port Vell (Old Port). From the top, visitors can look out over the new promenades and quays that have revitalized the area.*

| 0 kilometres | | 1 |
| 0 miles | 0.5 | |

The Sagrada Família
(see pp80–1), *Gaudí's unfinished masterpiece, begun in 1882, rises above the streets of the Eixample. Its poly-chrome ceramic mosaics and sculptural forms inspired by nature are typical of his work.*

EIXAMPLE
(see pp70–83)

OLD TOWN
(see pp52–69)

Barcelona cathedral (see pp58–9) *is a magnificent 14th-century building in the heart of the Barri Gòtic (Gothic Quarter). It has 28 side chapels which encircle the nave and contain some splendid Baroque altarpieces. The keeping of white geese in the cloisters is a centuries-old tradition.*

Parc de la Ciutadella (see pp64-5), *between the Old Town and the Vila Olímpica, has something for everyone. The gardens full of statuary offer relaxation, the boating lake and the zoo are fun, while the two museums within its gates cover geology and zoology.*

La Rambla (see pp60–1) *is the most famous street in Spain, alive at all hours of the day and night. A stroll down its length to the seafront, taking in its palatial buildings, shops, cafés and street vendors, makes a perfect introduction to Barcelona life.*

OLD TOWN

The old town, traversed by the city's most famous avenue, La Rambla, is one of the most extensive medieval city centres in Europe. The Barri Gòtic contains the cathedral and a maze of streets and squares. Across from the Via Laietana, the El Born neighbourhood is dominated by the Santa Maria del Mar church and is replete with 14th-century mansions. This area is bounded by the leafy Parc de la Ciutadella, home to the city's zoo. The revitalized seafront is a stimulating mix of old and new. Trendy shops and restaurants make up the fashionable marina, contrasted with the old maritime neighbourhood of Barceloneta and the new Olympic port.

SIGHTS AT A GLANCE

Museums and Galleries
Aquarium ㉔
Museu d'Art Contemporani ❿
Museu d'Historia de Catalunya ㉕
Museu Frederic Marès ❷
Museu de Geologia ⓳
Museu Marítim and
  Drassanes ㉘
Museu Picasso ⓭
Museu de la Xocolata ⓯
Museu de Zoologia ⓲

Harbour Sights
Golondrinas ㉗
Port Olímpic ㉑
Port Vell ㉓

Streets and Districts
Barceloneta ㉒
La Rambla ❼
El Raval ❾

Churches
Basílica de Santa Maria
  del Mar ⓮
Cathedral (pp58–9) ❻

Historic Buildings
Casa de l'Ardiaca ❶
Casa de la Ciutat ❹
La Llotja ⓬
Palau de la Generalitat ❺
Palau de la Música Catalana ⓫
Palau Güell ❽
Museu d'Història de
  la Ciutat ❸

Monuments
Arc del Triomf ⓰
Monument a Colom ㉖

Parks and Gardens
Parc de la Ciutadella ⓱
Parc Zoològic ⓴

GETTING THERE
The area is well served by Metro lines 1, 3 and 4; Jaume I station is in the heart of the Barri Gòtic. Many buses pass through the Plaça de Catalunya on the edge of the Barri Gòtic.

KEY
- Street-by-Street map *pp54–5*
- Ⓜ Metro station
- Train station
- Main bus stop
- Tramway stop
- Tourist information

| 0 metres | 500 |
| 0 yards | 500 |

◁ **Els Quatre Gats café in one of the narrow streets of Barcelona's Barri Gòtic**

Street-by-Street: Barri Gòtic

**Wax candle,
Cereria
Subirà**

The Barri Gòtic (Gothic Quarter) is the true heart of
Barcelona. The oldest part of the city, it was the
site chosen by the Romans in the reign of
Augustus (27 BC–AD 14) on which to found a
new *colonia* (town), and has been the location
of the city's administrative buildings ever since.
The Roman forum was on the Plaça de Sant
Jaume, where now stand the medieval Palau
de la Generalitat, the seat of
Catalonia's government, and the
Casa de la Ciutat, the city's town
hall. Close by are the Gothic
cathedral and royal palace,
where Columbus was received by
Fernando and Isabel on his return from
the New World in 1492 *(see p44)*.

Casa de l'Ardiaca
*Built on the Roman city wall,
the Gothic-Renaissance
archdeacon's residence
now houses Barcelona's
historical archives* ❶

To Plaça de Catalunya

★ Cathedral
*The façade and
spire are 19th-
century additions
to the original
Gothic building.
Among the artistic
treasures inside are
medieval Catalan
paintings* ❻

SANT SEVER

CARRER DEL BISBE

PIETAT

SANT DOMÈNEC DEL CALL

SANT HONORAT

**Palau de la
Generalitat**
*Catalonia's seat of
government has
superb Gothic
features, such as the
chapel and a stair-
case to an open-air,
arcaded gallery* ❺

CARRER DE FERRAN

PLAÇA DE
SANT JAUME

CARRER DE LA CIUTAT

To La Rambla

Casa de la Ciutat
*Barcelona's town hall was built in
the 14th and 15th centuries. The
façade is a Neo-Classical addition.
In the entrance hall stands* Three
Gypsy Boys *by Joan Rebull (1899–
1981), a 1976 copy of a sculpture
he originally created in 1946* ❹

KEY

- - - Suggested route

Museu Frederic Marès
This medieval doorway is from an extensive display of Spanish sculpture – the mainstay of this museum's extraordinarily eclectic and high-quality collections ❷

Roman city wall

Saló del Tinell

LOCATOR MAP
See Street Finder map 5

EIXAMPLE

OLD TOWN

MONTJUÏC

★ **Palau Reial**
The 14th-century Capella Reial de Santa Àgata, with a 1466 altarpiece, is one of the best surviving sections of the palace ❸

Capella Reial de Santa Àgata

Plaça del Rei

Palau del Lloctinent

Cereria Subirà candle shop

TAPINERIA

CARRER DELS COMTES DE BARCELONA

VIA LAIETANA

CARRER DE JAUME I

Jaume I
Metro

CARRER DAGUERIA

SOTS–TINENT NAVARRO

The Museu d'Història de la Ciutat features the most extensive subterranean Roman ruins in the world. Accessed through this 14th-century mansion, visitors can view the streets and squares of Roman Barcelona. The ruins extend underground, through to the exit at the Palau Reial.

The Centre Excursionista de Catalunya, housed in a medieval mansion, displays Roman columns from the Temple of Augustus, whose site is marked by a millstone in the street outside.

STAR SIGHTS

★ Cathedral

★ Palau Reial

0 metres   100
0 yards   100

Decorated marble mailbox, Casa de l'Ardiaca

Casa de l'Ardiaca ❶

Carrer de Santa Llúcia 1. **Map** 5 B2.
Tel 93 318 11 95. 🔲 Jaume I.
🟧 9am–8pm Mon–Fri, 9am–1pm
Sat. ⬤ public hols.
www.bcn.es/arxiu/arxiuhistoric

Standing beside what was originally the Bishop's Gate in the Roman wall is the Archdeacon's House. It was built in the 12th century, but its present form dates from around 1500 when it was remodelled, including the addition of a colonnade. In 1870 this was extended to form the Flamboyant Gothic patio around a fountain. The Modernista architect Domènech i Montaner (1850–1923) added the fanciful marble mailbox, carved with three swallows and a tortoise, beside the Renaissance portal. Upstairs is the Arxiu Històric de la Ciutat (City Archives).

Museu Frederic Marès ❷

Plaça de Sant Iu 5. **Map** 5 B2.
Tel 93 310 58 00. 🔲 Jaume I.
🟧 10am–7pm Tue–Sat, 10am–3pm
Sun. ⬤ 1 Jan, Good Fri, 1 May, 25 &
26 Dec. 🎫 (free to under 16s, also
Wed after 3pm & 1st Sun of every
month). ♿ 🅿 by appointment.
www.museumares.bcn.es

The sculptor Frederic Marès i Deulovol (1893–1991) was also a traveller and collector, and this museum is a monument to his eclectic taste. As part of the Royal Palace, it was occupied by 13th-century bishops, 14th-century counts

of Barcelona, 15th-century judges and 18th-century nuns, who lived here until they were expelled in 1936.

Virgin, Museu Frederic Marès

Marès, who had a small apartment in the building, opened this museum in 1948. It is one of the most fascinating in the city, and has an outstanding collection of Romanesque and Gothic religious art. In the crypt there are stone sculptures and two complete Romanesque portals. Exhibits on the three floors above range from clocks, crucifixes and costumes to antique cameras, pipes, tobacco jars and postcards. There is also a room full of children's toys.

Museu d'Història de la Ciutat ❸

Plaça del Rei. **Map** 5 B2.
Tel 93 315 11 11. 🔲 Jaume I.
🟧 Jun–Sep: 10am–8pm Tue–Sat,
10am– 3pm Sun; Oct–May: 10am–
2pm, 4–8pm Tue–Sat, 10am–3pm
Sun. ⬤ 1 Jan, 1 May, 24 Jun, 25
& 26 Dec. 🎫 🅿 by appointment.
www.museuhistoria.bcn.es

The Royal Palace was the residence of the count-kings of Barcelona from its foundation in the 13th century. The complex includes the 14th-century Gothic Saló del Tinell, a vast room with arches spanning 17 m (56 ft). This is where Isabel and Fernando (see p44) received Columbus after his triumphal return from America. It is also where the Holy Inquisition sat, believing the walls would move if lies were told.

Gothic nave of the Capella de Santa Àgata, Palau Reial

BARCELONA'S EARLY JEWISH COMMUNITY

From the 11th to the 13th centuries Jews dominated Barcelona's commerce and culture, providing doctors and founding the first seat of learning. But in 1243, 354 years after they were first documented in the city, violent anti-Semitism led to the Jews being consigned to a ghetto, El Call. Ostensibly to provide protection, the ghetto had only one entrance, which led into the Plaça de Sant Jaume. Jews were viewed by the monarch, who viewed them as "royal serfs"; but in return they also received privileges, as they handled most of Catalonia's lucrative trade with North Africa. However, official and popular persecution finally led to the disappearance of the ghetto in 1401, 91 years before Judaism was fully outlawed in Spain (see p44).

Originally there were three synagogues, the main one being in Carrer Sant Domènec del Call, but only the foundations are left. A 14th-century Hebrew tablet is embedded in the wall at No. 5 Carrer de Marlet, which reads: "Holy Foundation of Rabbi Samuel Hassardi, for whom life never ends".

Hebrew tablet

On the right, built into the Roman city wall, is the royal chapel, the Capella de Santa Àgata, with a painted wood ceiling and an altarpiece (1466) by Jaume Huguet *(see p28)*. Its bell tower is formed by part of a watchtower on the Roman wall. Stairs on the right of the altar lead to the 16th-century tower of Martí the Humanist (who reigned from 1396–1410), the last ruler of the 500-year dynasty of the count-kings of Barcelona. From the top of the tower there are fine views.

The main attraction of the Museu d'Història lies underground. Entire streets and squares of old Barcino are accessible via a lift and walkways suspended over the ruins of Roman Barcelona. The site was discovered when the Casa Clariana-Padellàs, the Gothic building from which you enter, was moved here stone by stone in 1931, as demonstrated by an extraordinary photo of the original dig towards the end of the exhibit. The water and drainage systems, baths, homes with mosaic floors, dye works, laundries and even the old forum now make up the most extensive and complete subterranean Roman ruins in the world.

Casa de la Ciutat ❹

Plaça de Sant Jaume 1. **Map** 5 A2. *Tel 93 402 73 00.* Ⓜ *Jaume I or Liceu.* ☐ *10am–1:30pm Sun (12 Feb & 23 Apr: 10am–8pm), or by appointment (93 402 73 64).*

The magnificent 14th-century city hall *(ajuntament)* faces the Palau de la Generalitat. Flanking the entrance are statues of Jaume I *(see p43)*, who granted the city rights to elect councillors in 1249, and Joan Fiveller, who levied taxes on court members in the 1500s. Inside is the huge council chamber, the 14th-century Saló de Cent, built for the city's 100 councillors. The Saló de les Cròniques was commissioned for the 1929 International Exhibition and decorated by Josep-Maria Sert *(see p29)* with murals of events in Catalan history.

Palau de la Generalitat ❺

Plaça de Sant Jaume 4. **Map** 5 A2. *Tel 93 402 46 00.* Ⓜ *Jaume I.* ☐ *23 Apr (St Jordi's Day), Sat by appointment only (call 93 402 46 17), 2nd & 4th Sun of every month: 10:30am–1:30pm.* **www.gencat.es**

Since 1403 the Generalitat has been the seat of the Catalonian Government. Above the entrance, in its Renaissance

The Italianate façade of the Palau de la Generalitat

façade, is a statue of Sant Jordi (St George) – the patron saint of Catalonia – and the Dragon. The late Catalan-Gothic courtyard is by Marc Safont (1416).

Among the fine interiors are the Gothic chapel of Sant Jordi, also by Safont, and Pere Blai's Italianate Saló de Sant Jordi. The building is open to the public only on the saint's feast day. At the back, one floor above street level, lies the *Pati dels Tarongers*, the Orange Tree Patio, by Pau Mateu, which has a bell tower built by Pere Ferrer in 1568.

The Catalan president has offices here as well as in the Casa dels Canonges. The two buildings are connected across Carrer del Bisbe by a bridge built in 1928 and modelled on the Bridge of Sighs in Venice.

The magnificent council chamber, the Saló de Cent, in the Casa de la Ciutat

Barcelona Cathedral ⑥

This compact gothic cathedral, with a
Romanesque chapel (the Capella de
Santa Llúcia) and beautiful cloister, was
begun in 1298 under Jaume II, on the
foundations of a Roman temple and
Moorish mosque. It was not finished
until the early 20th century, when the
central spire was completed. A white
marble choir screen, sculpted in the
16th century, depicts the martyrdom
of St Eulàlia, the city's patron.
Next to the font,
a plaque records
the baptism
of six native
Caribbeans, brought back
from the Americas by
Columbus in 1493.

**Statue of
St Eulàlia**

**The twin
octagonal bell
towers** date
from 1386–93.
The bells
were installed
in this tower
in 1545.

The main façade
was not completed
until 1889, and the
central spire until 1913.
It was based on the
original 1408 plans of
the French architect
Charles Galters.

Nave Interior
*The Catalan-style Gothic
interior has a single wide
nave with 28 side chapels.
These are set between the
columns supporting the
vaulted ceiling, which
rises to 26 m (85 ft).*

★ Choir Stalls
*The top tier of the beautifully
carved 15th-century stalls
contains painted coats of
arms (1518) of several
European kings.*

**Capella del Santíssim
Sagrament**
*This small chapel houses
the 16th-century Christ
of Lepanto crucifix.*

Capella de Sant Benet
This chapel, dedicated to the founder of the Benedictine Order and patron saint of Europe, houses a magnificent altarpiece showing The Transfiguration *by Bernat Martorell (1452).*

VISITORS' CHECKLIST

Plaça de la Seu. **Map** 5 A2. **Tel** *93 315 15 54.* ✈ *Jaume I.* 🚌 *17, 19, 45.* ⬜ *8am–7:30pm daily, guided tours 1–5pm.* 📷 *(free from 8am–12:45pm & 5:15–7:30pm daily).* ♿ **Sacristy Museum** ⬜ *9am–1pm, 4–7pm daily.* 📷 **Choir** ⬜ *daily.* 📷 ✝ *numerous services daily.*

★ **Crypt**
In the crypt, beneath the main altar, is the alabaster sarcophagus (1339) of St Eulàlia, martyred for her beliefs by the Romans during the 4th century AD.

★ **Cloisters**
The fountain, set in a corner of the Gothic cloisters and decorated with a statue of St George, provided fresh water.

Porta de Santa Eulàlia, entrance to cloisters

STAR SIGHTS

★ Choir Stalls
★ Crypt
★ Cloisters

The Sacristy Museum has a small treasury. Pieces include an 11th-century font, tapestries and liturgical artifacts.

Capella de Santa Llúcia

TIMELINE						
	559 Basilica dedicated to St Eulàlia and Holy Cross	**1339** St Eulàlia's relics transferred to alabaster sarcophagus			**1913** Central spire completed	
	877 St Eulàlia's remains brought here from Santa Maria del Mar	**1046–58** Romanesque cathedral built under Ramon Berenguer I		**1889** Main façade completed, based on plans dating from 1408 by architect Charles Galters		
400	**700**	**1000**	**1300**	**1600**		**1900**
4th century Original Roman (paleo-Christian) basilica built	**985** Building destroyed by the Moors	**1257–68** Romanesque Capella de Santa Llúcia built	**1493** Indians brought back from the Americas are baptized			
		1298 Gothic cathedral begun under Jaume II		*Plaque of the Caribbeans' baptism*		

La Rambla ❼

The historic avenue of La Rambla, leading to the sea, is busy around the clock, especially in the evenings and at weekends. Newsstands, caged bird and flower stalls, tarot readers, musicians and mime artists throng the wide, tree-shaded central walkway. Among its famous buildings are the Liceu Opera House, the huge Boqueria food market and some grand mansions.

Exploring La Rambla

The name of this long avenue, also known as Les Rambles, comes from the Arabic *ramla*, meaning the dried-up bed of a seasonal river. The 13th-century city wall followed the left bank of such a river that flowed from the Collserola hills to the sea. Convents, monasteries and the university were built on the other bank in the 16th century. As time passed, the riverbed was filled in and those buildings demolished, but they are remembered in the names of the five consecutive Rambles that make up the great avenue between the Port Vell and Plaça de Catalunya.

Mercat de Sant Josep Plaza de la Boqueria. **Map** 2 F3. **Tel** 93 318 20 17. Ⓜ *Liceu.* ◯ *8am–8:30pm Mon–Sat.*
Palau de la Virreina La Rambla 99. **Map** 5 A2. **Tel** 93 316 10 00. Ⓜ *Liceu.* ◯ *11am–2pm, 4–8:30pm Mon–Fri, 11am–8:30pm Sat, 11am–3pm Sun.*
Museu de Cera Pg de la Banca 7. **Map** 2 F4. **Tel** 93 317 26 49. Ⓜ *Drassanes.* ◯ *Jul–Sep: 10am–10pm daily; Oct–Jun: 10am–1:30pm & 4–7:30pm Mon–Fri, 11am–2pm & 4:30–8:30pm Sat, Sun & public hols.* 🅿 ♿

The busy, tree-lined avenue of La Rambla

Mercat de Sant Josep ⑤
Popularly known as "La Boqueria", the Mercat de Sant Josep is Barcelona's most colourful food market.

Gran Teatre del Liceu ⑦
Barcelona's opera house has had to be restored twice following damage caused by fires in 1861 and 1994.

Palau Güell ⑨
This Neo-Gothic palace, completed in 1889, is considered to be one of Gaudí's most important works (*see p62*).

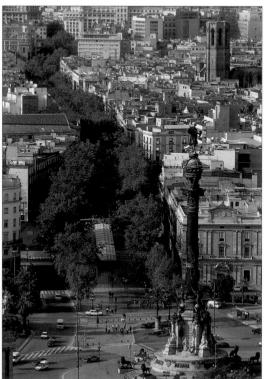

The monument to Columbus at the bottom of the tree-lined Rambla

Font de Canaletes ①
This 19th-century fountain has four taps from which to drink. Saying that someone "drinks the waters of Canaletes" indicates he or she is from Barcelona.

Reial Acadèmia de Ciències i Arts ②
Converted to a theatre in 1910, this building is the home of Barcelona's first official public clock.

Palau Moja ③
This Classical building dates back to 1790. The Baroque first-floor salon of Palau Moja is used for exhibitions.

Palau de la Virreina ④
The first person to live in this great palace in 1777, was the widowed *virreina* (viceroy's wife) of Spain in Peru.

Plaça de la Boqueria ⑥
This square features a colourful mosaic pavement by Joan Miró (1976) and an Art Deco dragon designed for a former umbrella shop.

Plaça Reial ⑧
Barcelona's most lively square was built in the 1850s and is adorned with palms. Its Neo-Classical carriage lamps were designed by Gaudí.

Museu de Cera ⑩
This waxwork museum is housed in an atmospheric, 19th-century stately home. The museum was established in 1973 and contains over 300 exhibits.

KEY

🚈	FGC train station
Ⓜ	Metro station
🅿	Parking
✚	Church

0 metres   100

0 yards   100

Palau Güell ❽

Nou de la Rambla 3–5.
Map 2 F3. **Tel** 93 317 39 74.
Liceu. ● closed until end
2006.

Gaudí's first major work in
Barcelona's city centre was
commissioned by his wealthy
patron Eusebi Güell. Güell
made it known that, even
if he was investing in an
inexperienced architect, there
would be no limit to the
budget at Gaudís disposal.

Gaudí took his patron at his
word as can be seen in the
quality of the materials used
for what was a dispropor-
tionately grand building raised
on a narrow plot in a narrow
street. The stone
work is clad with marble
and inside, high quality
woods are employed
throughout.

As in his other buildings,
Gaudí designed furniture,
lights, stained glass, and many
other fittings, working closely
with craftsmen to realise his
ideas. The house was finished
in 1889 and was used not
only as a luxurious family
home for a wealthy man but
also a place to hold political
meetings, chamber concerts
and to put up important
guests.

From the street there is little
hint of the colour and
playfulness to come in
Gaudí's mature work, except
in the spire-like chimneys
behind the parapet on the
roof. The austere façade of
Palau Güell is symmetrical
and character-ised mostly by
straight lines, both horizontal
and vertical. The only
indication of Gaudí's later
preference for curves is in the
two doorways, each formed
by a parabolic arch – a
geometric shape that he
would subsequently employ
to great effect.

Inside, the most notable
feature of the house is its very
high central room on the main
floor. Something between a
sitting room and a covered
courtyard, this central room
rises fully three floors (of a six
floor building) and is spanned
by a cupola. The other rooms
are grouped around it.

**Palau Güell's spire-like
roof chimneys**

El Raval ❾

Map 2 F3. Catalunya, Liceu.

The district of El Raval lies
west of La Rambla and
includes the old red-light area
near the port, once known as
Barri Xinès (Chinese quarter).

From the 14th century, the
city hospital was in Carrer de
l'Hospital, which still has
several herbal and medicinal
shops. Gaudí *(see p78)* was
brought here after being
fatally hit by a tram in 1926.
The buildings now house
the Biblioteca de Catalunya
(Catalonian Library), but the
elegant former dissecting
room has been fully restored.

Towards the port in Carrer
Nou de la Rambla is Gaudí's
Palau Güell. At the end of
Carrer Sant Pau is the city's
most complete Romanesque
church, the 12th-century
Sant Pau del Camp, where
resident Franciscan monks
still sing a plainsong mass.

Museu d'Art Contemporani ❿

Plaça dels Angels 1. **Map** 2 F2. **Tel** 93
412 08 10. Universitat, Catalunya.
☐ 11am–7:30pm Mon & Wed–Fri,
10am–8pm Sat, 10am–3pm Sun &
public hols. ● 1 Jan, 25 Dec.
6pm Wed & Sat, noon Sun.
www.macba.es **Centre de Cultura
Contemporània** Montalegre 5. **Tel**
93 306 41 00. **www**.cccb.org

This dramatic, glass-fronted
building was designed by the
American architect Richard
Meier. Its light, airy galleries act
as the city's contemporary art
mecca. The permanent collection of predominantly Spanish
painting, sculpture and installation from the 1950s onwards
is complemented by temporary
exhibitions from foreign artists
such as the US painter Susana
Solano and South African pho-
tojournalist David Goldblatt.

Next to the MACBA is the
**Centre de Cultura Contem-
porània**, a lively arts centre
that hosts major arts festivals
and regular shows of cutting
edge contemporary culture.

Façade of the Museu d' Art Contemporani

Although the Orfeó is now based at the more state-of-the-art L'Auditori in Plaça de les Glòries *(see p162)*, there is a concert at the Palau nearly every night; it is the main venue for the city's jazz and guitar festivals and national and international symphony orchestras regularly grace its flamboyant stage.

The Palau's new era is beginning with the completion of the work carried out by the top local architect Oscar Tusquets. An underground concert hall and an outdoor square for summer concerts are being added, consolidating the Palau's reputation as Barcelona's most loved music venue.

La Llotja ⑫

Carrer del Consolat de Mar 2. **Map** 5 B3. **Tel** *93 319 24 12 or 90 244 84 48.* ⓜ *Barceloneta.* ⬤ *closed to public.*

La Llotja (meaning commodity exchange) was built in the 1380s as the headquarters of the Consolat de Mar *(see p43)*. It was remodelled in Neo-Classical style in 1771 and housed the city's stock exchange until 1994, the original Gothic hall acting as the main trading room. It can still be seen through the windows.

The upper floors housed the Barcelona School of Fine Arts from 1849 to 1970, attended by the young Picasso and Joan Miró *(see p29)*. It is now occupied by local government offices.

Glorious stained-glass dome, Palau de la Música Catalana

Palau de la Música Catalana ⑪

Carrer de Sant Francesc de Paula 2. **Map** 5 B1. **Tel** *90 244 28 82.* ⓜ *Urquinaona.* ⬤ *Sep–Jun: 10am–3:30pm daily; Jul–Aug: 10am–6pm daily; and for concerts.* 🎫♿📷 *on the hour in English. Booking recommended.* **www.**palaumusica.org

This is a real palace of music, a Modernista celebration of tilework, sculpture and glorious stained glass. It is the only concert hall in Europe lit by natural light. Designed by Lluís Domènech i Montaner, it was completed in 1908. Although a few extensions have been added, the building still retains its original appearance. The elaborate red-brick façade is hard to appreciate fully in the confines of the narrow street. It is lined with mosaic-covered pillars topped by busts of the great composers Palestrina, Bach and Beethoven. The large stone sculpture of St George and

other figures at the corner of the building portrays an allegory from Catalan folksong by Miquel Blay.

But it is the interior of the building that is truly inspiring. The auditorium is lit by a huge inverted dome of stained glass depicting angelic choristers. The sculptures of composers Wagner and Clavé on the proscenium arch that frames the stage area were designed by Domènech but finished by Pau Gargallo. The stunning "Muses of the Palau", the group of 18 highly stylized, instrument-playing maidens are the stage's backdrop. Made of terracotta and trencadís (broken pieces of ceramic) they have become the buildings most admired feature.

The work of Josep Anselm Clavé (1824–74) in promoting Catalan song led to the creation of the Orfeó Català choral society in 1891, a focus of Catalan nationalism and the inspiration behind the Palau.

Statue of Poseidon in the courtyard of La Llotja

A wedding service in the Gothic interior of Santa Maria del Mar

Museu Picasso ⓭

Carrer Montcada 15–23. **Map** 5 B2.
Tel 93 319 63 10. Ⓜ Jaume I.
☐ 10am–7:30pm Tue–Sat & public
hols, 10am–2:30pm Sun. ◑ 1 Jan,
Good Fri, 1 May, 24 Jun, 25 & 26 Dec.
🎫 free 1st Sun of month. ♿
www.museupicasso.bcn.es

The popular Picasso Museum
is housed in five adjoining
medieval palaces on Carrer
Montcada: Berenguer d'Aguilar,
Baró de Castellet, Meca, Mauri
and Finestres.
  The museum opened in 1963
showing works donated by
Jaime Sabartes, a friend of
Picasso. Following Sabartes'
death in 1968, Picasso himself
donated paintings, including
early examples. He also left
graphic works in his will and
ceramics were given by his
widow, Jacqueline.
  The strength of the 3,000-
piece collection are Picasso's
early works. These show how,
even at the age of 15, he was
painting major works such as
The First Communion (1896)
and *Science and Charity* (1897).
There are a few works from his
Blue and Rose periods. Most
famous is his series of 44 paintings, *Las Meninas*, inspired by
Velázquez's masterpiece.

Basílica de Santa Maria del Mar ⓮

Pl Sta Maria 1. **Map** 5 B3. *Tel* 93
310 23 90. Ⓜ Jaume I. ☐ 9am–
1:30pm & 4:30–8pm daily (10am Sun).

This beautiful building, the
city's favourite church with
superb acoustics for concerts, is
the only example of a church
entirely in the Catalan Gothic
style. It took just 55 years to
build, with money donated by
merchants and shipbuilders.
The speed – unrivalled in the
Middle Ages – gave it a unity
of style both inside and out.

Pablo Picasso, *Self-Portrait* in
charcoal (1899–1900)

PABLO PICASSO IN BARCELONA

Picasso (1881–1973) was 13 when he arrived in Barcelona,
where his father, José Ruiz y Blasco, had found work
teaching in the city art school situated above the Llotja. The
city was rich, but it also possessed a large, poor working
class which was becoming organized and starting to rebel.
Shortly after the family's arrival, a bomb was thrown into a
Corpus Christi procession. They settled at No 3 Carrer de
la Mercè, a gloomy, five-storeyed house not far from the
Llotja. Picasso's precocious talent gave him admittance to the
upper school, where all the other pupils were aged at least
20. Here he immediately made friends with another artist,
Manuel Pallarès Grau, and the two lost their virginity to the
whores of Carrer d'Avinyó, who were to inspire *Les
Demoiselles d'Avignon* (1906–7), considered by many art
critics to be the wellspring of modern art. Picasso travelled
with Pallarès to the Catalan's home town of Horta, where he
painted some early landscapes, now in the Museu Picasso.
The two remained friends for the rest of their lives.

The west front has a 15th-century rose window of the Coronation of the Virgin. More stained glass, dating from the 15th to the 18th centuries, lights the wide nave and high aisles.

When the choir and furnishings were burned in the Civil War *(see p46)*, it added to the sense of space and simplicity.

Museu de la Xocolata 🟦

Comerç 36. **Map** 5 C2. *Tel 93 268 78 78.* 🚇 *Jaume I, Arc de Triomf.* ☐ 10am–7pm Mon, Wed–Sat, 10am–3pm Sun & pub hols. ☐ 1 Jan, 1 May, 25 & 26 Dec. 🎟 free 1st Sun of month. 🅮 🅲 by appointment. ☐ **www.**museudelaxocolata.com

Founded by Barcelona's chocolate and pastry-makers union, this museum takes you through the history of one of the most universally-loved foodstuffs: from the discovery of cocoa in South America to the invention of the first chocolate machine in Barcelona. This is done using old posters, photographs and footage. The real thing is displayed in a homage to the art of the *mona*. A Catalan invention, this was a traditional easter cake that over the centuries evolved into an edible sculpture. Every year, pastissers compete for the most imaginative piece, decorating their chocolate versions of well-known buildings or folk figures with jewels, feathers and other materials.

Arc del Triomf 🟦

Passeig Lluís Companys. **Map** 5 C1. 🚇 *Arc de Triomf.*

The main gateway to the 1888 Universal Exhibition, which filled the Parc de la Ciutadella, was designed by Josep Vilaseca i Casanovas. It is built of brick in Mudéjar (Spanish Moorish) style, with sculpted allegories of crafts, industry and business. The frieze by Josep Reynés on the main façade represents the city welcoming foreign visitors.

The pink brick façade of the late 19th-century Arc del Triomf

Parc de la Ciutadella 🟦

Avda del Marquès de l'Argentera. **Map** 6 D2. 🚇 *Barceloneta, Ciutadella-Vila Ollmpica.* ☐ 8am–10:30pm daily. 🅮

This popular park has a boating lake, orange groves and parrots living in the palm trees. It was once the site of a massive star-shaped citadel, built for Felipe V between 1715 and

1720 following a 13-month siege of the city *(see p45).* The fortress was intended to house soldiers to keep law and order, but was never used for this purpose. Converted into a prison, the citadel became notorious during the Napoleonic occupation *(see p45),* and, during the 19th-century liberal repressions, it was hated as a symbol of centralized power. In 1878, under General Prim, whose statue stands in the middle of the park, the citadel was pulled down and the park given to the city, to become, in 1888, the venue of the Universal Exhibition *(see p46).* Three buildings survived: the Governor's Palace, now a school; the chapel; and the arsenal, which continues to be occupied by the Catalan parliament.

The park offers more cultural and leisure activities than any other in the city and is particularly popular on Sunday afternoons when people gather to play instruments, dance and relax, or visit the museums and zoo. A variety of works by Catalan sculptors such as Marès, Arnau, Carbonell, Clarà, Llimona, Gargallo, Dunyac and Fuxà, can be seen in the park, alongside work by modern artists such as Tàpics and Botero.

The gardens in the Plaça de Armes boast a triumphal arch designed by architect Josep Fontseré, with the help of Antoni Gaudí, then still a young student.

Ornamental cascade in the Parc de la Ciutadella designed by Josep Fontseré and Antoni Gaudí

Museu de Zoologia ⑱

Passeig de Picasso. **Map** 5 C2.
Tel 93 319 69 12. 🚇 *Arc de Triomf*
or Jaume I. ⬚ *10am–3pm Tue–Sun*
& public hols (Thu till 6:30pm). 🖼
♿ 📷 *by appointment.*
www.museuzoologia.bcn.es

At the entrance to the Parc
de la Ciutadella is the fortress-
like Castell dels Tres Dragons
(Castle of the Three Dragons),
named after a play by Frederic
Soler that was popular at the
time it was built.

This crenellated brick edifice
was built by Lluís Domènech
i Montaner for the 1888
Universal Exhibition. His inspiration was Valencia's Gothic
commodities exchange. He
later used the building as a
workshop for Modernista
design, and it became a focus
of the movement. The building
served as a cafe-restaurant
during the Universal Exhibition.
Shortly afterwards it housed
the History Museum and it

**One of the galleries inside the
spacious Museu de Zoologia**

was not until 1910, when a
fishing exhibition was held
here, that specimens from the
natural sciences began to
appear. In 1917 it became the
Museum of Catalonia, where
flora, fauna and geological
collections were displayed. It
later housed the Biology
Museum and since 1937 the
building has been home to
the Zoological Museum. The
Museu de Zoologia and the
Museu de Geologia collectively
form Barcelona's Museum of
Natural Science.

Children peering into an animal enclosure at the Parc Zoològic

Museu de Geologia ⑲

Parc de la Ciutadella.
Map 5 C3. **Tel** 93 319 68 95.
🚇 *Arc de Triomf, Jaume I.*
⬚ *10am–3pm Tue–Sun & public*
hols (Thu till 6:30pm). ⬤ *1 Jan,*
Good Fri, 1 May, 25 & 26 Dec.
🖼 📷 *10:30am Sun.*
www.museugeologia.bcn.es
The Museu de Geologia,
Barcelona's oldest museum,
opened in 1882, the same
year the Parc de la Ciutadella
became a public space. The
origin of the museum goes
back to the Martorell
Museum, founded in 1878
to house the natural science
and archaeological collection
bequeathed by Francesc
Martorell i Peña to the city
of Barcelona. This Neo-
Classical building, designed
by architect Antoni Rovira
i Trias, was the city's first
public museum.

Today, the museum boasts
a large collection of fossils
and minerals, including specimens from Catalonia. Beside
it is the Hivernacle,
a glasshouse by Josep
Amargós now used for
concerts, and the Umbracle, a
brick and wood conser-
vatory by the park's architect,
Josep Fontseré. Both date
from 1884.

Parc Zoològic ⑳

Parc de la Ciutadella. **Map** 6 D3.
Tel 93 225 67 80. 🚇 *Ciutadella-Vila*
Olímpica. ⬚ *Oct–Feb: 10am–5pm,*
Mar: 10am–6pm, Apr & Sep: 10am–
7pm, May–Aug: 9:30am–7:30pm.
🖼 ♿ **www**.zoobarcelona.com

This zoo was laid out in the
1940s to a relatively enlight-
ened design – the animals
are separated by moats
instead of bars. Dolphin
and whale shows are held

Hivernacle glasshouse, Museu de Geologia

Yachts at the Port Olímpic overlooked by Spain's two tallest skyscrapers

in one of the aquariums. The zoo is very child-friendly with pony rides, electric cars and a train. Roig i Soler's 1885 sculpture by the entrance, *The Lady with the Umbrella (see p17)*, has become a symbol of Barcelona.

Port Olímpic ㉑

Map 6 F4. Ⓜ *Ciutadella-Vila Olímpica.*

The most dramatic rebuilding for the 1992 Olympics was the demolition of the old industrial waterfront and the laying out of 4 km (2 miles) of promenade and pristine sandy beaches. Suddenly Barcelona seemed like a seaside resort. At the heart of the project was a 65-ha (160-acre) new estate of 2,000 apartments and parks called Nova Icària. The area is still popularly known as the Vila Olímpica because the buildings originally housed the Olympic athletes.

The sole building of Barcelona's Old Port still standing is the former General Stores building. The Stores were designed in 1881 by the engineer Maurici Garrán and were intended for use as trading depots. They were refurbished in 1992 and today house the Museu d'Història de Catalunya *(see pp68–9)*.

On the sea front there are twin 44-floor buildings,

Spain's tallest skyscrapers, one occupied by offices, the other by the Arts hotel *(see p135)*. They stand beside the Port Olímpic, which was also built for 1992. This has shops and nightclubs, but the main reasons for visiting are two levels of restaurants around the marina which have made it the latest popular place to eat out. The wonderful outdoor setting attracts business people at lunchtime and pleasure seekers in the evenings and at weekends.

Lunch can be walked off along the string of beaches that is edged by a palmfringed promenade with

Sandy, palm-fringed beach at Barcelona's Port Olímpic

cafés. Behind it, the new coastal road heads around a park that lies beside the last three beaches, divided by rocky breakwaters. Swimming is safe on the gently sloping, sandy strands.

Barceloneta ㉒

Map 5 B5. Ⓜ *Barceloneta.*

Barcelona's fishing "village", which lies on a triangular tongue of land jutting into the sea just below the city centre, is renowned for its little restaurants and cafés. Its beach is also the closest to the city centre and is well equipped with lifeguards, disabled access, showers and play areas for children.

The area was designed in 1753 by the architect and military engineer Juan Martín de Cermeño to rehouse people made homeless by the construction, just inland, of the Ciutadella fortress *(see pp64–5)*. Since then it has housed largely workers and fishermen. Laid out in a grid system with narrow two- and three-storey houses, in which each room has a window on the street, the area has a friendly, intimate air.

In the small Plaça de la Barceloneta, at the centre of the district, is the Baroque church of Sant Miquel del Port, also by Cermeño. A market is often held in the square here.

Today, Barceloneta's fishing fleet is still based in the nearby Moll del Rellotge (the clock dock), by a small clock tower. On the opposite side of this harbour is the Torre de Sant Sebastià, terminus of the cable car that runs right across the port, via the World Trade Centre, to Montjuïc.

Fishing boat moored in Barceloneta harbour

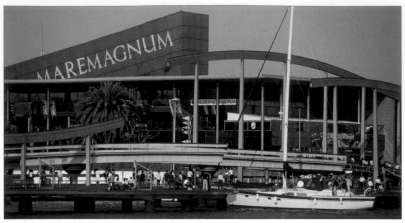

Maremàgnum shopping complex on the Moll d'Espanya, Port Vell

Port Vell ㉓

Map 5 A4.
Ⓜ Barceloneta, Drassanes.

Barcelona's marina is located at the foot of La Rambla, just beyond the old customs house. This was built in 1902 at the Portal de la Pau, the city's former maritime entrance. To the south, the Moll de Barcelona, with a new World Trade Centre, serves as the passenger pier for visiting liners. In front of the customs house, La Rambla is connected to the yacht clubs on the Moll d'Espanya by a swing bridge and a pedestrian jetty, known as La Rambla de Mar. The Moll d'Espanya boasts a vast new shopping and restaurant complex known as the Maremàgnum. Also on the Moll d'Espanya is an IMAX cinema and one of the largest aquariums in Europe.

On the shore, the Moll de Fusta (Timber Wharf), with terrace cafés, has red structures inspired by the bridge at Arles painted by Van Gogh. At the end of the wharf is *El Cap de Barcelona (Barcelona Head)*, a 20-m (66-ft) tall sculpture by Pop artist Roy Lichtenstein.

The attractive Sports Marina on the other side of the Moll d'Espanya was once lined with warehouses. The only one left, built by Elies Rogent in the 1880s, has been given a new lease of life as the Palau de Mar. Restaurants provide alfresco dining, but the building is otherwise given over to the Museu d'Història de Catalunya.

Spectacular glass viewing tunnel at the aquarium, Port Vell

Aquarium ㉔

Moll d'Espanya. **Map** 5 B4. Ⓜ Barceloneta, Drassanes. **Tel** 93 221 74 74. ◯ 9:30am–9pm daily (to 9:30pm Sat, Sun & Jun, Sep). 🖼 ♿ 🗹 www.aquariumbcn.com

Populated by over 11,000 organisms belonging to 450 different species, Barcelona's aquarium is one of the biggest in Europe. Occupying three levels of a glass building, the aquarium focusses particularly on the local Mediterranean coast. Two nature reserves, for instance, the Delta del Ebro and the Medes isles off the Costa Brava, are given a tank apiece. Tropical seas are also represented and moving platforms ferry visitors through a glass tunnel under an "ocean" of sharks, rays and sunfish. A large hall of activities for children includes an irregularly shaped tank of rays built around an island which is reached through crawl-through glass tunnels.

Museu d'Història de Catalunya ㉕

Plaça Pau Vila 3. **Map** 5 A4. Ⓜ Barceloneta, Drassanes. **Tel** 93 225 47 00. ◯ 10am–7pm Tue, Thu–Sat, 10am–8pm Wed, 10am–2:30pm Sun & public hols. 🖼 except 1st Sun every month. ♿ 🗹 by appointment (93 225 42 44). www.mhcat.net

This intelligently planned museum charts the history of Catalonia, from Lower Palaeolithic times through to the region's heydays as a maritime power and industrial pioneer. Second floor exhibits

Café-lined façade of the Museu d'Història de Catalunya

include the Moorish invasion, Romanesque architecture, medieval monastic life and the rise of Catalan seafaring. Third floor exhibits cover the industrial revolution and the impact of steam power and electricity on the economy. There is also a glass floor laid over a relief map of Catalonia which visitors can walk over. The first floor is reserved for temporary exhibits. All captions are helpfully in Catalan, Spanish and English.

A *golondrina* tour boat departing from the Portal de la Pau

The Columbus Monument lit by fireworks during La Mercè fiesta

Monument a Colom ㉖

Plaça del Portal de la Pau. **Map** 2 F4.
Tel 93 302 52 24. Ⓜ *Drassanes.* ☐
Oct–Mar: 10am–1:30pm & 3:30–6:30pm Mon–Fri, 10am–6:30pm Sat, Sun & public hols; Apr–May: 10am–1:30pm & 3:30–7:30pm Mon–Fri, 10am–7:30pm Sat, Sun & public hols; Jun–Sep: 9am–8:30pm daily. 🎦

The Columbus monument at the bottom of La Rambla was designed by Gaietà Buigas for the 1888 Universal Exhibition *(see p46)*. At that time Catalans considered Columbus to be Catalan rather than Italian.

The 60-m (200-ft) monument marks the spot where Columbus stepped ashore in 1493 after discovering America, bringing with him six Caribbean Indians. He was given a state welcome by the Catholic Monarchs in the Saló del Tinell *(see p56)*. The Indians' subsequent conversion to Christianity is commemorated in the cathedral *(see pp58–9)*.

A lift leads to a viewing platform at the top of the monument. The bronze statue was designed by Rafael Arché.

Golondrinas ㉗

Plaça del Portal de la Pau.
Map 2 F5. *Tel 93 442 31 06.*
Ⓜ *Drassanes.* **Departures:**
variable (phone for details). 🎦
www.lasgolondrinas.com

Sightseeing trips around Barcelona's harbour and to the Port Olímpic can be made on *golondrinas* ("swallows") – small double-decker boats that moor in front of the Columbus Monument at the foot of La Rambla.

Half-hour tours go out beneath the castle-topped hill of Montjuïc towards the industrial port. They usually stop off at the breakwater, which reaches out to sea from Barceloneta, to allow passengers to disembark for a stroll. A one-and-a-half hour trip takes in Barcelona harbour, the local beaches and finally Port Olímpic.

Museu Marítim and Drassanes ㉘

Avinguda de les Drassanes.
Map 2 F4. *Tel 93 342 99 20.*
Ⓜ *Drassanes.* ☐ *10am–7pm Mon–Sun.* ⬤ *1 & 6 Jan, 25 & 26 Dec.* 🎦 🅱 🎦 *by appointment.*
www.diba.es/mmaritim

The great galleys that were instrumental in making Barcelona a major seafaring power were built in the sheds of the Drassanes (shipyards) that now house the maritime

museum. These royal dry docks are the largest and most complete surviving medieval complex of their kind in the world. They were founded in the mid-13th century, when dynastic marriages uniting the kingdoms of Sicily and Aragón meant that better maritime communications between the two became a priority. Three of the yards' four original corner towers survive.

Among the vessels to slip from the Drassanes' vaulted halls was the *Real*, flagship of Don Juan of Austria, who led the Christian fleet to the famous victory against the Turks at Lepanto in 1571. The highlight of the museum's collection is a full-scale replica decorated in red and gold.

The *Llibre del Consolat de Mar*, a book of nautical codes and practice, is a reminder that Catalonia was once the arbiter of Mediterranean maritime law *(see p43)*. There are pre-Columbian maps, including one from 1439 that was used by Amerigo Vespucci.

Stained-glass window in the Museu Marítim

EIXAMPLE

Barcelona claims to have the greatest collection of Art Nouveau buildings of any city in Europe. The style, known in Catalonia as Modernisme, flourished after 1854, when it was decided to tear down the medieval walls to allow the city to develop into what had previously been a construction-free military zone.

The designs of the civil engineer Ildefons Cerdà i Sunyer (1815–76) were chosen for the new expansion *(eixample)* inland. These plans called for a rigid grid system of streets, but at each intersection the corners were chamfered to allow the buildings there to overlook the junctions or squares. The few exceptions

Jesus of the Column, Sagrada Família

to this grid system include the Diagonal, a main avenue running from the wealthy area of Pedralbes down to the sea, and the Hospital de la Santa Creu i de Sant Pau by Modernista architect Domènech i Montaner (1850–1923). He hated the grid system and deliberately angled the hospital to look down the diagonal Avinguda de Gaudí towards Antoni Gaudí's church of the Sagrada Família, the city's most spectacular Modernista building *(see pp80–3)*. The wealth of Barcelona's commercial elite, and their passion for all things new, allowed them to give free rein to the age's most innovative architects in designing their residences as well as public buildings.

SIGHTS AT A GLANCE

Museums and Galleries
Fundació Antoni Tàpies **3**

Churches
Sagrada Família pp80-3 **7**

Modernista Buildings
Casa Batlló **1**
Casa Milà, "La Pedrera" **4**
Casa Terrades, "Casa de les Punxes" **5**
Hospital de la Santa Creu i de Sant Pau **6**
Mansana de la Discòrdia **2**

GETTING THERE
Metro line 3 has stations at either end of the Passeig de Gràcia (Catalunya and Diagonal), and one in the middle, at the Illa de la Discòrdia (Passeig de Gràcia). Metro line 5 takes you straight to the Sagrada Família and Hospital de Sant Pau (a long walk from other sights).

KEY

- Street-by-Street map pp194-5
- Ⓜ Metro station
- 🚆 Train station
- 🚌 Main bus stop
- ℹ Tourist information

0 metres 500
0 yards 500

◁ Nativity façade of the Sagrada Família – the only façade to be more or less completed in Gaudí's lifetime

Street-by-Street: Quadrat d'Or

The hundred or so city blocks centring on the Passeig de Gràcia are known as the Quadrat d'Or, "Golden Square", because they contain so many of the best Modernista buildings *(see pp24–5)*. This was the area within the Eixample favoured by the wealthy bourgeoisie, who embraced the new artistic and architectural style with enthusiasm, not only for their residences, but also for commercial buildings. Most remarkable is the Mansana de la Discòrdia, a single block with houses by Modernisme's most illustrious exponents. Many interiors can be visited by the public, revealing a feast of stained glass, ceramics and ornamental ironwork.

Perfume bottle, Museu del Perfum

Diagonal Metro

Vinçon home decor store *(see p155)*

Passeig de Gràcia, the Eixample's main avenue, is a showcase of highly original buildings and smart shops. The graceful street lamps are by Pere Falqués (1850–1916).

RAMBLA DE CATALUNYA

PASSEIG DE GRÀCIA

Fundació Tàpies
Topped by Antoni Tàpies' wire sculpture Cloud and Chair, *this 1879 building by Domènech i Montaner houses a wide variety of Tàpies' paintings, graphics and sculptures* ❷

Casa Amatller

Museu del Perfum

Casa Ramon Mulleras

★ **Mansana de la Discòrdia**
In this city block, four of Barcelona's most famous Modernista houses vie for attention. All were created between 1900 and 1910. This ornate tower graces the Casa Lleó Morera by Domènech i Montaner ❶

To Plaça de Catalunya

Casa Batlló

Casa Lleó Morera

Passeig de Gràcia Metro

Palau Baró de Quadras was designed by Puig i Cadafalch in 1904 in a neo-Gothic style. The ornate façade is riddled with grotesque sculptures including this one, which adorns the doorway.

LOCATOR MAP
See Street Finder map 3

EIXAMPLE

OLD TOWN

AVINGUDA DIAGONAL

CARRER DE PAU CLARIS

CARRER DE PROVENÇA

CARRER DE LLÚRIA

CARRER DE MALLORCA

CARRER DE ROGER DE LLÚRIA

CARRER DEL BRUC

CARRER DE VALÈNCIA

CARRER D'ARAGÓ

Casa Thomas

To Sagrada Família

Palau Ramon de Montaner

Casa Terrades "Les Punxes"
Built in red brick with carved stone ornamentation, this 1905 house by Puig i Cadafalch echoes the Gothic buildings of northern Europe ❹

★ Casa Milà
Gaudí put all his architectural daring into this, his most famous house. The result is a remarkable wave-like façade and a roofscape of chimneys and vents resembling abstract sculptures ❸

0 metres 100
0 yards 100

KEY
— — — Suggested route

STAR SIGHTS

★ Mansana de la Discòrdia

★ Casa Milà

Casa Batlló ❶

Unlike Gaudí's other works, this block of flats, commissioned by Josep Batlló i Casanovas on the prestigious Passeig de Gracia, was a conversion of an existing building. With its reworked façade in stunning organic forms and its fantastic chimneys and rooftop, it looks as bold and convention-defying today as it did when it was finished in 1906. Inside, Gaudí's integral approach to architecture can be seen in the ventilators incorporated into the doors and windows. The building has been said to symbolise the legend of St George killing the dragon, whose scaly back arches above the main façade.

View of façade and Dragon's Back

★ **The Chimneys**
Extraordinary chimneys, usually the unseen and functional parts of a building, have become Gaudí's trademark. These fine examples are tightly-packed and covered in abstract patterns.

Terrace and Rear Façade
This outdoor space at the back of the house allows a view of the rear façade which has cast iron balconies and superbly colourful trencadis *work at the top.*

Attics
The closely-packed brick arches supporting the roof are plastered and painted white giving the sensation of being inside the skeleton of a large animal.

Stairs to main floor

Dining Room
The bulbous forms in the ceiling of the Battló family's dining room are thought to represent the splash caused by a drop of water.

STAR SIGHTS

★ Main Drawing Room

★ The Chimneys

★ The Dragon's Back

★ The Dragon's Back
One of the most extra-ordinary innovations to the house is this steep, narrow, colourfully-tiled cap above the façade which it is difficult to see as anything other than the spine of a reptile. Inside it is a white domed room which was used as a water deposit.

VISITORS' CHECKLIST

Passeig de Gràcia 43.
Map 3 A4.
Tel 93 216 03 06.
Ⓜ *Passeig de Gracia.*
🕐 9am–8pm daily. 🎫 🎧
www.casabatllo.es

Patio
The patio of the original building was enlarged to provide maximum natural light.

The cross
The ceramic cross was made in Mallorca but was damaged in transit. Gaudí liked the cracked effect and refused to send it back for repair. The arms point to the four cardinal points of the compass.

Dragon's belly room

The iron balconies have been likened to masks in carnival processions.

Trencadis decorations

Façade
Salvador Dali saw the curving walls and windows as "representing waves on a stormy day". The spindly, individually shaped columns across the first floor windows were also compared to tibias, earning Casa Batlló the nickname, "House of Bones".

Entrance

Fireplace room
Josep Batlló's former office has a mushroom-shaped fireplace tiled in earthy colours.

★ Main Drawing Room
One side of this room is formed by stained-glass windows looking out over the Passeig de Gracia. The ceiling plaster is moulded into a spiral and the doors and window-frames undulate playfully.

Sumptuous interior of the Casa Lleó Morera, Mansana de la Discòrdia

Mansana de la Discòrdia ➋

Passeig de Gràcia, between Carrer d'Aragó and Carrer del Consell de Cent. **Map** 3 A4. ⓜ *Passeig de Gràcia.* **Centre del Modernisme** Casa Amatller, Passeig de Gràcia 41. *Tel 93 488 01 39.* ⏰ *10am–7pm Mon–Sat, 10am–2pm Sun & public hols.* 🖼

Barcelona's most famous group of Modernista *(see pp24–5)* buildings illustrates the wide range of styles used by the movement's architects. They lie in an area known as the Mansana de la Discòrdia (Block of Discord), after the startling visual argument between them. The three finest were remodelled in the Modernista style from existing houses early in the 20th century. No. 35 Passeig de Gràcia is Casa Lleó Morera (1902–6), the first residential work of Lluís Domènech i Montaner. A shop was installed in the ground floor in 1943, but the Modernista interiors upstairs, with their magnificent stained glass bay windows, still exist. The house is not open to the public but if the door is open

it is possible to see the painted ceiling of the hallway.

Beyond the next two houses is Casa Amatller, designed by Puig i Cadafalch in 1898. Its façade, under a stepped gable roof, features a harmonious blend of Moorish and Gothic windows. The ground floor of the house contains the reception desk and shop for the Ruta del Modernisme

(see pp26–7). The entrance patio, with its spiral columns, and the staircase covered by a stained glass skylight can be seen but the rest of the building, including the beautiful wood-panelled library, is occupied by the Institut Amatller d'Art Hispànic and is not open to the public. The third house in the block is Antoni Gaudí's Casa Batlló *(see pp76–7)* with its fluid façade evoking marine or natural forms.

Fundació Antoni Tàpies ➌

Carrer d'Aragó 255. **Map** 3 A4. *Tel 93 487 03 15.* ⓜ *Passeig de Gràcia.* ⏰ *10am–8pm Tue–Sun & public hols.* ⬤ *1 & 6 Jan, 25 & 26 Dec.* 🎫 *(free to under 16s).* ♿ **www**.fundaciotapies.org

Antoni Tàpies *(see p29),* born in 1923, is Barcelona's best-known living artist. Inspired by Surrealism, his abstract work is executed in a variety of materials, including concrete and metal *(see pp72–3).* Difficult to appreciate at first, the exhibits should help viewers obtain a clearer perspective of Tàpies' work. The collection is housed in Barcelona's first domestic building to be constructed with iron (1880), designed by Domènech i Montaner for his brother's publishing firm.

ANTONI GAUDÍ (1852–1926)

Born in Reus (Tarragona) into an artisan family, Antoni Gaudí i Cornet was the leading exponent of Catalan Modernisme. After a blacksmith's apprenticeship, he studied at Barcelona's School of Architecture. Inspired by a nationalistic search for a romantic medieval past, his work was supremely original. His first major achievement was the Casa Vicens (1888) at No. 24 Carrer de les Carolines *(see p26).* But his most celebrated building is the church of the Sagrada Família *(see pp80–83),* to which he devoted his life from 1914. When he had put all his money into the project, he went from house to house begging for more. He was killed by a tram in 1926 *(see p60).*

Decorated chimneypot, Casa Vicens

The rippled façade of Gaudí's apartment building, Casa Milà

and gables are influenced in particular by the Gothic architecture of northern Europe. However, the deeply carved, floral stone ornamentation of the exterior, in combination with red brick used as the principal building material, are typically Modernista.

Hospital de la Santa Creu i de Sant Pau ❻

Carrer de Sant Antoni Maria Claret 167, 08025 Barcelona. **Map** 4 F1. **Tel** 93 291 91 99. Ⓜ *Hospital de Sant Pau.* **Grounds** ☐ *daily; write in advance for permission to visit pavilions not in medical use.* ♿ ✔ *93 488 20 78.* www.hspau.com

Lluis Domènech i Montaner began designing a new city hospital in 1902. His innovative scheme consisted of 26 attractive Mudéjar-style pavilions set in large gardens, as he believed that patients would recover better among fresh air and trees. All the connecting corridors and service areas were hidden underground. Also believing art and colour to be therapeutic, he decorated the pavilions profusely.

The turreted roofs were tiled with ceramics, and the reception pavilion embellished with mosaic murals and sculptures by Pau Gargallo. After his death, the project was completed in 1930 by Domènech's son, Pere.

Casa Milà ❹

Passeig de Gràcia 92. **Map** 3 B3. **Tel** 90 240 09 73. Ⓜ *Diagonal.* ☐ *10am–8pm daily.* ● *1 & 6 Jan, 25 & 26 Dec.* ▨ ✔ *daily at 4pm in English.* www.obrasocial.caixacatalunya.es

Usually called *La Pedrera* (the Stone Quarry), the Casa Milà is Gaudí's greatest contribution to Barcelona's civic architecture, and his last work before he devoted himself entirely to the Sagrada Família *(see pp80–83)*.

Built between 1906–10, *La Pedrera* departed from established construction principles and, as a result, was ridiculed by Barcelona's intellectuals.

Gaudí designed this eight floor apartment block around two circular courtyards. It features the city's first underground car park. The ironwork balconies, by Josep Maria Jujol, are like seaweed against the wave-like walls of white stone. There are no straight walls anywhere in the building.

The Milà family had an apartment on the first floor, which now features a typical *Modernista* interior. The museum, "El Espai Gaudí", on the top floor, includes models and explanations of Gaudí's work. From here, visitors can access the extraordinary roof. The sculptured ducts and chimneys have such a threatening appearance they are known as *espanta-bruixes*, or witch-scarers.

Casa Terrades ❺

Avinguda Diagonal 416. **Map** 3 B3. Ⓜ *Diagonal.* ● *to public.*

This free-standing, six-sided apartment block by Modernista architect Josep Puig i Cadafalch gets its nickname, *Casa de les Punxes* (House of the Points), from the spires on its six corner turrets. It was built between 1903 and 1905 by converting three existing houses on the site and was Puig's largest work. It is an eclectic mixture of medieval and Renaissance styles. The towers

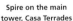

Spire on the main tower, Casa Terrades

Statue of the Virgin, Hospital de la Santa Creu i de Sant Pau

Sagrada Família ❼

Bell Towers
Eight of the 12 spires, one for each apostle, have been built. Each is topped by Venetian mosaics.

A carved whelk

Europe's most unconventional church, the Temple Expiatori de la Sagrada Família, is an emblem of a city that likes to think of itself as individualistic. Crammed with symbolism inspired by nature and striving for originality, it is the greatest work of Gaudí *(see pp24–5)*. In 1883, a year after work had begun on a Neo-Gothic church on the site, the task of completing it was given to Gaudí who changed everything, extemporizing as he went along. It became his life's work and he lived like a recluse on the site for 16 years. He is buried in the crypt. At his death only one tower on the Nativity façade had been completed, but work resumed after the Civil War and several more have since been finished to his original plans. Work continues today, financed by public subscription.

THE FINISHED CHURCH

Gaudí's initial ambitions have been scaled down over the years, but the design for the completion of the building remains impressive. Still to come is the central tower, which is to be encircled by four large towers representing the Evangelists. Four towers on the Glory (south) façade will match the existing four on the Passion (west) and Nativity (east) façades. An ambulatory – like an inside-out cloister – will run round the outside of the building.

Tower with lift

The apse was the first part of the church Gaudí completed. Stairs lead down from here to the crypt below.

The altar canopy, designed by Gaudí, is still waiting for the altar.

★ Passion Façade
This bleak façade was completed in the late 1980s by artist Josep Maria Subirachs. A controversial work, its sculpted figures are angular and often sinister.

Main entrance

Spiral Staircases
Steep stone steps – 400 in each – allow access to the towers and upper galleries. Majestic views reward those who climb or take the lift.

VISITORS' CHECKLIST

C/ Mallorca 401. **Map** 4 E3. *Tel* 93 207 30 31. Ⓜ *Sagrada Família.* 🚌 *19, 34, 43, 50, 51, 54.* ⏰ *Apr–Sep: 9am–8pm (to 6pm Nov–Feb, to 7pm Mar–Oct) daily (25 & 26 Dec: 9am–2pm).* 🔔 *1 & 6 Jan.* ✝ *numerous services daily.* 📷 🚫 ♿ *except crypt & towers.* **www**.sagradafamilia.org

★ Nativity Façade
The most complete part of Gaudí's church, finished in 1904, has doorways which represent Faith, Hope and Charity. Scenes of the Nativity and Christ's childhood are embellished with symbolism, such as doves representing the congregation.

Tower with lift

★ Crypt
The crypt, where Gaudí is buried, was built by the original architect, Francesc de Paula Villar i Lozano, in 1882. This is where services are held. On the lower floor a museum traces the careers of both architects and the church's history.

Nave
In the nave, which is still under construction, a forest of fluted pillars will support four galleries above the side aisles, while skylights let in natural light.

Entrance to Crypt Museum

STAR FEATURES

★ Passion Façade

★ Nativity Façade

★ Crypt

Passion Façade

It has been said that the Sagrada Família is like a book in stone: meant to be read in the same way as a medieval cathedral, with each element representing a Biblical event or aspect of Christian faith. This was certainly Gaudí's intent: his architecture was inseparable from the profound Catholicism which inspired it. The temple is dedicated to the Sagrada Família, the Holy Family.

Gargoyle on Sagrada Família

Detail on brass door of the Passion façade

The two existing façades are detailed, visual accounts of two key Bible passages. The Glory façade (yet to be built) will address the theme of judgement of sinners.

Main entrance to the Passion façade

Christ's Passion

The Passion façade depicts the sufferings and execution of Jesus, and its style reflects its subject matter. The statuary by Catalan sculptor Josep Maria Subirachs has attracted much criticism for its chunky, angular, "dehumanised" carving but Gaudí would probably have approved. He is known to have favoured an Expressionist style to give the story of Christ's Passion maximum impact.

A great porch whose roof is held up by six inclined buttress-like swamp tree roots shades the 12 groups of sculptures, arranged in three tiers and to be viewed from bottom to top, left to right in an inverted "S". The first scene, bottom left-hand corner, is the Last Supper at which Jesus (standing) announces his impending betrayal. Next to this is the arrest in the Garden of Gethsemane. An olive trunk's grain mimics the shape of the high priest's servant's ear that Peter cut off. The kiss of betrayal by Judas follows. The numbers of the cryptogram to the side of Jesus add up to 33 in every direction: his age at the time of his death.

The Flagellation

In the flagellation (between the central doors) Jesus is shown tied to a column at the top of a flight of three steps representing the three days of the Passion. Peter denying Christ is indicated by the cock that will crow 3 times in fulfilment of Jesus' prophecy. Behind this group of figures is a labyrinth, a metaphor for the loneliness of Jesus' path to the cross.

The sculptural group on the bottom right is in two parts. First is Ecce Homo (Christ bound with ropes and crowned with thorns). Pilate, overlooked by the Roman eagle, is shown washing his hands, freeing himself of responsibility for Jesus' death. Above, the "Three Marys" weep as Simon the Cyrene, a passer-by, is compelled by the Romans to pick up Christ's cross.

Knights sculpture on the Passion façade

The Holy Shroud

The central sculpture depicts an event not described in the Bible but added to the story of the Passion by later tradition. A woman named Veronica holds up her head cloth which she has offered to Jesus to wipe the blood and sweat from his face. It has been returned impressed with his likeness.

Next comes the solitary figure of the Roman centurion on horseback piercing the side of Jesus with his sword. Above him, three soldiers beneath the cross cast lots for Jesus' tunic. The largest sculpture (top centre) shows Christ hanging from a horizontal cross. At his feet is a skull referring to the place of the Crucifixion, Golgotha. Above him is the veil of the Temple of Jerusalem. The final scene is the burial of Jesus. The figure of Nicodemus, who is anointing the body, is thought to be a self-portrait of the sculptor Subirachs.

Nativity Façade

The northern, Nativity façade (overlooking Carrer Marina), finished according to Gaudí's personal instructions before his death, is far more subdued than the Passion façade. So much so that many of the sculptures barely rise out of the surface of the wall, making them difficult to identify. A great many natural forms are incorporated into the work confusing interpretation further. Gaudí intended the whole work to be coloured but his wishes are unlikely ever to be carried out.

Detail of sculpture on Nativity façade

Faith, Hope and Charity
The lavish ornamentation of the façade is arranged around three doors dedicated to Hope (left), Faith (right) and Charity or Christian Love in the middle. The two columns between the door-ways rest on a turtle and a tortoise signifying the permanence and stability of Christianity. In contrast, the two chamaeleons on either extreme of the façade, represent forces of change. The four angels on top of the columns are calling to the four winds and announcing the proximity of the end of the world.

Detail of a spire, Nativity façade

Hope Doorway
The lowest carvings of the Hope Doorway show the Flight into Egypt (left) and the Slaughter of the Innocents (right). Above the door are Joseph and the child Jesus watched over by Mary's parents (Jesus' grandparents), St Ann and St Joachim. The lintel of the door is composed of a woodcutter's two-handled saw and various other tools such as a hammer, axe, square and mallet - all indicative of Joseph's profession as a craftsman. Further above is a triangular grouping showing the betrothal of Mary and Joseph. The spire above the doorway is in the form of an elongated boulder which is an allusion to the holy Catalan mountain of Montserrat *(see pp122–3)*. At the base of this boulder sits Joseph in a boat, bearing a close resemblance to Gaudí himself and is very likely a posthumous homage by the masons who put the final touches to the façade after the master's death.

Faith Doorway
The Faith Doorway illustrates passages from the gospels and Christian theology. The heart of Jesus can be seen set into the lintel above the door. The scene on the lower left is the Visitation by Mary to Elizabeth, her cousin and mother of John the Baptist. On the right, Jesus wields a hammer and chisel in his father's workshop. Above the door is Jesus in the temple with John the Baptist (left) and John's father Zachariah (right). Higher up, the baby Jesus is presented in the temple, held by Simeon. As it rises, the stonework forms an intricate pinnacle recording the fundamentals of Catholicism including a lamp with 3 wicks for the trinity, bunches of grapes and ears of wheat for the Eucharist, and a hand set with an eye, showing God's omniscience and infinite care.

Charity Doorway
The double doors of the central Charity Doorway are separated by a column recording Jesus' genealogy. The three magi are on the lower left of the door with the shepherds opposite them. Out of nativity emerges the spiky tail of a many-pointed star (or comet). Around it are a children's choir and musicians. Above the star is the Annunciation and the Coronation of the Virgin Mary by Jesus. Above is a pelican sitting on a crown next to a glass egg bearing the JHS anagram of Jesus.

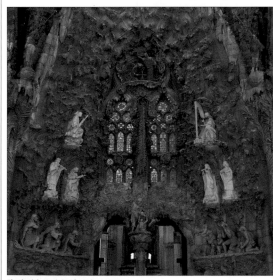

The lavish Nativity façade entrance

MONTJUÏC

The hill of Montjuïc, rising to 213 m (699 ft) above the commercial port on the south side of the city, is Barcelona's biggest recreation area. Its museums, art galleries, gardens and nightclubs make it a popular place in the evenings as well as during the day.

There was probably a Celtiberian settlement here before the Romans built a temple to Jupiter on their Mons Jovis, which may have given Montjuïc its name – though another theory suggests that a Jewish cemetery on the hill inspired the name Mount of the Jews.

The absence of a water supply meant that there were few buildings on Montjuïc until the castle was erected on the top in 1640.

Statue, gardens of the Palau Nacional

The hill finally came into its own as the site of the 1929 International Fair. With great energy and flair, buildings were erected all over the north side, with the grand Avinguda de la Reina Maria Cristina, lined with huge exhibition halls, leading into it from the Plaça d'Espanya. In the middle of the avenue is the Font Màgica (Magic Fountain), which is regularly illuminated in colour. Above it is the Palau Nacional, home of the city's historic art collections. The Poble Espanyol is a crafts centre housed in copies of buildings from all over Spain. The last great surge of building on Montjuïc was for the 1992 Olympic Games, which left Barcelona with international-class sports facilities.

SIGHTS AT A GLANCE

Historic Buildings
Castell de Montjuïc **7**

Modern Architecture
Estadi Olímpic de Montjuïc **8**
Pavelló Mies van der Rohe **4**

Museums and Galleries
Fundació Joan Miró **1**
Museu Arqueològic **2**
Museu Nacional d'Art de Catalunya **3**

Squares
Plaça d'Espanya **6**

Theme Parks
Poble Espanyol **5**

GETTING THERE

Apart from the exhibition halls near Espanya Metro station, reaching most of Montjuïc's attractions on foot involves a steep climb. However, buses 13 and 50 will take you up the hill from Plaça d'Espanya. For the castle, take the funicular from Metro Paral·lel, then the cable car. These run daily from 9am–8pm in winter and daily in summer to 10pm.

0 metres 500
0 yards 500

KEY

Street-by-Street map *pp86–7*

Ⓜ Metro station

Cable car station

Funicular station

Main bus stop

◁ **Changing colours of the Font Màgica (Magic Fountain) on the grand avenue leading up to Montjuïc**

Street-by-Street: Montjuïc

Montjuic is a spectacular vantage point
from which to view the city. It has
a wealth of art galleries and museums, as
well as theatres. Many of the buildings were
designed for the 1929 International Exhibition,
and the 1992 Olympics were held on its
southern slopes. Montjuïc is approached from
the Plaça d'Espanya between brick pillars
based on the campanile of St Mark's in
Venice. They give a foretaste of the
eclecticism of building styles
from the Palau Nacional,
which houses magnificent
Romanesque art, to the
Poble Espanyol, which
illustrates the architecture
of Spain's regions.

**Pavelló Mies van
der Rohe**
*This elegant statue
by Georg Kolbe
stands serenely in
the steel, glass, stone
and onyx pavilion
built in the Bauhaus
style as the German
contribution to the
1929 International
Exhibition* ❹

AVINGUDA DEL MARQUÈS DE COMILLAS

AVINGUDA DELS MONTANYANS

PASSEIG DE LES CASC

**★ Poble
Espanyol**
*Containing
replicas of build-
ings from many
regions of Spain, this
"village" provides a
fascinating glimpse of
vernacular styles* ❺

AVINGUDA DE L'ESTADI

**★ Museu Nacional
d'Art de Catalunya**
*On show in the Palau
Nacional (National
Palace), the main
building of the 1929
International Exhi-
bition, is Europe's
finest collection of
Romanesque frescoes.
These were a great
source of inspiration
for Joan Miró* ❸

**To Montjuïc castle and
Olympic stadium**

STAR SIGHTS

★ Poble Espanyol

★ Museu Nacional d'Art
de Catalunya

★ Fundació Joan Miró

Fountains and cascades descend in terraces from the Palau Nacional. Below them is the Font Màgica (Magic Fountain). On Thursday to Sunday evenings in summer and Friday and Saturday evenings in winter, its jets are programmed to a multi-coloured music and light show. This marvel of engineering was built by Carles Buigas (1898–1979) for the 1929 International Exhibition.

LOCATOR MAP
See Street Finder map 1

To Plaça d'Espanya

Museu Arqueològic
The museum displays important finds from prehistoric cultures in Catalonia and the Balearic Islands. The Dama d'Evissa, *a 4th-century sculpture, was found in Ibiza's Carthaginian necropolis* ❷

Museu Etnològic displays artifacts from Oceania, Africa, Asia and Latin America.

Mercat de les Flors theatre *(see p162)*

Teatre Grec is an open-air theatre set among gardens.

★ Fundació Joan Miró
This tapestry by Joan Miró hangs in the centre he created for the study of modern art. In addition to Miró's works in various media, the modern building by Josep Lluís Sert is of architectural interest ❶

To Montjuïc castle and cable car

KEY

– – – Suggested route

| 0 metres | 100 |
| 0 yards | 100 |

Flame in Space and Naked Woman (1932) by Joan Miró

Fundació Joan Miró **①**

Parc de Montjuïc. **Map** 1 B3. **Tel** 93
443 94 70. Ⓜ *Pl. Espanya then bus
50 or 55, or Paral·lel then funicular to
Montjuïc.* ◯ *Jul–Sep: 10am–8pm
Tue–Sat (till 9:30pm Thu); Oct– Jun:
10am–7pm Tue–Sat (till 9:30pm Thu),
10am–2:30pm Sun & public hols.*
● *1 Jan, 25 & 26 Dec.* 🅿️ ♿
www.bcn.fjmiro.es

Joan Miró (1893–1983) went
to La Llotja's art school *(see
p62)*, but from 1919 spent
much time in Paris. Though
opposed to Franco, he
returned to Spain in 1940 and
lived mainly in Mallorca, where
he died. An admirer of Catalan art and Modernisme *(see
pp24–5)*, Miró remained a
Catalan painter *(see pp28–9)*
but invented and developed a
Surrealistic style, with vivid
colours and fantastical forms.
During the 1950s he concen-
trated on ceramics.

In 1975, after the return of
democracy to Spain, his friend,
the architect Josep Lluís Sert,
designed this stark, white

building to house a permanent
collection of graphics, paintings, sculptures and tapestries
lit by natural light. Miró himself
donated the works and some
of the best pieces on display
include his *Barcelona Series*
(1939–44), a set of 50 black-
and-white lithographs. Exhibitions of other artists' work are
also held regularly.

Museu Arqueològic **②**

Passeig Santa Madrona 39–41. **Map**
1 B3. **Tel** 93 424 65 77. Ⓜ *Espanya,
Poble Sec.* ◯ *9:30am–7pm Tue–Sat,
10am–2:30pm Sun & public hols.*
● *1 Jan, 25, 26 Dec.* 📷 *except 11
Feb, 23 Apr, 18 May, 11 & 24 Sep.*
♿ 📷 **www**.mac.es

Housed in the 1929 Palace
of Graphic Arts, the
museum has artifacts from
prehistory to the Visigothic
period (AD 415–711). Highlights are finds from the Greco-
Roman town of Empúries *(see
p120)*, Hellenistic Mallorcan
and Visigothic jewellery and
Iberian silver treasure.

Museu Nacional d'Art de Catalunya **③**

Parc de Montjuïc, Palau Nacional. **Map**
1 A2. **Tel** 93 622 03 60. Ⓜ *Espanya.*
◯ *10am–7pm Tue–Sat, 10am–
2:30pm Sun & public hols.* ● *1 Jan,
1 May, 25 & 26 Dec.* 📷 *(free 1st Thu
of month).* 🚫 ♿ 📷 *by appointment
on 93 622 03 75).* **www**.mnac.es

The austere Palau Nacional
was built for the 1929 International Exhibition, but since
1934, it has housed the city's
most important art collection.

The museum has probably
the greatest display of Romanesque *(see pp22–3)* items in
the world, centred around a
series of magnificent 12th-
century frescoes. The most remarkable are the wall paintings
from Sant Climent de Taüll and
Santa Maria de Taüll *(see p113)*.

There is also an expanding
Gothic collection. Notable
artists include the 15th-century
Spanish artists Lluís Dalmau
and Jaume Huguet *(see p28)*.

Works by El Greco, Zurbarán
and Velázquez are on display
in the Cambó Rooms, a collection of notable Baroque and
Renaissance works from all
over Europe. The museum has
recently expanded and now
houses the entire body of 20th-
century art, furniture and sculpture previously at the Museu
d'Art Modern in the Parc de la
Ciutadella. It is also houses the
Thyssen-Bornemisza collection,
with works by Tiepolo, Titian,
Lotto, Canaletto and Velázquez.

**12th-century *Christ in Majesty*,
Museu Nacional d'Art de Catalunya**

Morning by Georg Kolbe (1877–1945), Pavelló Mies van der Rohe

Pavelló Mies van der Rohe ❹

Avinguda del Marquès de Comillas. **Map** 1 B2. **Tel** *93 423 40 16*. Ⓜ *Espanya*. 🚌 *50*. ◻ *10am–8pm daily* ⬤ *1 Jan, 25 Dec*. 🎫 *free to under 18s*. 🛈 *5–7pm Wed & Fri (in English)*. **www**.miesbcn.com

If the simple lines of this glass and polished stone pavilion look modern today, they must have shocked visitors at the 1929 International Exhibition. Designed by Ludwig Mies van der Rohe (1886–1969), director of the Bauhaus school, it included his world famous *Barcelona Chair*. The building was demolished after the exhibition, but an exact replica was built for the centenary of his birth.

Poble Espanyol ❺

Avinguda del Marquès de Comillas. **Map** 1 A2. **Tel** *93 508 63 30*. Ⓜ *Espanya*. ◻ *9am–8pm Mon, 9am–2am Tue–Thu, 9am–4am Fri & Sat, 9am–midnight Sun*. 🎫 ♿ 🛈 **www**.poble-espanyol.com

The idea behind the Poble Espanyol (Spanish Village) was to illustrate and display local Spanish architectural styles and crafts. It was laid out for the 1929 International Exhibition, but has proved to be enduringly popular.

Building styles from all over Spain are illustrated by 116 houses, arranged on streets radiating from a main square and created by many well-known architects and artists of the time. The village was refurbished at the end of the 1980s and is a favourite destination for tourists and locals alike.

Resident artisans produce crafts including hand-blown glass, ceramics, Toledo damascene and Catalan sandals *(espardenyes)*. The Torres de Avila, which form the main entrance, have been converted into a nightspot, with an interior by designers Alfredo Arribas and Javier Mariscal *(see p19)*. There are also shops, bars and a children's theatre.

Looking down from the Palau Nacional towards Plaça d'Espanya

Plaça d'Espanya ❻

Avinguda de la Gran Via de les Corts Catalanes. **Map** 1 B1. Ⓜ *Espanya*.

The fountain in the middle of this road junction, the site of public gallows until they were transferred to Ciutadella in 1715, is by Josep Maria Jujol, one of Gaudí's followers. The sculptures are by Miquel Blay. The 1899 bullring to one side is by Font i Carreras, but Catalans have never taken to bullfighting and the arena was once used as a music venue.

On the Montjuïc side of the roundabout is the Avinguda de la Reina Maria Cristina. This is flanked by two 47-m (154-ft) high brick campaniles by Ramon Raventós, modelled on the bell towers of St Mark's in Venice and built as the entrance way to the 1929 International Exhibition. The avenue, lined with exhibition buildings, leads up to Carles Buïgas's illuminated *Font Màgica* (Magic Fountain) in front of the Palau Nacional.

Castell de Montjuïc ❼

Parc de Montjuïc. **Map** 1 B5. **Tel** *93 329 86 13*. Ⓜ *Paral·lel, then funicular & cable car*. **Museum** ◻ *Nov–15 Mar: 9:30am–5pm Tue–Sun; 16 Mar–Oct: 9:30am–8pm*. ⬤ *1 Jan, Good Fri, 1 May, 25 & 26 Dec*. 🎫

The summit of Montjuïc is occupied by a huge, 18th-century castle with views over the port. The first castle was built in 1640, but destroyed by Felipe V in 1705. The present star-shaped fortress was built for the Bourbon family. During the War of Independence it was taken by French troops. After the Civil War it became a prison and the Catalan leader Lluís Companys *(see p47)* was executed here in 1940. It is now a military museum displaying ancient weaponry and model castles.

Estadi Olímpic de Montjuïc ❽

Passeig Olimpic, S/N. **Map** 1 A3. **Tel** *93 426 20 89*. Ⓜ *Espanya, Poble Sec*. 🚌 *50, 61*. ◻ *Jun–Sep: 10am–8pm; Oct–May: 10am–6pm; daily*. ⬤ *1 Jan, 25 Dec*. ♿ 🎫

The original Neo-Classical façade has been preserved from the stadium built by Pere Domènech i Roura for the 1936 Olympics, cancelled at the onset of the Spanish Civil War. The arena's capacity was raised to 70,000 for the 1992 Olympics. Nearby are the steel-and-glass Palau Sant Jordi stadium by Japanese architect Arata Isozaki, and swimming pools by Ricard Bofill.

Entrance to the Olympic Stadium, refurbished in 1992

Altar frontal of the 13th century dedicated to the Virgin, Museu Nacional d'Art de Catalunya ▷

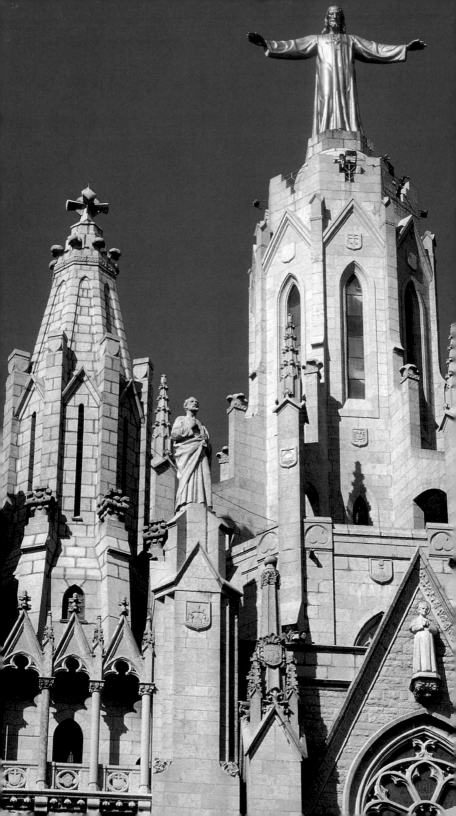

FURTHER AFIELD

Radical redevelopments throughout Barcelona in the late 1980s and 1990s have given it a wealth of new buildings, parks and squares. Sants, the city's main station, was rebuilt and the neighbouring Parc de l'Espanya Industrial and Parc de Joan Miró were created containing futuristic sculpture and architecture. In the east, close to the revitalized area of Poblenou, the city now has a new national theatre and concert hall. In the west, where the streets climb steeply, are the historic royal palace and monastery of Pedralbes, and Gaudí's Torre Bellesguard and Parc Güell. Beyond, the Serra de Collserola, the city's closest rural area, is reached by two funiculars. Tibidabo, the highest point, has an amusement park, the Neo-Gothic church of the Sagrat Cor and a nearby steel-and-glass communications tower. It is a popular place among *barcelonins* for a day out.

Parc Güell gateway sign

SIGHTS AT A GLANCE

Museums and Galleries
CaixaForum ⑫
Cosmocaixa ⑨
Museu del Futbol Club Barcelona ③

Historic Buildings
Monestir de Pedralbes ⑤
Palau Reial de Pedralbes ④
Torre Bellesguard ⑩

Modern Buildings
Torre de Collserola ⑥

Parks and Gardens
Parc de l'Espanya Industrial ②
Parc Güell ⑦
Parc de Joan Miró ①
Parc del Laberint d'Horta ⑪

Squares and Districts
Estació del Nord ⑬
Plaça de les Glòries Catalanes ⑭
Poblenou ⑮

Theme Parks
Tibidabo ⑧

KEY

	Street-by-Street maps
	Built-up area
🚉	Train station
🚡	Funicular station
═	Motorway (highway)
▬	Major road
═	Minor road

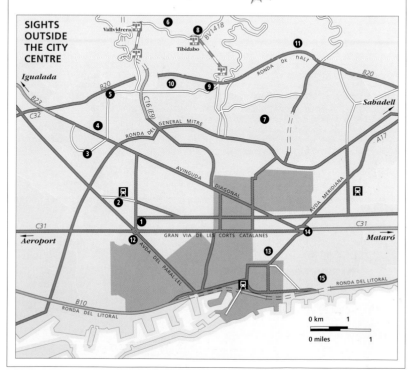

SIGHTS OUTSIDE THE CITY CENTRE

Vallvidrera
Tibidabo
Igualada
Sabadell
Aeroport
Mataró

GENERAL MITRE
RONDA DE DALT
AVINGUDA DIAGONAL
GRAN VIA DE LES CORTS CATALANES
AVDA DEL PARAL·LEL
AVDA MERIDIANA
RONDA DEL LITORAL
RONDA DEL LITORAL

0 km   1
0 miles   1

◁ The Neo-Gothic Temple Expiatori del Sagrat Cor dominating the summit of Tibidabo

Dona i Ocell (1983) by Joan Miró in the Parc de Joan Miró

Parc de Joan Miró ❶

Carrer d'Aragó 1. Ⓜ *Tarragona.*

Barcelona's 19th-century slaughterhouse *(escorxador)* was transformed in the 1980s into this unusual park, hence its alternative name, Parc de l'Escorxador.

It is constructed on two levels, the lower of which is devoted to football pitches interspersed with landscaped sections of palms, pines, eucalyptus trees and flowers. The upper level is completely paved and is dominated by a magnificent 1983 sculpture by the Catalan artist Joan Miró *(see p29)* entitled *Dona i Ocell (Woman and Bird)*. Standing 22 m (72 ft) high in the middle of a pool, its surface is covered with colourful glazed tiles.

Parc de l'Espanya Industrial ❷

Plaça de Joan Peiró. Ⓜ *Sants-Estació.*

This modern park, designed by the Basque architect Luis Peña Ganchegui, owes its name to the textile mill that used to stand on the 5-hectare (12-acre) site.

Laid out in 1986 as part of Barcelona's policy to provide more open spaces within the city, the park has canals and a rowing lake – with a Classical statue of Neptune at its centre. Tiers of steps rise around the lake like an amphitheatre and on one side a row of ten futuristic watchtowers dominates the entire area. Their only function is to serve as public viewing platforms and lamp standards.

Six contemporary sculptors are represented in the park, among them Andrés Nagel, whose enormous metal dragon incorporates a children's slide.

Museu del Futbol Club Barcelona ❸

Avda de Arístides Maillol (7, 9). **Tel** *93 496 36 08.* Ⓜ *Maria Cristina, Collblanc.* ◯ *10am–6:30pm Mon––Sat, 10am–2pm Sun & public hols.* ◼ *1 & 6 Jan, 24 Aug, 25 Dec.* 🖼️ ♿ 🗗 **www**.fcbarcelona.com

Camp Nou, Europe's largest football stadium, is home to the city's famous football club, Barcelona FC (Barça, as it is known locally). Founded in 1899, it is one of the world's richest soccer clubs, and has more than 100,000 members.

The stadium is a magnificent, sweeping structure, built in 1957

Line of watchtowers in the Parc de l'Espanya Industrial

to a design by Francesc Mitjans. An extension was added in 1982 and it can now comfortably seat 100,000 fans.

The club's museum, which displays club memorabilia and trophies on two floors, and has a souvenir shop, is one of the most popular in Barcelona. There are also paintings and sculptures of famous club footballers commissioned for the Blau-grana Biennial, an exhibition held in celebration of the club in 1985 and 1987, and others donated by Catalan artists. *Blau-grana* (blue-burgundy) are the colours of Barça's strip. The club's flags were used as an expression of local nationalist feelings when the Catalan flag was banned during the Franco dictatorship.

As well as hosting its own high-profile matches (mainly at weekends), Camp Nou also accommodates affiliated local soccer clubs and promotes other sports in its sports centre, ice rink and mini-stadium.

View across Camp Nou stadium, prestigious home of the Futbol Club Barcelona

Palau Reial de Pedralbes ❹

Avda Diagonal 686. Ⓜ *Palau Reial.*
Museu de Ceràmica & Museu de Arts Decoratives *Tel 93 280 50 24.*
◯ *10am–6pm Tue–Sat, 10am–3pm Sun & public hols.* ● *1 Jan, 1 & 20 May, 24 Jun, 25 & 26 Dec.* ♿
🎫 *(free 1st Sun of month).* 📷 *by appointment.*

The Palace of Pedralbes was once the main house on the estate of Count Eusebi Güell. In 1919 he offered it to the Spanish royal family. The first visit was from Alfonso XIII in 1926, before which the interior was refurbished and a new throne, supported by golden lions, was created for him.

The building opened to the public in 1937 and the Museu de Arts Decoratives installed. Exhibits include period furniture from other great houses and fine household items from the Middle Ages to the present. A genealogical tree traces the 500-year dynasty of the count-kings of Barcelona *(see p42).*

The palace also houses the Museu de Ceràmica, which displays old Catalan and Moorish pottery and modern ceramics, including works by Miró and Picasso *(see p88).*

The palace gardens are well laid out with small ponds and paths. Just behind the gardens, in Avinguda de Pedralbes, is the entrance to the original Güell estate. It is guarded by a black wrought-iron gate, its top forged into a great, open-jawed dragon, and two gate houses, all by Gaudí *(see pp24–5).*

Madonna of Humility, Monestir de Santa Maria de Pedralbes

Monestir de Santa Maria de Pedralbes ❺

Baixada del Monestir 9.
Tel 93 203 92 82. 🚇 *Reina Elisenda.* ◯ *10am–2pm Tue–Sun.* ● *public hols.* 🎫 📷 *by appointment (93 315 11 11).*

Approached through an arch in its ancient walls, the lovely monastery of Pedralbes retains the air of an enclosed community. This is heightened by the good state of preservation of its furnished kitchens, cells, infirmary and refectory. But the nuns of the Order of St

Clare moved to an adjoining building back in 1983, when the building was opened to the public. The monastery was founded in 1326 by Elisenda de Montcada de Piños, fourth wife of Jaume II of Catalonia and Aragón. Her alabaster tomb lies in the wall between the church and the cloister. On the church side her effigy is dressed in royal robes; on the other, in a nun's habit.

The monastery is built around a spacious, three-story cloister. The main rooms encircling the cloister include a dormitory, a refectory, a chapterhouse, an abbey and day cells. Numerous works of art, as well as liturgical orana-ments, pottery, furniture, altar cloths and gold and silver work, are on display here.

The most important room in the monastery is the Capella (chapel) de Sant Miquel, with murals of the *Passion* and the *Life of the Virgin,* both painted by Ferrer Bassa in 1346, when Elisenda's niece, Francesca Saportella, was abbess.

Torre de Collserola ❻

Carretera de Vallvidrera al Tibidabo.
Tel 93 406 93 54. 🚋 *Peu del Funi-cular, then Funicular de Vallvidrera & bus 211.* ◯ *11am–2:30pm, 3:30–7pm Wed–Sun.* ● *1 & 6 Jan, 25 Dec.* 🎫♿
www.torredecollserola.com

In a city that enjoys thrills, the ultimate ride is offered by the communications tower near Tibidabo mountain *(see p98).* A glass-sided lift takes less than two minutes to reach the top of this 288-m (944-ft) tall structure standing on the summit of a 445-m (1,460-ft) hill. The tower was designed by English architect Norman Foster for the 1992 Olympic Games. Needle-like in form, it is a tubular steel mast on a concrete pillar, anchored by 12 huge steel cables. There are 13 levels. The top one has an observa-tory with a telescope and a public viewing platform with a 360° view of the city, the sea and the mountain chain on which Tibidabo sits.

BARCELONA *V* REAL MADRID

FC Barcelona

Més que un club is the motto of Barcelona FC: "More than a club". It has above all, however, been a symbol of the struggle of Catalan nationalism against the central government in Madrid. To fail to win the league is one thing. To come in behind Real Madrid is a complete disaster. Each season the big question is which of the two teams will win the title. Under the Franco regime in a memorable episode in 1941, Barça won 3–0 at home. At the return match in Madrid, the crowd was so hostile that the police and referee "advised" Barça to prevent trouble. Demoralized by the intimidation, they lost 11–1. Loyalty is paramount: one Barça player who left to join Real Madrid received death threats.

Real Madrid

Parc Güell ❼

In 1910 the industrialist Eusebio Güell commissioned Gaudi to lay out a private housing estate on a hillside above Barcelona. The plan was to create a mini-garden city with common amenities, leisure areas and decorative structures but only two of the houses were ever built. What was left after the project fell through, however, was one of the most original public spaces ever conceived. The layout is loosely based on the Sanctuary of Apollo at Delhi and Gaudi makes ingenious use of the contours to create arcades and viaducts all of natural stone. The most striking features of the park, however, are those covered with trencadis – mosaics made up of broken tiles – which are largely the work of the architect Josep Maria Jujol.

Hypostyle Hall
A total of 86 Classical columns – unusually conventional in style for gaudi's work – support the weight of the square above. Set into the ceiling are four mosaic representions of the sun.

Hill of the Crosses
A serpentine path leads up to this stone tower from which there is a panoramic view over the city from the port to the heights of Tibidabo and Collserola.

Güell House

Entrance

★ Double Staircase
Water trickles from the mouth of the park's emblematic multicoloured dragon that presides over this monumental flight of steps. Above is an ornamental brown tripod and below another fountain, this time the head of a snake.

★ Entrance Pavilions
The two fairy-tale like gatehouses have oval ground plans and intricately tiled trencadis exteriors. Inside are irregular rooms, odd shaped windows and narrow staircases.

★ The Square
A serpentine bench covered in *trencadis* – the world's first collage – curves all the way around the edge of this square intended for markets and public events. From here are impressive views over Barcelona.

VISITORS' CHECKLIST

Olot 7, Vallcarca. **Tel** 93 285 68 99. 🚇 1.3 km (1 mile) walk from Lesseps, along a main road and uphill. 🚌 24. 🕐 Nov–Feb: 10am–6pm; Mar & Oct: 10am–7pm; Apr & Sep: 10am–8pm; May–Aug: 10am–9pm; daily. ♿

Casa-Museu Gaudí
Tel 93 219 38 11. 🕐 Mar–Apr & Oct: 10am–6pm; May–Sep: 10am–8pm; Nov–Feb: 10am–6pm; daily. 📷
www.bcn.es/parcsijardins

The Trias house is one of only two houses to have been built in the would-be housing estate.

Upper Viaduct
This is one of three viaducts that carry snaking pathways on the east side of the park.

The perimeter wall follows the contours around the park. The Carretera El Carmel entry is formed by a swivelling section of wall executed in wrought iron.

0 meters 40

0 yards 40

STAR SIGHTS

★ Entrance Pavilions

★ Double Staircase

★ The Square

Casa Museu Gaudí
This house, which Gaudí lived in until he moved to the Sagrada Família, contains furniture designed by the architect, including benches and cupboards from Casa Mila.

Merry-go-round, Tibidabo

Tibidabo ⓭

Plaça del Tibidabo 3–4. *Tel 93 211 79 42.* ⓐ *Avda Tibidabo, then Tramvia Blau & Funicular; or Peu del Funicular, then Funicular & bus 111; or bus 17, 60, 73; or Tibi Bus from Plaça Cata-lunya.* **Amusement Park** ☐ *ring to confirm.* ⓞ *Oct–Apr: Mon–Fri.* ♿ **Temple Expiatori del Sagrat Cor** *Tel 93 417 56 86.* ☐ *10am–8pm Mon–Fri, 10:30am–7pm Sat, 10:30am–2pm Sun.* ♿ **www**.tibidabo.es

The heights of Tibidabo can be reached by Barcelona's last surviving tram. The name, in-spired by Tibidabo's views of the city, comes from the Latin *tibi dabo* (I shall give you) – a reference to the Temptation of Christ when Satan took Him up a mountain and offered Him the world spread at His feet.

The hugely popular Parc d'Atraccions (Amusement Park, *see p163*) first opened in 1908. The rides were renovated in the 1980s. While the old ones retain their charm, the newer ones provide the latest in vertiginous experiences. Their location at 517 m (1,696 ft) adds to the thrill. Also in the park is the Museu d'Autòmats displaying automated toys, juke boxes and slot machines.

Tibidabo is crowned by the Temple Expiatori del Sagrat Cor (Church of the Sacred Heart), built with religious zeal but little taste by Enric Sagnier between 1902 and 1911. A lift takes you up to the feet of an enormous figure of Christ.

Just a short bus ride away is another viewpoint – the Torre de Collserola *(see p95)*.

CosmoCaixa ⓽

Teodor Roviralta 47–51. *Tel 90 222 30 540.* ⓐ *Avinguda del Tibidabo.* ☐ *10am–8pm Tue–Sun.* ♿ **www**.fundacio.lacaixa.es

Barcelona's revamped science museum is even more stimu-lating and interactive than its popular predecessor which was housed in the Modernista building that still stands on site. Beside it now is a new wing on nine levels, six of them are underground. Its particular boast is a glasshouse contain-ing a recreated section of a flooded Amazon forest inhabited by fish, amphibians, insects, reptiles, mammals, birds and plant species. Other exhibition spaces include the Matter Room which takes a look at the big bang theory, a Geological Wall which examines different types of rock, and a planetarium.

Torre Bellesguard ⓾

Carrer de Bellesguard 16. ⓐ *Avinguda del Tibidabo.* ⓞ *closed to public.*

Bellesguard means "beautiful spot" and here, half way up the Collserola hills, is the place chosen by the medieval Catalan kings as their summer home. Their castle, built in 1408, was in particular a favourite residence of Barcelona's Martí the Humanist *(see p57)*.

The surrounding district of Sant Gervasi was developed in the 19th century after the coming of the railway. In 1900 Gaudí built the present

Wrought-iron entrance door at Antoni Gaudí's Torre Bellesguard

house on the site of the castle, which had fallen badly into ruin. Its castellated look and the elongated, Gothic-inspired windows refer clearly to the original castle. Gaudí kept the vestiges of its walls in his structure. The roof, with a walkway behind the parapet, is topped by a distinctive Gaudí tower. Ceramic fish mosaics by the main door symbolize Catalonia's past sea power.

Parc del Laberint d'Horta ⓫

Germans Desvalls, Passeig Castanyers. *Tel 93 428 39 34.* ⓐ *Mundet.* ☐ *10am–6pm daily (winter); 10am–9pm daily (summer).* ♿ *(free Wed & Sun).* ♿ **www**.bcn.es/parcsijardins

As its name suggests, the centrepiece of the city's oldest public park, created in the 18th century for Joan Antoni Desvalls, Marqués de Llúpia i d'Alfarràs, is a cypress maze. Even without this Horta would be an agreeable place to escape the bustle of the city.

The semi-wild garden slopes steeply uphill from the entrance beside the marquis' semi-derelict palace which now houses a gardening school. It is a veritable compendium of aristocratic Baroque fantasies. Classical temples dedicated to Ariadne (who helped Theseus escape from the Minotaur's labyrinth) and Danae (mother of Perseus) stand at either side of a broad paseo which oversees the maze. From here a monumental flight of steps leads up to a Neo-Classical temple. Elsewhere there is a "romantic garden", a faux cemetery and, in the woodland into which the garden eventu-ally leads, a hermit's cave.

CaixaForum ⓬

Avinguda del Marquès de Comillas 6–8, Montjuïc. *Tel 93 476 86 00.* ⓐ *Espanya.* ☐ *10am–8pm Tue–Sun.* **www**.lacaixa.es/caixaforum

Barcelona is growing ever stronger in the field of con-temporary art and this new exhibition centre can only

Catalonia's new National Theatre near the Plaça de les Glòries Catalanes

enhance its reputation further. The "la Caixa" Foundation's collection of 700 works by Spanish and international artists, is housed in the Antiga Fàbrica Casaramona, a restored textile mill in Mondernista style. The mill was built by Josep Puig i Cadafalch after he had completed the Casa de los Punxes. Opened in 1911, it was intended to be a model factory – light, clean and airy – but had only a short working life unil the buisness closed down in 1920. The building then became a storehouse and later, after the Civil War, stables for police horses. The collection is displayed according to changing themes but one permanent exhibit is Joseph Beuy's *Lead Room (Chamber of pain)*. There are also temporary exhibitions.

Estació del Nord ⓭

Avinguda de Vilanova. **Map** 6 D1. Ⓜ *Arc de Triomf.*

Only the 1861 façade overlooking a park and the grand 1915 entrance remain of this former railway station. The rest has been remodelled as a sports centre, a police headquarters, and the city's bus station. Two elegant, blue-tiled sculptures, *Espiral arbrada (Branched Spiral)* and *Cel obert (Open Sky)* by Beverley Pepper (1992) sweep through the pleasant park. In front of the station, at Avinguda de Vilanova 12, is a carefully restored building occupied by Catalonia's power generating company. It was built as a power station in 1897 by the architect Pere Falqués. Though the great machinery inside is not visible, the exterior of this iron and brick structure is unmistakably Modernista.

Plaça de les Glòries Catalanes ⓮

Gran Via de les Corts Catalanes. **Map** 4 F5. Ⓜ *Glòries.*

This whole area, where the Diagonal crosses the Gran Via de les Corts Catalanes, has recently been redeveloped as the city expands northeastwards and the Diagonal is extended down to the sea, completing the vision of the Eixample's planner Ildefons Cerdà *(see p71)*. On the north side, a new shopping centre contrasts with the Encants Vells flea market *(see p155)*, which sprawls beside the highway heading north out of town. It is open 8am–8pm four days a week, and much of the merchandise of furniture, clothes, and bric-à-brac is simply laid out on the ground. It is busiest early in the day and bartering is all part of the fun.

To the south of the *plaça* is the new Teatre Nacional de Catalunya, a vast temple to culture by the Barcelona architect Ricard Bofill. Beside it is the Auditori de Barcelona, with two concert halls by Rafael Moneo which were inaugurated in 1999. The Museu de la Música *(see p73)* will probably move here in mid-2005.

La Rambla del Poblenou, a good place for a stroll and a cup of coffee

Poblenou ⓯

Rambla del Poblenou. Ⓜ *Poblenou.*

Poblenou is the trendy part of town where artists have built their studios in the defunct warehouses of the city's former industrial heartland. The area is centred on the Rambla del Poblenou, a quiet avenue which extends from Avinguda Diagonal down to the sea. Here palm trees back a stretch of sandy beach. A walk around the quiet streets leading from the Rambla will reveal a few protected pieces of industrial architecture, legacies from the time Barcelona was known as "the Manchester of Spain".

Along the parallel Carrer del Ferrocarril is the Plaça de Prim with low, whitewashed houses reminiscent of a small country town. See pages 106–7 for a guided walk through Poblenou.

Blue-tiled sculpture by Beverley Pepper, Parc de l'Estació del Nord

THREE GUIDED WALKS

There is no shortage of good places to take a stroll in Barcelona. Each of the Street-by-Street maps in the book (the Old Town, the Eixample and Montjuïc) has a short walk marked on it which takes in the well-known sights in the area. Other classic walks are down La Rambla *(see pp60–61)* and around Parc Güell *(see pp96–7)*. The walks described on the next six pages, however, take you to three less-explored districts, each with a distinct flavour.

The first walk is around the Born, once a run-down area to stay clear of but now an appealing quarter mixing old streets and modern shops. Next comes Gràcia which could be thought of as "village Barcelona": a proud working-class area of low-rise houses, tiny boutiques and charming squares

Trueta memorial, Poblenou walk

which host a busy nightlife. The final walk is around the post-industrial heartland of Poblenou whose buildings are being restored and put to new uses, and whose skyline is punctuated by a few surviving slender brick chimneys. Each route avoids heavy traffic as far as possible and makes the most of quiet or pedestrianised streets and squares. While there are monuments to be seen along the way, the appeal here is as much in the atmosphere of the areas and the unusual shops, characterful cafes and architectural oddities encountered. All three walks begin and end with a metro station. As in any big city, care should be taken with personal belongings and although it is safe to walk at any time, be aware that the character of areas can change when the bars open.

CHOOSING A WALK

The Three Walks
This map shows the location of the three guided walks in relation to the main sightseeing areas of Barcelona.

Market sweet shop, Poblenou walk

Gracia *(pp104–5)*

Santa Maria del Mar, Born walk

Eixample

Poblenou *(pp106–7)*

Born *(pp102–3)*

Old Town

Montjuïc

| 0 kilometres | | 4 |
| 0 miles | | 2 |

KEY
······· Walk route

◁ Plaça del Sol Café, Gràcia walk

A One-Hour Walk Around the Born

The tiny district of El Born, across the Via Laietana from the Barrí Gotic, is now making a comeback after long years of neglect. Close to the waterfront, this area flourished in Catalonia's mercantile heyday from the 13th century. The narrow streets still bear the names of the craftsmen and guilds that set up here, for instance, hatters in Carrer dels Sombrerers, mirror-makers in Carrer dels Mirallers, silversmiths in Carrer de la Argentaria. While it still has something of a medieval air, El Born has become the hip and arty place to be.

left into Placeta de Montcada which becomes Carrer Montcada *(see p64)*, an immaculate collection of Gothic mansions dating from the 14th century with later Renaissance refurbishments. Most of the buildings are now museums and galleries. The Casa Cervelló-Guidice at 25 ⑥ is the only

Passeig del Born, the main street of El Born area ⑮

The Carrer de Montcada

From Jaume I metro station in Plaça de l'Angel ① set off down Carrer de La Argentaria but turn left almost at once at the tobacconist's (marked "Tabac") into Carrer del Vigatans. After passing the youth hostel on your left, note the carved head protruding from the wall on the right at the corner of Carrer dels Mirallers ②. At the end of the street you have no choice but to turn sharp left into Carrer de la Carassa to meet Carrer de Barra de

Ferro. Turn right and right again into Carrer de Banys Vells. Halfway down this street on the left at 9 is a large church charity shop, Farcells Caritas ③, where you may be able to pick up a bargain. At the end of the street you meet the side wall of the church of Santa Maria del Mar ④. Turn left along Carrer Sombrerers. On your left at 23 is Casa Gispert ⑤ a famous old shop selling coffee roasted on the premises, nuts and dried fruit. When you can go no further, turn

building on the street still with its original façade. Opposite it, at 20 ⑦, is the Palau Dalames, whose patio has an ornately carved staircase. Its neighbour at 22 is El Xampanyet *(see p.???)* ⑧, the city's best known bar for *cava* (Catalan sparkling wine) and tapas.

Much of the right-hand side of Montcada is taken up by five palaces including the Museu Picasso ⑨ *(see pp64–5)*. Opposite this are two more museums. The first you come to at 14 is the Museu Barbier-Mueller ⑩, in the Palau Nadal. This collection of pre-Columbian sculptures, fabrics, ceramics and ritual

TIPS FOR WALKERS

Starting point: *Plaça de l'Angel*
Length: *1.5 km (1 mile)*
Getting there: *Go to Jaume I metro station in the Plaça de l'Angel on Line 4.*
Stopping off points: *There are many bars and eateries along the route including the Café del Born (Plaça Comercial) and Origens 99,9% (Carrer Vidrieria 6–8), a Catalan restaurant and shop. You'll find lots on Carrer de La Argentaria, notably Xocalateria Xador (for hot chocolate; 61–3), and Taller de Tapas (51).*

Visitors flocking to the popular Museu Picasso ⑨

Enjoying the café culture in Plaça de Comercial in front of Mercat del Born ⑯

[Map]

CARRER DE LA PRINCESA

CARRER DE CREMAT GRAN

C CREMAT XIC

CARRER DE CORRETGER

C DE L'HOSTAL DE SANT ANTONI

C DEL SABATERET

CARRER DE LA FUSINA

C DE MONTCADA

CARRER DELS FLASSADERS

C DE LA CIRERA

CARRER DEL REC

CARRER DEL COMERÇ

CARRER DE COMERCIAL

C DE L'ARC DE SANT VICENÇ

DE LA SECA

PLAÇA DE COMERCIAL ⑯

CARRER DE LES MOSQUES

PASSEIG DEL BORN

C DE VIDRIERA

CARRER DE L'ESPARTERIA

C ANTIC DE SANT JOAN

CARRER DEL REC

CARRER DE RIBERA

CALDERS

CARRER DEL BONAIRE

RERA PALAU

PLAÇA DE LES OLLES

0 meters 50
0 yards 50

KEY

• • • Walk route

Ⓜ Metro station

---

into the arch at the start of Carrer de l'Hostal de Sant Antoni (on your right) ⑭ to see an unusual hieroglyphic-like frieze. Carrer Triangle leads you into Carrer del Rec and before long you meet the Passeig del Born ⑮. It was the jousts held in this broad avenue from the 13th to 17th centuries that gave the name to the Born quarter of which it forms the heart. To the left, the Passeig opens out into the Plaça de Comercial, which is dominated by the Mercat del Born ⑯, the former wholesale market. This old iron and glass building was modelled on Les Halles in Paris but is now being turned into a library. Excavations on the site have helped archaeologists piece together a clear picture of life in 18th-century Barcelona. Continue on Carrer del Rec on the other side of the Passeig del Born and turn right at the next junction into Carrer de l'Esparteria. Turn left at Carrer de Vidriera to reach Plaça de les Olles. Turn right here and follow the wide pavement which skirts the Plaça del Palau. It also passes an old ironmonger's with giant paella pans.

When you reach the Café La Bolsa – across the road from La Llotja (see pp62–3) ⑰ – turn right into Carrer dels Canvis Vells. Bear right into the Carrer de l'Anisadeta, which is so short that it is over almost as soon as it is begun, and you find yourself back in the charming Plaça de Santa Maria ⑱, facing the church of the same name (see p64–5). Pop inside to admire the beautiful Catalan Gothic interior. Bear left across the square to the start of Carrer de La Argentaria, the busiest street in El Born, lined with bars and eateries. Follow this back to your starting point at the metro in Plaça de l'Angel.

---

objects was assembled by the great Swiss art collector, Josef Mueller (1887–1977) with the aid of his son-in-law Jean Paul Barbier, who felt that "primitive" art deserved to be more admired and appreciated. The courtyard is dominated by a reproduction of a giant Olmec head from Mexico. Just after is the Museu Tèxtil i

d'Indumentària in Palau del Marquès de Lió (or Mora) ⑪, which has displays of textiles and clothing from the 4th century. At the end of Montcada turn right along Carrer de la Princesa, where you'll find several tempting shops. First you pass the windows of Brunells chocolate shop at 22 ⑫, then the *turrón* and sweet shop of La Campana (founded in 1890) at 36 ⑬.

The Passeig del Born

Take the next small street to the right, Carrer del Corretger, which turns a sharp corner. Turn right at the cake shop into Carrer Triangle. Look up

Brunells chocolate shop ⑫

A 90-Minute Walk Through Gràcia

When you cross the Avinguda Diagonal and plunge into the maze of sinuous streets and small squares on the other side, it is easy to get the impression that you have left the city behind and entered a village. Since Gràcia became part of Barcelona in 1897 it has never lost its sense of independence and identity. During the day, it feels calmly removed from the pace of modern metropolitan life just a few blocks away. In August and in the evening, however, expect a hullabaloo as the district draws crowds to its exotic shops and nightlife.

façade, Carrer Gràcia. Turn left and quickly right down Carrer Domènech. Turn left at the end up Carrer de Francisco Giner and this will lead you into Plaça de Rius I Taulet ⑤, where a 33-m (108-ft) clock tower is overlooked by the sky blue façade of Gràcia's local government

The façade of Casa Fuster, a Modernista building ③

The Passeig de Gràcia

From Plaça Joan Carles I ① the famous Passeig de Gràcia continues briefly as a modest, plane tree-shaded avenue. On your left, almost immediately, you come to Casa Bonaventura Ferrer ②, a Modernista building by Pere Falqués I Urpi, with stonework sculpted into swirling leaves and a façade finished off with an iron crown. A short way along, the road narrows to go round another Modernista building (although its inspiration is

clearly Neo-Gothic). The last work of architect Lluis Domènech i Montaner, Casa Fuster ③ has been converted into a hotel. The Café Vienés on the ground floor is open to non-residents.

The squares of Gràcia

A few steps beyond Casa Fuster up the Passeig de Gràcia's well-to-do continuation, Gran de Gràcia, you can see the handsome stained-glass *miradores* (upper-floor bay windows) above La Colmena *patisseria* at 15 ④. Then go back to Casa Fuster and turn down the road behind its rear

TIPS FOR WALKERS

Starting point: *Plaça Joan Carles I*
Length: *2.5 km (1.5 miles)*
Getting there: *Diagonal metro station in Plaça Joan Carles I is on Line 3 or reached by FCG train.*
Stopping-off points: *Most of Gràcia's squares have bars and restaurants. Try Miria (modern Mediterranean food) in Plaça Rius i Taulet; Café del Sol (drinks and music) or Mirasol (classic bar) in Plaça de Sol; Niu Toc (fish) on Plaça Revolució de Setembre de 1868 or Virreina Bar (sandwiches and beer) in Plaça de la Virreina.*

A performance of *castellers* at fiesta time ⑤

Nightlife at the Plaça del Sol ⑥

0 meters 125
0 yards 125

KEY

··· Walk route

Ⓜ Metro station

streets, and stroll along Carrer Xiquets de Valls, named after a renowned team of *castellers*. This brings you into the Plaça del Sol ⑥, a nightlife hub popularly known Plaça dels Encants. Turn left to leave by Carrer Maspons. Straight ahead, on the other side of Carrer del Torrent l'Olla, is the Plaça Revolució de Setembre de 1868 ⑦. The name commemorates the *coup d'état* led by General Prim, which unseated Spain's ruling Bourbon dynasty, who were so antagonistic to the Catalans they ushered in the first republican government in Spain's history. Turn left into the square and leave by Carrer de Verdi that sprouts from the top of it. This is a busy but pleasant street of modern shops. After passing Cinemes Verdi (on your right), which often shows original-version foreign films, turn right down Carrer de l'Or. You soon arrive in one of Gràcia's most agreeable squares, the Plaça Virreina ⑧, where the church of Sant Joan faces downhill towards two fine buildings: one is a residence with a tower and the other a redbrick house in Modernista style with a graphic red and cream façade and wrought iron balconies.

Casa Vincens

Leave Virreina by the shady Carrer de Astúries and stay on

Stained-glass windows in *miradores* ④

it across the top of Plaça Diamant ⑨. This is where a civil war air-raid shelter has been discovered, and it is planned to open it to the public as a museum of peace. Turn right up Carrer Torrent l'Olla and left down Santa Agata. When you reach Gran de Gràcia cross over it into Carrer de les Carolines. At the bottom of this street at 24 is one of Antoni Gaudí's early works, Casa Vicens ⑩. It is privately owned but well worth admiring from the outside. Commissioned as a summer house by a brick and tile maker, it took the inexperienced Gaudí five years to build (1883–8). Inspired by Moorish architecture, the house was a bold break with tradition and the lavish use of colour and ornament clearly indicate where Gaudí's interests lay. The exterior of the house is a checkerboard of green and white tiles and other tiles with a marigold motif. The riotous ironwork shows off with extravagant loops and intriguing beasts. Now retrace your steps to Gran de Gràcia. If you are in the mood for more Gaudí, go uphill to Plaça Lesseps and from there follow the signs to Parc Güell *(see pp96–7)*. If not, go downhill past pretty Plaça Trilla ⑪. You can either finish the walk at Fontana metro station or continue on back to your starting point.

headquarters. A plaque on the wall commemorates the achievements of Catalonia's *castellers*, teams of amateur gymnasts who can often be seen building human towers up to eight people high on fiesta days in Gràcia. Cross the square and leave by Carrer Mariana Pineda. Cross Travessera de Gràcia, one of the district's main shopping

The interior and stained-glass windows at Casa Vicens ⑩

A Two-hour Walk Through Poblenou

It's hard to believe today but the trendy district of Poblenou once had the highest concentration of smoke-belching factories in Catalonia. By the 1960s these had gone out of business or moved to the outskirts, leaving their old buildings to decay. With the 1992 Olympic Games came an impetus for recovery and since then Poblenou's warehouses have been spruced up and converted into chic studios for artists and photographers. New developments brought hotels, discos and restaurants, creating a fascinating mix of industrial archaeology and contemporary culture.

right) ⑥, a handsome salmon-coloured building by Josep Masdeu dating from 1914, which is decorated with Modernista floral motifs.

At the next junction with Carrer Joncar, turn left between El Tio Che ⑦, a well-known shop founded in 1912, selling ice cream and *turrón* (a typical Spanish sweet made of almonds) and, opposite it, the Casino de l'Alliança de Poblenou ⑧, a concert hall (not a gambling enterprise as its name might suggest). Turn right at the first

The controversial Torre Agbar ③

The Avinguda Diagonal
Leave the metro station in Plaça de Les Glòries Catalanes ① (a recently redeveloped area; *see p99)* by the Carrer Badajoz exit, which will lead you on to the wide, new seaward extension of Avinguda Diagonal ②. This takes you directly beneath a tall, unusual and much-criticised building that breaks up the city skyline, the Torre Agbar ③. A domed cylindrical tower of 33 floors, unkindly

described as an upended blue cigar, it was built by French architect Jean Nouvel for the local water company, Aguas de Barcelona.

Continue on down Diagonal, which has a wide *paseo* in the middle flanked by traffic lanes, tramways that link Glòries with Sant Adrià del Besòs as well as cycle tracks. About 700 m (half a mile) down Diagonal turn right into Rambla del Poblenou ④, the main street of Poblenou that leads eventually to the sea. After crossing Carrer de Pere IV, the Rambla narrows and becomes more attractive. In the middle is a memorial to Doctor Josep Trueta ⑤. This pioneering surgeon was born in Poblenou in 1897 and, after working to save lives during the bombardments of the Civil War, went into a 30-year exile in England on the fall of democracy in 1939.

Rambla del Poblenou
Keep straight on down the Rambla over the next three circular road junctions. Along the way are several buildings worth stopping to look at, such as 51 (on the

see p99)

TIPS FOR WALKERS

Starting point: *Plaça de Les Glories Catalanes*
Length: *3.5 km (2 miles)*
Getting there: *Glòries metro station is on metro line 1*
Stopping off points: *There are bars on Rambla de Poble Nou, swish new restaurants on Carrer Taulat and a few cheaper bars on Carrer Maria Aguilo. Go for an ice cream at El Tio Che.*

Memorial to civil-war hero, Dr Josep Trueta ⑤

El Tio Che, the renowned ice cream and *turrón* parlour ⑦

junction you come to down Carrer Maria Aguilo, a lively but humanly-scaled pedestrianized shopping street. On the left, up a short street, is the district's market, the Mercat de la Unió (under restoration) ⑨. Beside it is a handsome building, 24 Plaça de la Unió, with Art Nouveau white and green ceramic festoons draped over the windows. On the right of Maria Aguilo, at 120 ⑩, is the shop of the artist Chema

Vidal who makes scale models of monuments in Poblenou, both existing and demolished. Cross over Carrer del Taulat (the junction is slightly staggered) into Carrer del Ferrocarril and turn left into the old square of Plaça del Prim ⑪. Here, you'll see gnarled, leaning, fat-rooted ombu trees (an Argentinian species) and low whitewashed houses. Now somewhat lost amid the modernity around it, this square is the original heart of Poblenou, from which all else grew. It is said that among the fishermen and workers who lived on this square were many followers of the mid-19th century Icaria Utopian movement, which militated against capitalism and attempted to create a world of "universal brotherhood". Return to Carrer del Taulat and turn right. If you wish to end your walk here, turn left up Carrer de Bilbao to reach Poblenou metro

station. Otherwise, continue along Taulat, a strip of gardens through modern residential developments. A short detour to the corner of Carrer de Ramon Turró and Espronceda takes you to a garden ⑫ dedicated to the Indian social reformer and philosopher Mahatma Gandhi, with a sculpture of him by the Nobel Peace Prize winner Adolfo Pérez Esquivel.

Returning to Passeig del Taulat, ahead of you all the while rises the most characteristic surviving industrial building in Poblenou, the Torre de les Aigües ⑬. Turn left into Carrer de la Selva to get to the base of this structure, which

Torre de les Aigües ⑬

stands in the middle of Plaça Ramon Calsina. This round, red-brick tower, 63 m (207 ft) high, was built to raise and store water from the nearby Besos river. Near the top of it is a vertigo-inducing metal staircase that leads round the brickwork to a balcony.

From here continue up Carrer de la Selva to Selva del Mar metro station on the corner of Carrer de Pujades. On the way you might like to wander a few steps to your left along Carrer de Llull. On the corner with Carrer de Provençals rises the highest chimney in Barcelona ⑭. This graceful flat-topped 65-m (213-ft) spire used to form part of the now-defunct Macosa steelworks. Return to Carrer de la Selva and end your walk at the Selva de Mar metro stop.

0 meters   250

0 yards   250

KEY

••• Walk route

M Metro station

The unusual ombu trees in the village-like Plaça del Prim ⑪

CATALONIA

LLEIDA · ANDORRA · GIRONA
BARCELONA PROVINCE · TARRAGONA

There is a wealth of natural beauty in Catalonia's four provinces, plus the small Catalan-speaking country of Andorra. They offer rocky coasts and mountains, fertile plains and sandy shores. Many who visit don't stray far from the coast, but the rewards for venturing further afield are immense.

Beyond the constant bustle of Barcelona, Catalonia is essentially a rural region, with no large cities and few industrial blights. Of the four provinces, all named after their principal city, Lleida is the largest and least populated. Among its jewels are the Romanesque churches of the Boí valley and the Aigüestortes National Park.

Santa Maria, Ripoll

The province of Girona is blessed with mountains and sea. This eastern end of the Pyrenees has the magical Cerdanya valley and the ancient monasteries of Ripoll and Sant Joan de les Abadesses, as well as medieval villages and a handsome and too-often overlooked capital city. Its coast, the Costa Brava, is rocky and full of delights.

Barcelona province has its own coasts; the Maresme to the north is rather spoiled by the railway running beside the sea, but the Garraf to the south is more exciting – Sitges is a highly fashionable spot. Inland are the Holy Mountain of Montserrat (Catalonia's spiritual heart), the Penedès winelands, and the country town of Vic.

Tarragona, the most southerly of the provinces, has one of the peninsula's former Roman capitals. Here the land rolls more gently, supporting fruit and nut orchards and the monastic communities of Poblet and Santes Creus, before falling away towards the rice lands of the Ebre. The coastline is more gentle, too, with long, sandy beaches.

Aigüestortes y E. Sant Maurici National Park in the central Pyrenees, in the province of Lleida

◁ A fisherman inspects his nets in Cadaqués on the Costa Brava

Exploring Catalonia

Catalonia includes a long stretch of the
Spanish Pyrenees, whose green, flower-
filled valleys hide picturesque villages
with Romanesque churches. The Parc
Nacional d'Aigüestortes and Vall d'Aran
are paradises for naturalists, while Baqueira-
Beret offers skiers reliable snow. Sun-lovers
can choose between the rugged Costa
Brava or the long sandy stretches of the
Costa Daurada. Tarragona is rich in Roman
monuments. Inland are the monasteries
of Poblet and Santes Creus and the well-
known vineyards of Penedès.

**Isolated houses in the countryside
around La Seu d'Urgell**

KEY

▬▬▬	Motorway (highway)
▬▬▬	Other highway
▬▬▬	Main road
▭▭▭	Minor road
▬▬▬	Scenic route
┄┄┄	Main railway
────	Minor railway
▬▬▬	International border
▬▬▬	Regional border
△	Summit

GETTING AROUND

The motorway from France
enters Spain at La Jonquera
and, from Barcelona,
follows the coast via
Tarragona and Tortosa. As
Spain has recently changed
its road numbers some of
these numbers may not
correspond to new road
signs. Buses connect most
towns. The main north–
south railway hugs the coast
from Blanes southwards.
Other lines connect
Barcelona to Vic and Lleida
(*see inside back cover*).

SEE ALSO

• *Where to Stay* pp134–41

• *Restaurants* pp146–51

For additional map symbols *see back flap*

Church on the seafront of Sitges

Vineyards outside Gandesa, west of Tarragona

SIGHTS AT A GLANCE

The Vall d'Aran, surrounded by the snow-capped mountains of the Pyrenees

BUTTERFLIES OF THE VALL D'ARAN

A huge variety of butterflies and moths is found high in the valleys and mountains of the Pyrenees. The isolated Vall d'Aran is the home of several unique and rare subspecies. The best time of the year in which to see the butterflies is between May and July.

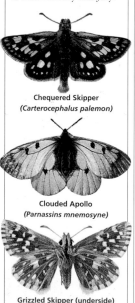

Chequered Skipper
(Carterocephalus palemon)

Clouded Apollo
(Parnassins mnemosyne)

Grizzled Skipper (underside)
(Pyrgus malvae)

Vall d'Aran ❶

Lleida N230. 🚌 *Vielha.*
🛈 *Vielha (973 64 01 10).*

This valley of valleys – *aran* means valley – is a lovely 600-sq km (230-sq mile) haven of forests and meadows filled with flowers, surrounded by towering mountain peaks.

The Vall d'Aran was formed by the Riu Garona, which rises in the area and flows out to France as the Garonne. With no proper link to the outside world until 1924, when a road was built over the Bonaigua Pass, the valley was cut off from the rest of Spain for most of the winter. Snow blocks the narrow pass from November to April, but today access is easy through the Túnel de Vielha from El Pont de Suert.

The fact that the Vall d'Aran faces north means that it has a climate similar to that on the Atlantic coast. Many rare wild flowers and butterflies flourish in the perfect conditions that are created by the shady slopes and damp breezes. It is also a famous habitat for many species of narcissus.

Tiny villages have grown up beside the Riu Garona, often around Romanesque churches, notably at **Bossòst, Salardú, Escunhau** and **Arties**. The valley is also ideal for outdoor sports such as skiing and is popular with walkers.

Vielha ❷

Lleida. 🏘 *2,700.* 🚌 🛈 *Carrer Sarriulera 10 (973 64 01 10).* 🚌 *Thu.* 🎉 *Festa de Vielha (8 Sep), Feria de Vielha (8 Oct).*

Now a modern ski resort, the capital of the Vall d'Aran holds on to its medieval past. The Romanesque church of **Sant Miquel** has an octagonal bell tower and a superb 12th-century crucifix, the *Mig Aran Christ*. It formed part of a larger carving representing the Descent from the Cross. The **Museu de la Vall d'Aran** is devoted to Aranese culture.

🏛 **Museu de la Vall d'Aran**
Carrer Major 26.
Tel *973 64 18 15.* ⭕ *10am–1pm, 5–8pm Tue–Sat, 11am–2pm Sun.* ⭕ *1 Jan, 17 Jul, 8 Sep, 25 Dec.* ♿
www.aran.org

Mig Aran Christ (12th-century), Sant Miquel church, Vielha

Baqueira-Beret ❸

Lleida. 🚠 100. 🚌 🛈 *Baqueira-Beret (973 63 90 00).* 🎪 *Romeria de Nostra Senyora de Montgarri (2 Jul).*

This extensive ski resort, one of the best in Spain, is popular with both the public and the Spanish royal family. There is reliable winter snow cover and a choice of over 40 pistes at altitudes from 1,520 m to 2,470 m (4,987 ft to 8,104 ft).

Baqueira and Beret were separate mountain villages before skiing became popular, but they have now merged to form a single resort. The Romans took full advantage of the thermal springs located here, which are nowadays appreciated by tired skiers.

Vall de Boí ❹

Lleida N230. 🚌 *La Pobla de Segur.* 🚌 *El Pont de Suert.* 🛈 *Barruera (973 69 40 00).* **www.**vallboi.com

This small valley on the edge of the Parc Nacional d'Aigüestortes is dotted with tiny villages, many of which are built around magnificent Catalan Romanesque churches.

Dating from the 11th and 12th centuries, these churches are distinguished by their tall belfries, such as the six-storey bell tower of the **Església de Santa Eulàlia** at Erill-la-Vall.

The two churches at Taüll, **Sant Climent** *(see pp22–3)* and **Santa Maria**, have superb frescoes. Between 1919 and 1923 the originals were taken for safekeeping to the Museu Nacional d'Art de Catalunya in Barcelona *(see p88).* Replicas now stand in their place. You can climb the towers of Sant Climent for superb views of the surrounding countryside.

Other churches in the area worth visiting include those at **Coll**, for its fine ironwork, **Barruera**, and **Durro**, which has another massive bell tower.

At the head of the valley is the hamlet of **Caldes de Boí**, popular for its thermal springs and ski facilities. It is also a good base for exploring the Parc Nacional d'Aigüestortes, the entrance to which is only 5 km (3 miles) from here.

The tall belfry of Sant Climent church at Taüll in the Vall de Boí

Parc Nacional d'Aigüestortes ❺

Lleida. 🚌 *La Pobla de Segur.* 🚌 *El Pont de Suert, La Pobla de Segur.* 🛈 *Barruera (973 69 61 89).*

The pristine mountain scenery of Catalonia's only national park is among the most spectacular to be seen anywhere in the Pyrenees.

Established in 1955, the park covers an area of 102 sq km (40 sq miles). Its full title is Parc Nacional d'Aigüestortes i Estany de Sant Maurici, named after the lake *(estany)* of Sant Maurici in the east and the Aigüestortes (literally, twisted waters) area in the west. The main village is the mountain settlement of Espot, on the park's eastern edge. Dotted around the park are waterfalls and the sparkling, clear waters of around 150 lakes and tarns which, in an earlier era, were scoured by glaciers to depths of up to 50 m (164 ft).

The finest scenery is around Sant Maurici lake, which lies beneath the twin shards of the Serra dels Encantats, (Mountains of the Enchanted). From here, there is a variety of walks, particularly along the string of lakes that leads north to the towering peaks of Agulles d'Amitges. To the south is the dramatic vista of Estany Negre, the highest and deepest tarn in the park.

Early summer in the lower valleys is marked by a mass of pink and red rhododendrons, while later in the year wild lilies bloom in the forests of fir, beech and silver birch.

The park is also home to a variety of wildlife. Chamois (also known as izards) live on the mountain screes and in the meadows, while beavers and otters can be spotted by the lakes. Golden eagles nest on mountain ledges, and grouse and capercaillie are found in the woods.

During the summer the park is popular with walkers, while in winter, the snow-covered mountains are ideal for cross-country skiing.

A crystal-clear stream, Parc Nacional d'Aigüestortes

LES QUATRE BARRES

The four red bars on the *senyera*, the Catalan flag, are said to represent the four provinces: Barcelona, Girona, Lleida and Tarragona. The design derives from a legend of Guifré el Pelós, first Count of Barcelona *(see p42)*. It relates how he received a call for help from Charles the Bald, who was King of the West Franks and grandson of Charlemagne. Guifré went to his aid and turned the tide of battle, but was mortally wounded. As he lay dying, Charles dipped his fingers in Guifré's blood and dragged them across his plain gold shield, giving him a grant of arms.

Catalonia's national emblem

Andorra ❻

Principality of Andorra. 🏛 *72,000.* 🚌 *Andorra la Vella.* ℹ️ *Plaça de la Rotonda, Andorra la Vella (376 82 7117).* **www**.andorra.ad

Andorra occupies 464 sq km (179 sq miles) of the Pyrenees between France and Spain. In 1993, it became fully independent and held its first ever democratic elections. Since 1278, it had been an autonomous feudal state under the jurisdiction of the Spanish bishop of La Seu d'Urgell and the French Count of Foix (a title adopted by the President of France). These are still the ceremonial joint heads of state.

Andorra's official language is Catalan, though French and Castilian are also spoken by most residents.

For many years Andorra has been a tax-free paradise for shoppers, a fact reflected in the crowded shops and super-markets of the capital **Andorra la Vella**. Les Escaldes (near the capital), as well as Sant Julià de Lòria and El Pas de la Casa (the towns nearest the Spanish and French borders), have also become shopping centres.

Most visitors never see Andorra's rural charms, which match those of other parts of the Pyrenees. The region is excellent for walkers. One of the main routes leads to the **Cercle de Pessons**, a bowl of lakes in the east, and past Romanesque chapels such as **Sant Martí** at La Cortinada. In the north is the picturesque Sorteny valley where traditional farmhouses have been converted into snug restaurants.

La Seu d'Urgell ❼

Lleida. 🏛 *13,000.* 🚌 ℹ️ *Avenida Valles de Andorra 33 (973 35 15 11).* 🛒 *Tue & Sat.* 🎉 *Festa major (last week of Aug).* **www**.laseu.org

This Pyrenean town was made a bishopric in the 6th century. Feuds between the bishops of Urgell and the Counts of Foix over land, gave rise to Andorra in the 13th century. The **cathedral** has a Romanesque statue of Santa Maria d'Urgell. The **Museu Diocesà** contains a 10th-century copy of St Beatus of Liébana's *Commentary on the Apocalypse*.

🏛 Museu Diocesà

Plaça del Deganat. **Tel** *973 35 32 42.* ⏰ *Oct–May: noon–1pm Mon–Fri, 11–1pm Sat & Sun; Jun–Sep: 10am–1pm & 4–7pm Mon–Sat, 10am–1pm Sun.* 🌙 *1 Jan, 25 Dec & public hols.* 📷 🚻

Carving, La Seu d'Urgell cathedral

Puigcerdà ❽

Girona. 🏛 *7,000.* 🚌 🚌 ℹ️ *Carrer Querol 1 (972 88 05 42).* 🛒 *Sun.* 🎉 *Festa de l'Estany (third Sun of Aug); Festa del Roser (third week of Jul).* **www**.puigcerda.com

Puig is Catalan for hill. Despite sitting on a relatively small hill compared with the encircling mountains, which

rise to 2,900 m (9,500 ft), Puigcerdà nevertheless has a fine view down the beautiful Cerdanya valley.

Puigcerdà was founded in 1177 by Alfons II as the capital of Cerdanya, an important agricultural region, which shares a past and its culture with the French Cerdagne. The Spanish enclave of **Llívia**, an attractive little town with a medieval pharmacy, lies 6 km (3.75 miles) inside France.

Cerdanya is the largest valley in the Pyrenees. At its edge is the **Cadí-Moixeró** nature reserve *(see p170)*, a place for ambitious walks.

Portal of Monestir de Santa Maria

Ripoll ❾

Girona. 🏛 *11,000.* 🚌 🚌 ℹ️ *Plaça del Abat Oliva (972 70 23 51).* 🛒 *Sat.* 🎉 *Festa major (11–12 May), La Llana y Casament a Pagès (Sun after Festa major).* **www**.elripolles.com

Once a tiny mountain base from which raids against the Moors were made, Ripoll is now best known for the **Monestir de Santa Maria** *(see p22)*, founded in 879. The town is called the "cradle of Catalonia" as the monastery was the power base of Guifré el Pelós (Wilfred the Hairy), founder of the House of Barcelona *(see p42)*. He is also buried here. In the later 12th century, the west portal was decorated with what are regarded as the finest Romanesque carvings in Spain. This and the cloister are the only parts of the medieval monastery to have survived.

Environs

In the mountains to the west is **Sant Jaume de Frontanyà** *(see p22)*, another superb Romanesque church.

The medieval town of Besalú on the banks of the Riu Fluvià

Sant Joan de les Abadesses ❿

Girona. 🏠 3,800. 🚌 🚉 ℹ️ *Plaça de Abadia 9 (972 72 05 99).* 🚌 *Sun.* 🎉 *Festa major (second week of Sep).* **www.**santjoandelesabadesses.com

A fine, 12th-century Gothic bridge arches over the Riu Ter to this unassuming market town, whose main attraction is its **monastery**.

Founded in 885, it was a gift from Guifré, first count of Barcelona, to his daughter, the first abbess. The church has little decoration except for a wooden calvary, *The Descent from the Cross*. Though made in 1150, it looks modern. The figure of a thief on the left was burnt in the Civil War and replaced so skilfully that it is hard to tell it is new. The museum has Baroque and Renaissance altarpieces.

12th-century calvary, Sant Joan de les Abadesses monastery

Environs
To the north are **Camprodon** and **Beget**, both with Romanesque churches *(see p23)*. Camprodon also has some grand houses, and its region is noted for sausages.

Olot ⓫

Girona. 🏠 28,000. 🚌 🚉 ℹ️ *Carrer Hospici 8 (972 26 01 41).* 🚌 *Mon.* 🎉 *Feria de mayo (1 May), Corpus Christi (Jun), Festa del Tura (8 Sep), Feria de Sant Lluc (18 Oct).* **www.**olot.org/turisme

This small market town is at the centre of a landscape pockmarked with extinct volcanoes. But it was an earthquake in 1474 that destroyed its medieval past.

During the 18th century the town's textile industry spawned the "Olot School" of art *(see p28)*: cotton fabrics were printed with drawings. In 1783 the Public School of Drawing was founded. Much of the school's work, which includes paintings such as Joaquim Vayreda's *Les Falgueres*, is in the **Museu Comarcal de la Garrotxa**. *Modernista* sculptor Miquel Blay's damsels support the balcony at No. 38 Passeig Miquel Blay.

🏛 Museu Comarcal de la Garrotxa
Calle Hospici 8. **Tel** 972 27 91 30. ⏰ *11am–2pm, 4–7pm Mon, Wed–Sat, 11am–2pm Sun & public hols.* ⏰ *1 Jan, 25 Dec.* 🅿️ 🚫 ♿

Besalú ⓬

Girona. 🏠 2,000. 🚌 🚉 ℹ️ *Plaça de la Llibertat 1 (972 59 12 40).* 🚌 *Tue.* 🎉 *Sant Vicenç (22 Jan), Festa major (weekend closest to 25 Sep).* **www.**ajuntamentbesalu.org

A magnificent medieval town, with a striking approach across a fortified bridge over the Riu Fluvià, Besalú has two fine Romanesque churches: **Sant Vicenç** and **Sant Pere** *(see p23)*. The latter is the sole remnant of a Benedictine monastery founded in 977, but pulled down in 1835.

In 1964 a **mikvah**, a Jewish ritual bath, was discovered by chance. It was built in 1264 and is one of only three of that period to survive in Europe. The tourist office has the keys to all the town's attractions.

To the south, the sky-blue lake of **Banyoles**, where the 1992 Olympic rowing contests were held, is ideal for picnics.

Shop selling *llonganisses* in the mountain town of Camprodon

GIRONA TOWN CENTRE

Banys Arabs ②
Catedral ④
Centre Bonastruc Ça Porta ⑦
Església de Sant Feliu ③
Església de Sant Pere de
    Galligants ①
Museu d'Art ⑤
Museu d'Història
    de la Ciutat ⑥

0 metres   250

0 yards   250

Key to Symbols *see back flap*

Girona ⑬

Girona. 🏛 *75,000.* ✈ 🚉 🚌
ℹ *Rambla de la Llibertat 1 (972 22
65 75).* 🚌 *Tue, Sat.* 🎉 *El Pedal
(bike race, last fortnight of Sep),
Sant Narcís (29 Oct for a week).*
www.ajuntament.gi/turisme

This handsome town puts on
its best face beside the Riu
Onyar, where tall, pastel-
coloured buildings rise above
the water. Behind them, in the
old town, the Rambla de la
Llibertat is lined with busy
shops and street cafés.

The houses were built in the
19th century to replace sections of the city wall damaged
during a seven-month siege
by French troops in 1809. Most
of the rest of the ramparts, first
raised by the Romans, are still
intact and have been turned
into the Passeig Arqueològic
(Archaeological Walk), which
runs right round the city.

The walk's starting point is
on the north side of the town,
near the **Església de Sant Pere
de Galligants** (St Peter of the
Cock Crows) *(see p23)*. The
church now houses the city's
archaeological collection.

From here, a narrow street
goes through the north gate,
where huge Roman foundation
stones are still visible. They
mark the route of the Via
Augusta, the road which once
ran from Tarragona to Rome.
The most popular place of
devotion in the town is the

Església de Sant Feliu. The
church, begun in the 14th
century, was built over the
tombs of St Felix and St
Narcissus, both patrons of the
city. Next to the high altar are
eight Roman sarcophagi.

Despite their name, the
nearby **Banys Àrabs** (Arab
Baths), lit by a fine octagonal
lantern, were built in the late
12th century, about 300 years
after the Moors had left.

🏛 **Centre Bonastruc Ça Porta**
Carrer de la Força 8. **Tel** *972 21 67
61.* ◯ *10am–6pm daily (to 3pm Sun).*
◼ *1 & 6 Jan, 25 & 26 Dec.* 🖼 ♿
This centre charts the history
of Jews in Girona. The
buildings it occupies in the
maze of alleyways and steps
in the old town were once
part of El Call, the Jewish
ghetto, which was inhabited
by the city's Jews from the
late 9th century until their
expulsion from Spain in 1492.

⛪ **Catedral**
Girona Cathedral's west face is
pure Catalan Baroque, but the
rest of the building is Gothic.
The single nave, built in 1416
by Guillem Bofill, possesses
the widest Gothic span in the
Christian world. Behind the
altar is a marble throne known
as "Charlemagne's Chair". It is
named after the Frankish king

Painted houses packed tightly along the bank of the Riu Onyar in Girona

whose troops took Girona in 785. In the chancel is a 14th-century jewel-encrusted silver and enamel altarpiece, the best example in Catalonia. Among the fine Romanesque paintings and statues in the cathedral's museum are a 10th-century illuminated copy of St Beatus of Liébana's *Commentary on the Apocalypse*, and a 14th-century statue of the Catalan king, Pere the Ceremonious.

The collection's most famous item is a tapestry, called *The Creation*, decorated with lively figures. The rich colours of this large 11th- to 12th-century work are well preserved.

Tapestry of *The Creation*

🏛 Museu d'Art
Pujada de la Catedral 12. *Tel* 972 20 95 36. ◯ 10am–7pm (to 6pm Oct–Feb) Tue–Sat, 10am–2pm Sun. ● 1 & 6 Jan, 25 & 26 Dec. 🎫 ♿
This gallery holds works from the Romanesque period to the 20th century. The many items from churches ruined by war or neglect tell of the richness of church interiors long ago.

🏛 Museu del Cinema
Carrer Sèquia 1. *Tel* 972 41 27 77. ◯ Tue–Sun. ● 1 & 6 Jan, 25 & 26 Dec. 🎫 🗂 ♿
Next to Església de Mercadel, this collection includes film and artifacts from the mid-19th century to the present day.

🏛 Museu d'Història de la Ciutat
Carrer de la Força 27. *Tel* 972 22 22 29. ◯ Tue–Sun. ● 1 & 6 Jan, 25 & 26 Dec. 🎫
The city's history museum is in an 18th-century former convent. Recesses where the decomposing bodies of members of the Capuchin Order were placed can still be seen. Exhibits include old *sardana* (see p129) instruments.

Figueres ⑭

Girona. 🏠 35,000. 🚉 🚌 ℹ️ *Plaça del Sol (972 50 31 55).* 🛍 *Thu.* 🎉 *Santa Creu (3 May), Sant Pere (29 Jun).* **www**.figueresciutat.com

Figueres is the market town of the Empordà plain. Beside the plane-tree-shaded Rambla is the former Hotel de Paris, now home to the **Museu de Joguets** (Toy Museum). At the bottom of the Rambla is a statue of Narcís Monturiol i Estarriol (1819–95) who, it is said, invented the submarine.

Figueres was the birthplace of Salvador Dalí, who in 1974 turned the town theatre into the **Teatre-Museu Dalí**. Under its glass dome are works by Dalí and other painters. The museum is a monument to Catalonia's most eccentric artist.

Environs
The **Casa-Museu Castell Gala Dalí**, 55 km (35 miles) south of Figueres, is the medieval castle Dalí bought in the 1970s. It contains some of his paintings. East of Figueres is the Romanesque monastery, **Sant Pere de Rodes** *(see p23).*

***Rainy Taxi,* a monument in the garden of the Teatre-Museu Dalí**

🏛 Museu del Joguet
C/ Sant Pere 1. *Tel* 972 50 45 85. ◯ Jun–Sep: daily; Oct–May: Tue–Sun. 🎫 ♿ **www**.mjc-figueres.net

🏛 Teatre-Museu Dalí
Pl Gala-Salvador Dalí S. *Tel* 972 67 75 00. ◯ Jul–Sep: daily; Oct–Jun: Tue–Sun. ● 1 Jan, 25 Dec. 🎫 🗂 by appointment. **www**.salvador-dali.org

🏛 Casa-Museu Castell Gala Dalí
C/ Gala Dalí, Púbol (La Pera). *Tel* 972 48 86 55. ◯ mid-Mar–Nov: Tue–Sun; Dec–mid-Mar: only for groups by appointment. 🎫

THE ART OF DALI

Salvador Dalí i Domènech was born in Figueres in 1904 and mounted his first exhibition at the age of 15. After studying at the Escuela de Bellas Artes in Madrid, and dabbling with Cubism, Futurism and Metaphysical painting, the young artist embraced Surrealism in 1929, becoming the movement's best-known painter.
Never far from controversy, the self-publicist Dalí became famous for his hallucinatory images – such as *Woman-Animal Symbiosis* – which he described as "hand-painted dream photographs". Dalí's career also included writing and film-making, and established him as one of the 20th century's greatest artists. He died in his home town in 1989.

Ceiling fresco in the Wind Palace Room, Teatre-Museu Dalí

Cadaqués ⑮

Girona. 🏛 *2,000*. 🚌 ℹ️ *Carrer Cotxe 2 (972 25 83 15)*. 🚌 *Mon.* 🎭 *Fiesta major de Verano (first week of Sep), Santa Esperança (18 Dec).*

This pretty resort is over-looked by the Baroque **Església de Santa Maria**. In the 1960s it was dubbed the "St Tropez of Spain", due to the young crowd that sought out Salvador Dalí in nearby Port Lligat. For six months of the year, from 1930 until his death in 1989, Dalí lived here with his wife Gala.

Today their much modified house, which expanded far beyond their original fisher-man's cabin, is known as the **Casa-Museu Salvador Dalí**. Managed by the Gala-Salvador Dalí Foundation, the museum and its contents provide a unique interpretation of the artist's life and inspiration.

🏛 **Casa-Museu Salvador Dalí** Port Lligat. **Tel** *972 25 10 15*. ☎ *972 25 10 83*. ⬜ *booking required.* ● *7 Jan–12 Mar.* 🎫

Empúries ⑯

Girona. 🚌 *L'Escala.* **Tel** *972 77 02 08*. ⬜ *Easter, Jun–Sep: 10am–8pm daily; Oct–May: 10am–6pm daily.* 🎫 *ruins.*

The extensive ruins of this Greco-Roman town *(see p41)* occupy an imposing site be-side the sea. Three separate settlements were built between the 7th and 3rd centuries BC: the old town (Palaiapolis); the new town (Neapolis); and the Roman town.

An excavated Roman pillar in the ruins of Empúries

Looking south along the Costa Brava from Tossa de Mar

The **old town** was founded by the Greeks in 600 BC as a trading port. It was built on what was a small island, and is now the site of the tiny hamlet of Sant Martí de Empúries. In 550 BC this was replaced by a larger new town on the shore which the Greeks named Emporion, meaning "trading place". In 218 BC, the Romans landed at Empúries and built a city next to the new town.

A nearby museum exhibits some of the site's finds, but the best are in Barcelona's Museu Arqueològic *(see p88)*.

Peratallada ⑰

Girona. 🏛 *150*. ℹ️ *C/Unió 3, Ajun-tament de Forallac, Vulpellac (972 64 55 22)*. 🎭 *Feria Peratallada (last week-end in Apr), Festa Major (6 & 7 Aug), Medieval Market (first weekend in Oct).*

This tiny village is the most spectacular of the many that lie a short inland trip from the Costa Brava. Together with Pals and Palau Sator it forms part of the 'Golden Triangle' of medieval villages. Its moun-tain-top position gives some dramatic views of the area. A labyrinth of cobbled streets wind up to the well-conserved castle and look out tower, whose written records date from the 11th century. Peratall-ada's counts and kings made doubly sure of fending off any attackers by constructing a sturdy wall enclosing the entire village that even today limits the nucleus from further expansion, ensuring it retains its medieval character.

Tossa de Mar ⑱

Girona. 🏛 *4,000*. 🚌 ℹ️ *Avinguda Pelegrí 25 (972 34 01 08)*. 🚌 *Thu.* 🎭 *Festa de hivern (22 Jan), Festa de estiu (29 Jun).* **www**.infotossa.com

At the end of a tortuous cor-niche, the Roman town of Turissa is one of the prettiest along the Costa Brava. Above the modern town is the **Vila Vella** (old town), a protected national monument. The medieval walls enclose fisher-men's cottages, a 14th-century church and countless bars.

The **Museu Municipal** in the old town exhibits local archaeology and modern art.

🏛 **Museu Municipal** Plaça Roig y Soler 1. **Tel** *972 34 07 09*. ⬜ *daily in summer.* ● *Mon in winter.* 🎫

Blanes ⑲

Girona. 🏛 *30,000*. 🚌 🚌 ℹ️ *Paseo de Catalunya 21 (972 33 03 48)*. 🚌 *Mon.* 🎭 *Santa Ana (26 Jul); Festa Ma-jor Petita (21 Aug).* **www**.blanes.net

The working port of Blanes has one of the longest beaches on the Costa Brava. The highlight of the town is the **Jardí Botànic Mar i Murtra**. These gardens, designed by Karl Faust in 1928, are spectacularly sited above cliffs. Their 7,000 species of Mediterranean and tropical plants include African cacti.

🌿 **Jardí Botànic Mar i Murtra** Pg Karl Faust 10. **Tel** *972 33 08 26*. ⬜ *daily.* ● *1 & 6 Jan, 24 & 25 Dec.* 🎫 ♿

◁ **Surrealist decoration on one of the buildings of the Teatre-Museu Dalí in Figueres**

The Costa Brava

The Costa Brava ("wild coast") runs for some 200 km (125 miles) from Blanes northwards to the region of Empordà, which borders France. It is a mix of rugged cliffs, pine-backed sandy coves, golden beaches and crowded, modern resorts. The busiest resorts – Lloret de Mar, Tossa de Mar and Platja d'Aro – are to the south. Sant Feliu de Guíxols and Palamós are still working towns behind the summer rush. Just inland there are medieval villages to explore, such as Peralada, Peratallada and Pals. Wine, olives and fishing were the mainstays of the area before the tourists came in the 1960s.

Cadaqués *retains an air of seclusion as it is accessible only by a steep road. It has an arty atmosphere and its small, stony beaches are relatively unspoiled and uncrowded.*

Roses lies at the head of a sweeping bay. Its sandy beach, the longest on the Costa Brava, has become a mecca for lovers of water sports.

L'Escala is a small resort, popular mainly with local tourists. It has fine beaches and a small port where fishing nets dry in the sun.

L'Estartit *is a good base for the Illes Medes, a former pirates' lair, which now form a marine reserve with clear waters perfect for skin diving.*

Begur is a hilltop town just inland. It has good views of the coast, and small coves are tucked at its feet.

Palamós is a working port with modern hotels to the south, and secluded beaches and coves lapped by clear water to the north.

Llafranc, a whitewashed resort, with a promenade leading to neighbouring Calella, is one of the coast's most pleasant resorts.

Platja d'Aro's long and sandy beach is lined with modern hotels. It is one of the most popular resorts on the coast.

Tossa de Mar has a golden beach in a small cove beneath the fortified old town.

Map labels: Cadaqués, Roses, L'Escala, L'Estartit, Illes Medes, Begur, Llafranc, Calella de Palafrugell, Palamós, Platja d'Aro, S'Agaró, Sant Feliu de Guixols, Tossa de Mar, Lloret de Mar, Blanes

0 kilometres   10

0 miles   5

Lloret de Mar *has more hotels than anywhere else on the coast. But there are unspoiled beaches nearby, such as Santa Cristina.*

Monestir de Montserrat ⑳

A Benedictine monk

The "serrated mountain" *(mont serrat)*, its highest peak rising to 1,236 m (4,055 ft), is a superb setting for Catalonia's holiest place, the Monastery of Montserrat, which is surrounded by chapels and hermits' caves. The monastery was first mentioned in the 9th century, enlarged in the 11th century, and in 1409 became independent of Rome. In 1811, when the French attacked Catalonia in the War of Independence *(see p45),* the monastery was destroyed. Rebuilt and repopulated in 1844, it was a beacon of Catalan culture during the Franco years. Today Benedictine monks live here. Visitors can hear the Escolania singing the *Salve Regina y Virolai* (the Montserrat hymn) at 1pm and 6:45pm every day (Sundays noon only), except in July and during the Christmas period, in the basilica.

Gothic cloister

Funicular to the holy site of Santa Cova

Plaça de Santa Maria
The focal points of the square are two wings of the Gothic cloister built in 1477. The modern monastery façade is by Francesc Folguera.

The Museum has a collection of 19th- and 20th-century Catalan paintings and many Italian and French works. It also displays liturgical items from the Holy Land.

The Way of the Cross
This path passes 14 statues representing the Stations of the Cross. It begins near the Plaça de l'Abat Oliba.

STAR FEATURES

★ Basilica Façade

★ Black Virgin

View of Montserrat
The complex includes cafés and a hotel. A second funicular transports visitors to nature trails above the monastery.

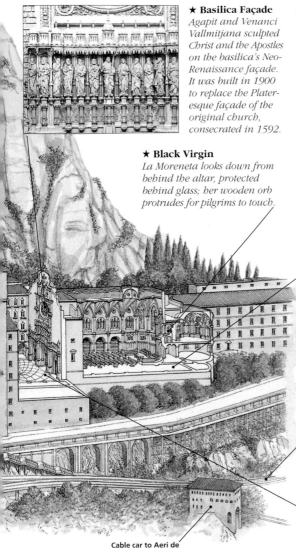

★ Basilica Façade

Agapit and Venanci Vallmitjana sculpted Christ and the Apostles on the basilica's Neo-Renaissance façade. It was built in 1900 to replace the Plateresque façade of the original church, consecrated in 1592.

★ Black Virgin

La Moreneta looks down from behind the altar, protected behind glass; her wooden orb protrudes for pilgrims to touch.

Cable car to Aeri de Montserrat station

VISITORS' CHECKLIST

Montserrat (Barcelona province).
Tel *93 877 77 75.* 🚠 *Aeri de Montserrat, then cable car; Monistrol-Enllaç, then rack railway.* 🚂 *from Barcelona.* **Basilica** ◯ *Oct–Jun: 7:30am–7:30pm daily; Jul–Sep: 7:30am–8:15pm daily.* ✝ *from 9am Mon–Fri, from 7:30am Sat, from 8am Sun & religious hols.* 📷 **Museum** ◯ *10am–6pm Mon–Fri, 9:30am–6:30pm Sat–Sun & public hols.* 📷 ♿ 📷
www.abadiamontserrat.net

Basilica Interior

The sanctuary in the domed basilica is adorned by a richly enamelled altar and paintings by Catalan artists.

The rack railway, opened in 2003, follows the course of a historic rail line built in 1880.

Inner Courtyard

On one side of the courtyard is the baptistry (1902), with sculptures by Carles Collet. A door on the right leads towards the Black Virgin.

THE VIRGIN OF MONTSERRAT

The small wooden statue of La Moreneta (the dark maiden) is the soul of Montserrat. It is said to have been made by St Luke and brought here by St Peter in AD 50. Centuries later, the statue is believed to have been hidden from the Moors in the nearby Santa Cova (Holy Cave). Carbon dating suggests, however, that the statue was carved around the 12th century. In 1881 Montserrat's Black Virgin became patroness of Catalonia.

The blackened Virgin of Montserrat

Vic ㉑

Barcelona. 🏠 *32,000.* 🚃 🚌 **ℹ** *C/ Ciutat 4 (93 886 20 91).* 🚌 *Tue & Sat.* 🎪 *Mercat del Ram (Sat before Easter), Sant Miquel (5–15 Jul), Música Viva (3 days mid-Sep), Mercat medieval (6–8 Dec).* **www**.victurisme.com

Market days are the best time to go to this small country town. This is when the excellent local sausages *(embotits),* for which the area is renowned, are piled high in the large Gothic Plaça Major, along with other produce from the surrounding plains.

In the 3rd century BC Vic was the capital of an ancient Iberian tribe, the Ausetans. The town was then colonized by the Romans – the remains of a Roman temple survive today. Since the 6th century the town has been a bishop's see. In the 11th century, Abbot Oliva commissioned El Cloquer tower, around which the cathedral was built in the 18th century. The interior is covered with vast murals by Josep-Maria Sert (1876–1945, *see p29).* Painted in reds and golds, they represent Biblical scenes.

Adjacent to the cathedral is the **Museu Episcopal de Vic** *(see p23),* which has one of the best Romanesque collections in Catalonia. The large display of mainly religious art and relics includes bright, simple murals and wooden carvings from rural churches. Also on display are 11th- and 12th-century frescoes and some superb altar frontals.

Twelfth-century altar frontal, Museu Episcopal de Vic

Cardona dominating the surrounding area from its hilltop site

🏛 **Museu Episcopal**
Plaça Bisbe Oliba, 3. **Tel** *93 886 93 60.* ⏰ *Tue–Sun.* ⬤ *1, 6 Jan, 25, 26 Dec.* 🎭 ♿ 🎬

Cardona ㉒

Barcelona. 🏠 *6,000.* 🚌 **ℹ** *Avinguda Rastrillo (93 869 27 98).* 🚌 *Sun.* 🎪 *Carnival (Feb), Festa major (second Sun of Sep).*

This 13th-century, ruddy-stoned castle of the Dukes of Cardona, constables to the crown of Aragón, is set on the top of a hill. The castle was rebuilt in the 18th century and is now a luxurious parador *(see p132).* Beside the castle is an elegant, early 11th-century church, the **Església de Sant Vicenç**.

The castle gives views of the town and of the Muntanya de Sal (Salt Mountain), a huge salt deposit beside the Riu Cardener that has been mined since Roman times.

Solsona ㉓

Lleida. 🏠 *7,000.* 🚌 **ℹ** *Carretera de Bassella 1 (973 48 23 10).* 🚌 *Tue & Fri.* 🎪 *Carnival (Feb), Sant Isidro (closest weekend to 15 May), Corpus Christi (May/Jun), Festa major (8–11 Sep).* **www**.elsolsonesinvita.com

Nine towers and three gateways remain of Solsona's fortifications. Inside is an ancient town of noble mansions. The cathedral houses a beautiful black stone Virgin. The **Museu Diocesà i Comarcal** contains Romanesque paintings and the **Museu Ganivets** has a fine knife collection.

🏛 **Museu Diocesà i Comarcal**
Plaça del Palau 1. **Tel** *973 48 21 01.* ⏰ *Tue–Sun.* ♿ ⬤ *1 Jan, 25, 26 Dec.*

🏛 **Museu del Ganivet**
Llobera 14. **Tel** *973 48 15 69.* ⏰ *Tue–Sun.* ⬤ *6 Jan, 25, 26 Dec.* 🎭 ♿

Lleida ㉔

Lleida. 🏠 *112,000.* 🚃 🚌 **ℹ** *Plaça Ramon Berenguer IV, s/n (973 24 88 40).* 🚌 *Thu & Sat.* 🎪 *Sant Anastasi (11 May), Sant Miquel (29 Sep).* **www**.lleidatur.es

Dominating Lleida, the capital of Catalonia's only inland province, is **La Suda**, a fort taken from the Moors in 1149. The cathedral, founded in 1203, lies within the fort's walls, above the town. It was transformed into barracks by Felipe V in 1707. Today it is desolate, but remains imposing, with magnificent Gothic windows.

A lift descends from La Seu Vella to the Plaça de

Sant Joan in the busy, pedestrianized shopping street that sweeps round the foot of the hill. The new cathedral is here, as is the reconstructed 13th-century town hall, the **Paeria**.

Poblet 25

See pp126–7.

Montblanc 26

Tarragona. 🏘 6,000. 🚃 🚌 ℹ️
*Antigua Iglesia de Sant Francesca
(977 86 17 33).* 🛍 *Tue & Fri.* 📷
Festa major (8–11 Sep).

The medieval grandeur of Montblanc lives on within its walls – possibly Catalonia's finest piece of military architecture. At the **Sant Jordi** gate St George allegedly slew the dragon. The **Museu Comarcal de la Conca de Barberà** has displays on local crafts.

🏛 **Museu Comarcal de la Conca de Barberà**
Carrer de Josa 6. **Tel** *977 86 03 49.*
⭕ *Tue–Sun & public hols.* 📷

Santes Creus 27

Tarragona. 🏘 150. 🚃 ℹ️ *Plaça de Sant Bernard 1 (977 63 81 41).* 🛍
Sat & Sun. 📷 *Santa Llúcia (13 Dec).*

The tiny village of Santes Creus is home to the prettiest of the "Cistercian triangle"

monasteries. The other two, Vallbona de les Monges and Poblet, are nearby. The **Monestir de Santes Creus** was founded in 1150 by Ramon Berenguer IV *(see p42)* during his reconquest of Catalonia. The Gothic cloisters are decorated with figurative sculptures, a style first permitted by Jaume II, who ruled from 1291 to 1327. His tomb is in the 12th-century church which features a rose window.

🔒 **Monestir de Santes Creus**
Tel *977 63 83 29.* ⭕ *Tue–Sun & public hols.* ◐ *1 Jan, 25 Dec.* 📷
♿ 📷 *by appointment.*

Vilafranca del Penedès 28

Barcelona. 🏘 35,000. 🚃 🚌
ℹ️ *Carrer Cort 14 (93 892 12 54).*
🛍 *Sat.* 📷 *Fira de Mayo (2nd week of May), Festa major (end Aug).*
www.turismevilafranca.com

This market town is set in the heart of Penedès, the main wine-producing region of Catalonia. The **Museu del Vi** (Wine Museum) documents the history of the area's wine trade. Local *bodegues* can be visited for wine tasting.

Sant Sadurní d'Anoia, the capital of Spain's sparkling wine, *cava (see pp32–3)*, is 8 km (5 miles) to the north.

🏛 **Museu del Vi**
Plaça de Jaume I. **Tel** *93 890 05 82.*
⭕ *Tue–Sun & public hols.* 📷

Anxaneta climbing to the top of a tower of *castellers*

HUMAN TOWERS

The province of Tarragona is famous for its *casteller* festivals, in which teams of men stand on each other's shoulders in an effort to build the highest human tower *(castell)*. Configurations depend on the number of men who form the base. Teams wear similar colours, and often have names denoting their home town. The small boy who has to undertake the perilous climb to the top, where he makes the sign of the cross, is called the *anxaneta. Castellers* assemble in competition for Tarragona province's major festivals throughout the year. In the wine town of Vilafranca del Penedès they turn out for Sant Fèlix (30 August), and in Tarragona city for Santa Tecla, its *festa major* on 23 September. Rival teams in Valls appear on St John's Day (24 June), but strive for their best achievement at the end of the tower-building season on St Ursula's Day (21 October), when teams from all over Catalonia converge on the town square.

Monestir de Santes Creus, surrounded by poplar and hazel trees

Monestir de Poblet ㉕

The monastery of Santa Maria de Poblet is a haven of tranquillity and a resting place of kings. It was the first and most important of three sister monasteries, known as the "Cistercian triangle" *(see p125)*, that helped to consolidate power in Catalonia after it had been recaptured from the Moors by Ramon Berenguer IV. In 1835, during the Carlist upheavals, it was plundered and seriously damaged by fire. Restoration of the impressive ruins, largely complete, began in 1930 and monks returned in 1940.

The dormitory is reached by stairs from the church. The vast 87-m (285-ft) gallery dates from the 13th century. Half of it is still in use by the monks.

The 12th-century refectory is a vaulted hall with an octagonal fountain and a pulpit.

View of Poblet
The abbey, its buildings enclosed by fortified walls that have hardly changed since the Middle Ages, is in an isolated valley near the Riu Francolí's source.

Museum

Wine cellar

Library
The Gothic scriptorium was converted into a library in the 17th century, when the Duke of Cardona donated his book collection.

Former kitchen

Royal doorway

Museum

Royal doorway

Royal tombs

TIMELINE

1100	1300	1500	1700	1900

1150 Santes Creus founded – third abbey in Cistercian triangle

1175 Founding of sister monastery at Vallbona de les Monges

14th century Main cloister finished

1479 Juan II, last king of Aragón, buried here

1812 Poblet desecrated by French troops

1940 Monks return

1196 Alfonso II is the first king to be buried here

1336–87 Reign of Pere the Ceremonious, who designates Poblet a royal pantheon

1952 Tombs reconstructed. Royal remains returned

1150 Poblet monastery founded by Ramon Berenguer IV

1835 Disentailment *(p45)* of monasteries. Poblet ravaged

Chapterhouse
This perfectly square room, with slender columns, has tiers of benches for the monks. It is paved with the tombstones of 11 abbots who died between 1393 and 1693.

VISITORS' CHECKLIST

Off N240, 10 km (6 miles) from Montblanc. **Tel** 977 87 00 89. L'Espluga de Francolí, then walk or taxi. 9:30am–1pm, 3:30–6pm daily. 1 Jan, 25 & 26 Dec. 8am daily; 10am, 1pm & 6pm Sun & public hols.

Parlour cloister

Sant Esteve cloister

New sacristy

★ High Altar Reredos
Behind the stone altar, supported by Romanesque columns, an impressive alabaster reredos fills the apse. It was carved by Damià Forment in 1527.

The Abbey Church, large and unadorned, with three naves, is a typical Cistercian building.

★ Royal Tombs
The tombs in the pantheon of kings were begun in 1359. In 1950 they were reconstructed by the sculptor Frederic Marès.

Baroque church façade

★ Cloisters
The evocative, vaulted cloisters were built in the 12th and 13th centuries and were the centre of monastic life. The capitals are beautifully decorated with carved scrollwork.

STAR FEATURES

★ High Altar Reredos

★ Royal Tombs

★ Cloisters

Palm trees lining the waterfront at Sitges

Sitges ㉙

Barcelona. 👤 20,000. 🚉 🚌
ℹ️ C/ Sínia Morera 1 (93 894 50 04).
🚢 Thu (in summer). 🎉 Festa major
(22–27 Aug).

There are no less than nine
beaches to choose from at
this seaside town. It has a
reputation as a gay resort but
is just as popular with
Barceloneses. Lively bars and
restaurants line its main boulevard, the Passeig Marítim, and
there are many examples of
modernista architecture
scattered amongst the '70s
apartment blocks. Modernista
artist Santiago Rusiñol (*see p29*)
spent much time here and bequeathed his quirky collection
of ceramics, sculptures, painting and ornate iron-work to
the **Museu Cau Ferrat**. It lies
next to Sitges's landmark, the
17th century church of **Sant
Bartomeu i Santa Tecla**.

🏛 **Museu Cau Ferrat**
Carrer Fonollar. **Tel** 93 894 03 64.
⬜ Tue–Sun. 🔵 public hols. 📷

Costa Daurada ㉚

Tarragona. 🚉 🚌 Calafell, Sant Vicenç
de Calders, Salou. ℹ️ Tarragona (977
23 34 15). www.costadaurada.org

The long. sandy beaches of
the Costa Daurada (Golden
Coast) run along the shores of
Tarragona provine. **El Vendrell**
is one of the area's active ports.
The **Museu Pau Casals** in Sant
Salvador (El Vendrell) is dedi-
cated to the famous cellist.

Port Aventura, south of
Tarragona, is one of Europe's
largest theme parks and has
many exotically-themed
attractions, such as Polynesia
and Wild West. **Cambrils** and
Salou to the south are the live-
liest resorts – the others are
low-key, family holiday spots.

🏛 **Museu Pau Casals**
Avinguda Palfuriana 59–61.
Tel 977 68 42 76. ⬜ Tue–Sun.

🎢 **Port Aventura**
Autovia Salou–Vila-seca. **Tel** 977 77
90 00. ⬜ mid-Mar–6 Jan. 📷 ♿

Tarragona ㉛

Tarragona. 👤 125,000. ✈️ 🚉 🚌
ℹ️ Carrer Fortuny 4 (977 25 07 95).
🚢 Tue & Thu. 🎉 Sant Magí (19
Aug), Santa Tecla (23 Sep).

Tarragona is now a major
industrial port, but it has
preserved many remnants of
its Roman past. As the capital

of Tarraconensis, the Romans
used it as a base for the conquest of the peninsula in the
3rd century BC (*see p41*).
   The avenue of Rambla
Nova ends abruptly on the
clifftop Balcó de Europa, in
sight of the ruins of the
Amfiteatre Romà and the
ruined 12th-century church of
Santa Maria del Miracle.
   Nearby is the Praetorium,
a Roman tower that was
converted into a palace in
medieval times. It now houses
the **Museu de la Romanitat**.
This displays Roman and
medieval finds, and gives
access to the cavernous
passageways of the excavated
Roman circus, built in the 1st
century AD. Next to the
Praetorium is the **Museu
Nacional Arqueològic**,
containing the most important
collection of Roman artifacts in
Catalonia. It has an extensive
collection of bronze tools and
beautiful mosaics, including a

The remains of the Roman amphitheatre, Tarragona

Head of Medusa. Among the most impressive remains are the huge pre-Roman stones on which the Roman wall is built. An archaeological walk stretches 1-km (1,100-yd) along the wall.

Behind the wall lies the 12th-century **cathedral**, built on the site of a Roman temple. This evolved over many centuries, as seen from the blend of styles of the exterior. Inside is an alabaster altarpiece of St Tecla, carved by Pere Joan in 1434. The 13th-century cloister has Gothic vaulting, but the doorway is Romanesque *(see pp22–3)*.

In the west of town is a 3rd- to 6th-century Christian cemetery (ask about opening times in the archaeological museum). Some of the sarcophagi were originally used as pagan tombs.

Ruins of the Palaeo-Christian Necropolis

Environs

The **Aqüeducte de les Ferreres** lies just outside the city, next to the A7 motorway. This 2nd-century aqueduct was built to bring water to the city from the Riu Gaià, 30 km (19 miles) to the north. The **Arc de Berà**, a 1st-century triumphal arch on the Via Augusta, is 20 km (12 miles) northeast on the N340.

The bustling, provincial town of **Reus** lies inland from Tarragona. Although its airport serves the Costa Daurada, it is often overlooked by holiday-makers. However there is some fine *modernista* architecture to be seen here, notably some early work by Antoni Gaudí who was born in Reus. The Pere Mata Psychiatric Institute was designed by Domènech i Montaner before his masterpiece, the Hospital de la Santa Creu i de Sant Pau *(see p79)*.

🏛 **Museu Nacional Arqueològic de Tarragona**
Plaça del Rei 5. **Tel** 977 23 62 09.
🕐 *Tue–Sun.* 📷♿
www.mnat.es

🏛 **Museu de la Romanitat**
Plaça del Rei. **Tel** 977 24 19 52.
🕐 *Tue–Sun.* 📷

Tortosa ⊕

Tarragona. 🏛 *30,000.* ℹ️ *Plaça del Bimil.lenari (977 51 08 22).* 🚌 *Mon.* 🎉 *Nostra Senyora de la Cinta (1st week Sep).* **www**.tortosa.altanet.org

A ruined castle and medieval walls are clues to Tortosa's historical importance. Sited at the lowest crossing point on the Riu Ebre, it has been strategically significant since Iberian times. The Moors held the city from the 8th century until 1148. The old Moorish castle, known as La Suda, is all that remains of their defences. It has now been renovated as a parador *(see p141)*. The Moors also built a mosque in Tortosa in 914. Its foundations were used for the present cathedral, on which work began in 1347. Although it was not completed for two centuries, the style is pure Gothic.

Tortosa was badly damaged in 1938–39 during one of the fiercest battles of the Civil War *(see p47)*, when the Ebre formed the front line between the opposing forces.

Delta de L'Ebre ⊕

Tarragona. 🚌 *Aldea.* 🚆 *Deltebre, Aldea.* ℹ️ *Deltebre (977 48 96 79).* **www**.ebre.com/delta

The delta of the Riu Ebre is a prosperous rice-growing region and wildlife haven. Some 70 sq km (27 sq miles) have been turned into a nature reserve, the **Parc Natural del Delta de L'Ebre**. In Deltebre there is an information centre and an interesting **Eco-Museu**, with an aquarium containing species found in the delta.

The main towns in the area are **Amposta** and **Sant Carles de la Ràpita**, both of which serve as good bases for exploring the reserve.

The best places to see the variety of wildlife are along the shore, from the Punta del Fangar in the north to the Punta de la Banya in the south. Everywhere is accessible by car except the Illa de Buda. Flamingoes breed on this island and, together with other water birds such as herons and avocets, can be seen from tourist boats that leave from Riumar and Deltebre.

🏛 **Eco-Museu**
Carrer Martí Buera 22. **Tel** 977 4896 79. 🕐 *daily.* 📷♿

THE SARDANA

Catalonia's national dance is more complicated than it appears. Its success depends on the dancers forming a circle and accurately counting the complicated short- and long-step skips and jumps. Music is provided by a *cobla*, an 11-person band consisting of a leader playing a three-holed flute *(flabiol)* and a little drum *(tamborí)*, five woodwind players and five brass players. The *sardana* is performed during most *festes* and at special day-long gatherings called *aplecs*. In Barcelona it is danced on Saturday evenings at 6 in front of the cathedral and every Sunday evening at 6 in the Plaça de Sant Jaume.

A group of *sardana* dancers captured in stone

TRAVELLERS'
NEEDS

WHERE TO STAY

Catalonia has an unrivalled variety of accommodation to offer visitors. The Barcelona and Catalonia tourist authorities have complete listings of hotels, country houses and camp sites as well as information on a range of other options. In Barcelona you can stay in the modern luxury of Spain's highest skyscraper,

Sign for a luxury five-star hotel

while on the coast you can try a self-catering holiday village (efficiencies) with all sorts of sports and entertainments provided. Family-run *cases de pagès*, which are stone-built farm or village houses or country manors, are Catalonia's most distinctive alternative. Some of the best hotels in every price range are listed on pages 134–41.

Façade of the Hotel Lloret in Barcelona's Rambla de Canaletes

HOTEL GRADING AND FACILITIES

The different types of hotel in Catalonia are denoted by the blue plaques near their doors. These show a star-rating which reflects the number and range of facilities available rather than quality of service. *Hotels* (H) and *hotel-residències* (HR) are graded from one to five stars; *motels* (M), *hostals* (H) and *hostal-residències* HR) from one to three stars; and *pensions* (P), with the simplest accommodation, have one or two stars. Hotels, *hostals*, *pensions* and motels have restaurants that are open to non-residents. *Hotel-residències* and *hostal-residències* do not have full dining rooms, but some serve breakfast.

PRICES AND PAYING

Spanish law requires all hotels to display their prices at reception and in every room. As a rule, the higher the star-rating, the greater the price. Rates are almost invariably quoted per room (but meal prices per person). A double room in a one-star *hostal* can be as little as 18 euros a night; one in a five-star hotel will cost more than 150 euros a night. Prices vary according to region, season, day of the week or special feature such as a view or balcony. The prices given on pages 116–21 are based on mid-season or high (tourist)-season rates. Prices for rooms and meals are usually quoted without including VAT *(IVA)*, currently seven per cent.

BOOKING AND CHECK-IN

Hotels in Barcelona can be very busy during the many trade fairs held all year round, so booking in advance is advisable. Off-season in rural Catalonia there is rarely any need to book ahead, but if you want a room in a busy season or in a particular hotel it is a good idea to do so. Resort hotels on the Costa Brava often close from autumn to spring. On the warmer Costa Daurada, hotels may have a shorter winter closing period. You will not normally be asked for a deposit when you book a room. However, a deposit of 20–25 per cent may be levied for bookings during peak periods or for a stay of more than a few nights. You may lose all or some of it if you cancel at less than a week's notice. Most hotels will honour a booking only until 8pm. If you are delayed, telephone to tell them when to expect you.

When checking in you will be asked for your passport or identity card to comply with police regulations. It will normally be returned as soon as your details have been copied.

PARADORS

There are seven paradors in Catalonia – at Aiguablava, Artíes, Cardona, Seu de Urgell, Vic, Vielha and Tortosa. They form part of Spain's chain of high-quality, government-run hotels in historic buildings, or in purpose-built, new buildings in spectacular settings. Reservations for paradors can be made through the **Central de Reservas** (Madrid), **Keytel International** (London) and **Marketing Ahead** (New York).

The spacious and comfortable interior of the parador at Vic

◁ **Christmas market in front of the cathedral, Barcelona**

Solid, stone-built architecture typical of traditional Catalan farmhouses

RURAL ACCOMMODATION

Cases de Pagès are Catalan farmhouses *(masies)* or country houses that accept visitors. Some do B&B, some an evening meal or full board. Tourist offices have the *Guia residèncias-casa de pagès*, published by the Generalitat de Catalunya. You can book directly or through **Turisverd**.

The **Associació Fondes de Catalunya** is a group of *cases fonda* (simple country hotels), offering wholesome regional cuisine). The facility closes for two weeks during August, so if you plan to visit Catalonia in that month, you should make a reservation before setting off.

The **Xarxa d'Albergs de Catalunya** runs youth hostels, which also cater for adults and families, and the **Federació d'Entitats Excursionistes de Catalunya** runs mountain refuges for hikers.

SELF-CATERING

Villas and apartments let by the week are plentiful on the Costa Daurada and Costa Brava. *Aparthotels (*or *hotels-apartment)* and *residèncias-apartament* are a new breed of self-catering accommodation (efficiencies). Ranked from one to four stars, each apartment has a kitchen, but each complex also has a restaurant and often a swimming pool and other facilities. Generalitat de Catalunya tourist offices *(see p174)* and most travel agents have details of all types of villas and apartments. Holiday (vacation) villages *(ciutats de vacances)*, such as Cala Montjoi and Club-Hotel Giverola on the Costa Brava, are similar, but accommodation is in bungalows and includes sports and entertainments.

Sign for a camp site

Gites de Catalunya are superior country houses rented out on a week-by-week basis by Turisverd or **The Individual Travellers' Spain**. Many *cases de pagès* are also self-catering (run as efficiencies).

CAMP SITES

Catalonia has over 300 camp sites, classified as deluxe (L), 1-star, 2-star, 3-star, or farm (M, *càmpings-masia*). All have basic amenities, guards and a safe. *Catalunya Càmpings*, published by the Generalitat *(see p174)*, is available from tourist offices. Many sites in Barcelona are grouped under the **Associació de Càmpings de Barcelona** (which closes for three weeks in August, so ring in advance). A camping carnet from your home camping association can be used instead of a passport at sites and also covers you for third-party insurance. Camping is permitted only at official sites.

DISABLED TRAVELLERS

Few hotels are well equipped for disabled guests, although some youth hostels are. The **Federació ECOM** and Viajes 2000 *(see p175)* will advise on hotels throughout Catalonia for visitors with special needs.

DIRECTORY

PARADORS

Central de Reservas
Calle Requena 3,
28013 Madrid.
Tel 91 516 66 66.
Fax 91 516 66 57/ 66 58.
www.parador.es

Keytel International
402 Edgware Road,
London W2 1ED.
Tel 020 7616 0300 in UK.
Fax 020 7616 0317 in UK.

Marketing Ahead
381 Park Av. Sth., Suite 718, New York, NY 10016.
Tel 800 223 1356 (toll free).
Fax (212) 686 0271 in NY.

RURAL ACCOMMODATION

Associació Fondes de Catalunya
Ramón Turró 63–65, 2
08005 Barcelona.
Tel 902 314 249.
Fax 93 300 16 58.
www.casafonda.com

Federació d'Entitats Excursionistes de Catalunya
La Rambla 41, 1er, 08002 Barcelona.
Tel 93 412 07 77.
Fax 93 412 63 53.
www.feec.org

Turisverd
Plaça Sant Josep Oriol 4,
08002 Barcelona.
Tel 93 412 69 84.
www.turisverd.com

Xarxa d'Albergs de Catalunya
Carrer Rocafort 116–122,
08015 Barcelona.
Tel 93 483 83 41.
Fax 93 483 83 47.
www.tujuca.com

SELF-CATERING

The Individual Travellers' Spain
Bignor, Pulborough,
West Sussex RH20 1QD.
Tel 08700 780 194.
Fax 08700 780 190.

CAMPING

Associació de Càmpings de Barcelona
Gran Via Corts Catalanes 608, 3ª, 08007 Barcelona.
Tel 93 412 59 55.
Fax 93 302 13 36.
www.campingsbcn.com

DISABLED TRAVELLERS

Federació ECOM
Gran Via de les Corts Catalanes 562, principal, 2a, 08011 Barcelona.
Tel 93 451 55 50.
Tel 93 451 69 04.
www.ecom.es

SPANISH TOURIST OFFICES

UK
22–23 Manchester Sq.,
London W1U 3PX.
Tel 020 7486 8077.
www.tourspain.co.uk

US
666 Fifth Ave, Floor 35,
New York, NY 10103.
Tel (212) 265 8822.
www.okspain.org

Choosing a Hotel

The choice of hotels in the following pages have been selected across a wide price range for the excellence of their facilities, location or character. The chart below first lists hotels in Barcelona by area, followed by a selection in the rest of Catalonia. Hotels within the same price category are listed alphabetically.

PRICE CATEGORIES
For a standard double room per night, with tax, breakfast and service included.

€ under 75 euros
€€ 75–125 euros
€€€ 125–200 euros
€€€€ 200–275 euros
€€€€€ over 275 euros.

OLD TOWN

Fontanella   🖼 P   €
Via Laietana 71, 2nd, 08002 **Tel** *93 317 59 43* **Fax** *93 317 59 43* *Rooms 11*   **Map** *5 B1*

This is a simple, family-run *hostal* where the owners do their best to make visitors feel at home. There's a wonderful antique lift, which creaks up to a knick-knack filled lobby and the basic rooms are made cosy and welcoming with flowery prints and lots of goodies in the bathrooms. Triple and quadruple rooms are also available.

Gat Raval   €
Carrer de Joaquín Costa 44, 08001 **Tel** *93 481 66 70* **Fax** *93 342 66 97* *Rooms 24*   **Map** *2 F1*

A hip, newish *hostal*, painted in an eye-catching lime green and brilliant white, this is an excellent budget choice in the heart of the trendy Raval district. Huge blown-up photographs of Barcelona give it a stylish edge. Rooms are plain, but crisp and modern, and there is Internet access for guests. **www.gataccommodation.com**

Hostal d'Avinyó   €
Carrer de Avinyo 42, 08002 **Tel** *93 318 79 45* **Fax** *93 318 68 93* *Rooms 28*   **Map** *5 A3*

This simple hotel has a very central position, near Port Vell, La Ramblas and the Picasso Museum. Best of all, it's on one of the Old Town's best shopping streets, with trendy fashion boutiques and hip bars and restaurants. The rooms are basic but clean. They are better value in the low season. **www.hostalavinyo.com**

Hostería Grau   €
Carrer de Ramalleres 27, 08001 **Tel** *93 301 81 35* **Fax** *93 317 68 25* *Rooms 27*

Close to the Museum of Contemporary Art (MACBA) and the nightlife of El Raval, this is a delightful little *hostal*. Rooms are simply decorated with floral prints and come with or without en suite facilities. They also rent apartments, a good choice for families or for longer stays. **www.hostalgrau.com**

Peninsular   🖼 ▤   €
Carrer de Sant Pau 34, 08001 **Tel** *93 302 31 38* **Fax** *93 412 36 99* *Rooms 59*   **Map** *2 F3*

Rooms are truly basic in this former Carmelite convent but good value. Just off La Rambla behind the Liceu opera house, its charms lie in its luminous, plant-filled inner courtyard and friendly staff. Breakfast is served in a high-ceilinged, old-fashioned dining room, but there is no restaurant.

Pensió 2000   €
Carrer de Sant Pere més Alt, 08003 **Tel** *93 310 7466* **Fax** *93 319 42 52* *Rooms 7*   **Map** *5 B1*

This welcoming little *hostal* has a perfect location overlooking the flamboyant Modernista Palau de la Música. The cosy bedrooms, some with shared bathroooms, lead off a large, comfortable sitting room with a big TV. Triple and quadruple rooms are also available. **www.pensio2000.com**

Pensión Francia   €
Carrer de Rera Palau 4, 08003 **Tel** *93 319 03 76* *Rooms 14*   **Map** *5 B3*

Right in the heart of the fashionable Born district, with its great shopping and nightlife, this offers basic, but immaculate, whitewashed rooms. All have TVs but some have shared bathrooms. The quietest overlook the narrow Passeig del Palau. There's also a cosy lounge area.

España   🖼 ⬛ ▤   €€
Carrer de Sant Pau 9–11, 08001 **Tel** *93 318 17 58* **Fax** *93 317 11 34* *Rooms 66*   **Map** *2 F3*

Lluís Domènech i Montaner, the outstanding Modernista architect, designed this hotel including the wonderful mural of mermaids in the dining room. The modern bedrooms don't live up to the promise of the gorgeous lobby with its swirling woodwork and lavish fireplace. **www.hotelespanya.com**

Jardí   🖼 ▤   €€
Plaça Sant Josep Oriol 1, 08002 **Tel** *93 301 59 00* **Fax** *93 342 57 33* *Rooms 40*   **Map** *5 A2*

A popular *hostal* overlooking a pretty leafy square in the heart of the Gothic Quarter. Some bedrooms have been renovated and have good views over the square and the handsome Gothic church of Santa María del Pi; others are cheaper but not as atmospheric. Best for night owls.

Key to Symbols *see back cover flap*

Lloret 🗺🗎 €€

Rambla de Canaletes 125, 08002 **Tel** *93 317 33 66* **Fax** *93 301 92 83 Rooms 58* **Map** *5 A1*

Right on La Rambla and close to the Plaça de Catalunya, this functional hotel has an excellent location but few frills. The lobby is charming, but rooms are rather dated. The best have balconies overlooking the action on the avenue below, but suffer from street noise. **www.hlloret.com**

Mesón de Castilla 🗺🅿🗎 €€

Carrer de Valdonzella 5, 08001 **Tel** *93 318 21 82* **Fax** *93 412 40 20 Rooms 57* **Map** *2 F1*

A comfortable hotel, but old-fashioned, in a building with a Modernista façade near the Museum of Contemporary Art (MACBA) in the bohemian Raval neighbourhood. The rooms are simple, but hand-painted furniture gives them some charm. It's in a quiet location, and there are family rooms available. **www.mesoncastilla.com**

Park Hotel 🗺🅿🍴🗎 €€

Carrer de Marquès de l'Argentera 11, 08003 **Tel** *93 319 60 00* **Fax** *93 319 415 19 Rooms 91* **Map** *5 C3*

A rare gem of 1950s architecture, designed by Antonio Moragas in 1951 and well preserved during his son's award-winning renovations in 1990. The slim wraparound staircase is a highlight. Rooms are small but smartly furnished and the best have balconies. The restaurant, Abac, is outstanding. **www.parkhotelbarcelona.com**

HCC Montblanc 🗺🅿🍴🏊🍸🗎 €€€

Via Laietana 61, 08003 **Tel** *93 343 55 55* **Fax** *93 343 55 58 Rooms 157* **Map** *5 B2*

A sleek modern hotel offering large rooms with attractive modern decor and good facilities including Internet connection. It also has a terrace with fabulous views, a small pool (summer only), a gym and a good restaurant. It's located on a busy street, but rooms are soundproofed. **www.hcchotels.es**

Jazz Hotel 🗺🅿🍴🏊🗎 €€€

Carrer Pelai 3, 08001 **Tel** *93 552 96 96* **Fax** *93 552 96 97 Rooms 108* **Map** *5 A1*

A glassy ultra-modern hotel near the Plaça de Catalunya, this offers better facilities than its three-star rating would suggest. There's a rooftop pool with sun-deck, and the rooms (all soundproofed) are stylishly decorated with contemporary furniture and fabrics. **www.hoteljazzbarcelona.com**

Metropol 🗺🅿🍴🗎 €€€

Carrer Ample 31, 08002 **Tel** *93 310 51 00* **Fax** *93 319 12 76 Rooms 71* **Map** *5 A3*

A handsome 19th-century hotel which has been thoroughly modernised but retains some old-fashioned charm. It's tucked away down a quiet street in the Barri Gòtic, and the streetside rooms, many with balconies, are bright and modern. Interior rooms can be a little gloomy. **www.hesperia-metropol.com**

Montecarlo 🗺🅿👥🗎 €€€

La Rambla 124, 08002 **Tel** *93 412 04 04* **Fax** *93 318 73 23 Rooms 55* **Map** *5 A2*

This beautiful hotel right on La Rambla in the centre of Barcelona occupies a former 19th-century palace. The lobby is a gorgeous whirl of gilt and marble, but rooms are smart and modern. Staff are particularly helpful here, and there are fantastic deals available on the website. **www.montecarlobcn.com**

Nouvel 🗺🍴🗎 €€€

Carrer de Santa Anna 18–20, 08002 **Tel** *93 301 82 74* **Fax** *93 301 83 70 Rooms 54* **Map** *5 A1*

In a pretty little shopping street off La Rambla, near the Plaça de Catalunya, this well-managed old-style hotel is tastefully decorated and furnished. The best rooms have curving Modernista-style balconies, and there's a charming lobby and lounge area with 1920s-style chandeliers. **www.hotelnouvel.com**

Oriente 🗺🍴🗎 €€€

La Rambla 45–7, 08002 **Tel** *93 302 25 58* **Fax** *93 412 38 19 Rooms 142* **Map** *2 F1*

A former Franciscan friary makes a romantic setting for the recently restored Oriente. The cloister has been converted into a glorious ballroom with gilded columns. The rooms are modern, with creamy fabrics and simple wooden furniture. The nicest (but noisiest) rooms offer views of La Rambla. **www.husa.es**

San Agustín 🗺🍴🗎 €€€

Plaça de Sant Agustí 3, 08001 **Tel** *93 318 16 58* **Fax** *93 317 29 28 Rooms 75* **Map** *2 F3*

One of the city's oldest hotels has a peach façade overlooking a handsome square. Rooms are modern and simply furnished, but those in the attic have charming wooden beams and fabulous views of the square. This arty neighbourhood has good galleries and restaurants. **www.hotelsa.com**

Colón 🗺🅿🍴🗎 €€€€

Avinguda de la Catedral 7, 08002 **Tel** *93 301 14 04* **Fax** *93 317 29 15 Rooms 145* **Map** *5 B2*

This traditional, rather formal hotel has a fabulous location opposite the Gothic cathedral. The best rooms have terraces overlooking the square, where guests can watch the *sardana*, the traditional Catalan folk dance, performed in the Plaça de Catedral on Sunday mornings. The hotel has two meeting rooms and Internet. **www.hotelcolon.es**

Neri 🗺🅿🍴🗎 €€€€

Carrer de Sant Sever 5, 08002 **Tel** *93 304 06 55* **Fax** *93 304 03 37 Rooms 22* **Map** *5 A2*

An enchanting hotel which combines the architectural features of the original 18th-century palace with sleek contemporary fittings. Airy, stylish rooms are draped in sensuous fabrics, and there's a magnificent rooftop terrace with views of the Gothic cathedral. Fabulous restaurant too serving Mediterranean cuisine. **www.hotelneri.com**

Arts

Carrer de Marina 19–21, 08005 **Tel** *93 221 10 00* **Fax** *93 221 10 70* *Rooms 455*

Map *6 E4*

Set in a soaring tower overlooking the Port Olímpic, this is one of Europe's most luxurious and glamorous hotels. Huge rooms boast spectacular views along with every imaginable modern convenience, and there are stunning suites on the upper floors for those with very deep pockets. **www.hotelartsbarcelona.com**

Le Méridien

La Rambla 111, 08002 **Tel** *93 318 62 00* **Fax** *93 301 77 76* *Rooms 212*

Map *5 A1*

A newly refurbished and very elegant hotel on La Rambla, this is popular with visiting film stars and opera singers from the nearby Liceu opera house. Rooms are handsomely furnished and the hotel is well equipped for business travellers. For a treat, book the extravagant Presidential Suite. **www.lemeridien-barcelona.com**

EIXAMPLE

Hostal Ciudad Condal

Carrer de Mallorca 255, 08008 **Tel** *93 215 10 40* **Fax** *93 487 04 59* *Rooms 15*

Map *3 A4*

A modest *hostal* located in a handsome Modernista building on one of the Eixample's most elegant streets. All rooms have mini-bars and air conditioning. Rear rooms on the second floor are quieter than those closer to street level. No breakfasts, but there are dozens of cafés close by. **www.hostalciudadcondal.com**

Hotel Paseo de Gracia

Passeig de Gràcia 102, 08008 **Tel** *93 215 58 24* **Fax** *93 215 37 24* *Rooms 33*

Map *3 B3*

There are few budget choices in the chi-chi Eixample district, but this modest little hotel is a good option. It has a fabulous location on the city's most desirable boulevard, close to the finest Gaudí buildings, and some of the simple rooms offer views of the Plaça de Catalunya.

Gran Via

Gran Via de les Corts Catalanes 642, 08010 **Tel** *93 318 19 00* **Fax** *93 318 99 97* *Rooms 53*

Map *3 B5*

A hotel in a late 19th-century building with an ageing grandeur, north of the Plaça de Catalunya adjoining the Passeig de Gràcia. The rooms are spacious and all have polished wooden floors and antique-style furnishings. Best of all is the terrace and garden, a delightful oasis in the heart of the city. **www.nnhotels.com**

Hostal Palacios

Rambla Catalunya 27, 1st, 08007 **Tel** *93 301 3079* **Fax** *93 301 3792* *Rooms 11*

Map *3 A3*

This friendly *hostal* is housed in a magnificent Modernista building. Many of the original fittings, including the huge carved doors and colourful tiles, have been retained, and stylishly complement the modern fabrics and contemporary bathrooms. Guests can use the piano in the lounge. **www.hostalpalacios.com**

Actual

Carrer Rosselló 238, 08008 **Tel** *93 552 05 50* **Fax** *93 552 05 55* *Rooms 29*

Map *3 B3*

This modern, stylish hotel is fashionably decorated in sleek minimalist style. It has a superb location on the same block as Gaudí's La Pedrera, and the upmarket boutiques of the Passeig de Gràcia are on the doorstep. Like many hotels in this area, it is geared towards business travellers, which means good weekend deals. **www.hotelactual.com**

Axel

Carrer Aribau 33, 08011 **Tel** *93 323 93 93* **Fax** *93 323 93 94* *Rooms 66*

This is Barcelona's best gay hotel, a stylish four-star establishment with a wealth of excellent facilities. The rooms are sleek and modern, there's a fabulous rooftop bar, and business facilities are available in the small library. There's also a dipping pool, and a good restaurant with drag shows. **www.hotelaxel.com**

Catalunya Plaza

Plaça de Catalunya 7, 08002 **Tel** *93 317 71 71* **Fax** *93 317 78 55* *Rooms 46*

Map *5 A1*

A reliable chain hotel in the city centre which is popular with business people. The 19th-century building has large sitting rooms decorated with some intricate frescoes. Rooms are attractively if generically decorated, and staff are very attentive and extremely helpful. **www.hotelcatalunyaplaza.com**

Prestige Paseo de Gracia

Passeig de Gracia 62, 08007 **Tel** *93 272 41 80* **Fax** *93 272 41 81* *Rooms 45*

Map *3 A4*

Zen meets Modernism in this tasteful, luxury hotel near Gaudí's most important buildings. Rooms are light-filled and stylish, with up-to-the-minute amenities including Bang and Olufsen TVs and music systems. In the chilled-out Zeroom, you can browse through art and design books. There's also an Oriental garden.

Claris

Carrer Pau Claris 150, 08009 **Tel** *93 487 62 62* **Fax** *93 215 79 70* *Rooms 124*

Map *3 B4*

Antique kilims and elegant English and French furniture ornament this hotel off the Passeig de Gràcia. It occupies the converted Vedruna Palace, and is scattered with fabulous artworks from around the world. There's a panoramic rooftop pool and sun-deck, and guests may use the hotel Smart cars. **www.derbyhotels.es**

Key to Price Guide *see p134* **Key to Symbols** *see back cover flap*

Condes de Barcelona

Passeig de Gràcia 73–75, 08008 **Tel** *93 445 00 00* **Fax** *93 445 32 32 Rooms 183*   **Map** *3 A4*

This hotel is located in two handsomely renovated Modernista palaces, with marble lobbies and creamy façades. The rooms in both locations are coolly contemporary and some have Jacuzzis. Choose a room with terrace to admire Gaudí's La Pedrera directly across the street. **www.condesdebarcelona.com**

Hispanos Siete Suiza

Carrer Sicilia 255, 08025 **Tel** *93 208 20 51* **Fax** *93 208 20 52 Rooms 19*   **Map** *4 D3*

This *aparthotel* has a stunning location next to Gaudí's Sagrada Família cathedral. The 18 two-bedroom apartments and one suite are traditionally decorated. Proceeds from the *aparthotel* go to the Dr Melchor Colet foundation for cancer research. Colet's collection of vintage cars is on permanent show. **www.barcelona19apartments.com**

Majèstic

Passeig de Gràcia 68, 08007 **Tel** *93 488 17 17* **Fax** *93 488 18 80 Rooms 303*   **Map** *3 A4*

A grand, traditional hotel in Neo-Classical style in a chic street (adjoining the Carrer de València). The stylish bedrooms are decorated with plush drapes and elegant prints, and are all equipped with five-star amenities. There are also some very luxurious suites, and a superb rooftop pool with spectacular views. **www.hotelmajestic.es**

Omm

Carrer Rosselló 265, 08008 **Tel** *93 445 40 00* **Fax** *93 445 40 04 Rooms 59*   **Map** *3 B3*

From the glistening ultra-modern façade with its peeled-back balconies, to the fluid, glassy public spaces, this hotel is the epitome of sleek Barcelona design. The fashionably minimalist rooms are very comfortable, and the slick bar and club make it popular with fashionistas. **www.hotelomm.es**

Ritz

Gran Via de les Corts Catalanes 668, 08010 **Tel** *93 510 11 30* **Fax** *93 318 01 48 Rooms 122*   **Map** *3 B5*

One of Barcelona's most elegant grand hotels has been recently refurbished. The large luxurious bedrooms are decorated in classical style and boast huge marble bathrooms inspired by Roman spas. There's a health club and beauty parlour. Famous guests include the Spanish royal family and Frank Sinatra. **www.ritzbcn.com**

FURTHER AFIELD

PEDRALBES Princesa Sofia Intercontinental

Plaça de Pius XII 4, 08028 **Tel** *93 508 10 00* **Fax** *93 508 10 01 Rooms 500*

A vast, luxury hotel decorated in marble, wood and bronze, with a restaurant, bar and facilities for conferences. There are both indoor and outdoor pools, and a host of extras including a beauty parlour and boutique. Rooms are cheaper on weekends and in summer. **www.intercontinental.com**

POBLENOU Hostal Poble Nou

Carrer Taulat 30, 08005 **Tel** *93 221 26 01* **Fax** *93 221 26 01 Rooms 5*

This charming, little *hostal* is located in a colourful 1930s townhouse in the traditional neighbourhood of Poblenou. It's close to the best city beaches and well connected by metro and tram to the city centre. The en suite rooms are simple, but there's a pretty breakfast terrace. Breakfast included in price. **www.hostalpoblenou.com**

SARRIA-SANT GERVASI Rekor'd

Carrer de Muntaner 352, 08021 **Tel** *93 200 19 53* **Fax** *93 414 50 84 Rooms 15 + 2 apartments*

A small, modern hotel oriented towards business travellers in the uptown shopping area. The large rooms are sleekly furnished with contemporary fabrics and fittings, and all come equipped with exercise bikes and office space. The facilites for business travellers are excellent. **www.hotelrekord.com**

VALLVIDRERA Gran Hotel La Florida

Carretera Vallvidrera al Tibidabo 83–93, 08035 **Tel** *93 259 30 00* **Fax** *93 259 30 01 Rooms 74*

In a beautiful palace in the hills above Barcelona, this hotel is set in beautiful gardens offering breathtaking views of the whole city. The suites are all equipped with every imaginable facility, and there is a wonderful spa and restaurant. A shuttle service takes you to the heart of the city in minutes. **www.hotellaflorida.com**

CATALONIA

ANDORRA LA VELLA Andorra Park Hotel

Les Canals 24, **Tel** *376 87 77 77* **Fax** *376 82 09 83 Rooms 40*

One of Andorra's most luxurious hotels, it is modern and built into a steep, wooded hillside. It has a library, a swimming pool hewn out of rock, and is situated beside a department store. **www.andorraparkhotel.com**

ARTIES Parador Don Gaspar de Portolà   €€€

*Ctra Bequeira-Beret, 25599 (Lleida) **Tel** 973 64 08 01 **Fax** 973 64 10 01 Rooms 57*

A modern, warm, comfortable parador built in the local traditional stone and slate. It's in one of the prettiest villages of the Vall d'Aran, with attractive narrow streets dotted with medieval chapels. It's handy for local ski resorts, and makes a good base for mountain walkers. **www.parador.es**

AVINYONET DE PUIGVENTÓS Mas Pau   €€

*Carretera de Besalúa Olot, 17742 (Girona) **Tel** 972 54 61 54 **Fax** 972 54 63 26 Rooms 20*

A beautiful hotel in a 16th-century house, surrounded by gardens and wooded farmland. Many of the luxurious bedrooms and suites are located in the 25-metre-high tower, and have splendid views. There's a spectacular restaurant too. **www.maspau.com**

BANYOLES Mirallac   €€€

*Passeig Darder 50, 17820 (Girona) **Tel** 972 57 10 45 **Fax** 972 58 08 87 Rooms 27*

A cheeful, old-style hotel overlooking the vast lake at Banyoles, they offer traditionally decorated rooms, a huge swimming pool and lots of lakeside activities. There's a good restaurant serving tasty local specialities. Mirallac is also an ideal place for adventure sports lovers.

BEGUR Aigua Blava   €€€

*Platja de Fornells, 17255 (Girona) **Tel** 972 62 20 58 **Fax** 972 62 45 62 Rooms 86*

This charming, whitewashed Mediterranean-style hotel overlooks Fornells Bay, one of the prettiest spots on the Costa Brava. Arches frame beautiful sea views, and it is surrounded by pine trees and gardens. The rooms are light and airy, and it also offers ten fully-equipped apartments. Closed from November to mid-February. **www.aiguablava.com**

BEQUEIRA-BERET Royal Tanau   €€€€€

*Ctra de Beret, 25598 (Lleida) **Tel** 973 64 44 46 **Fax** 973 64 43 44 Rooms 30*

This luxurious boutique hotel in the Tanau skiing area has several amenities, including indoor and outdoor Jacuzzis and a spa. In winter, a private ski lift whisks guests directly to the pistes. There are full après-ski facilities and it offers elegant, fully-equipped suites as well as rooms. **www.solmelia.com**

BEUDA Can Felicià   €€

*Segueró, 17851 (Girona) **Tel** 972 59 05 23 **Fax** 972 59 05 23 Rooms 6*

Beautiful views make this charming, rural hotel in a former school a good place to stay. The rooms are painted in fresh, light colours and overlook a lovely garden, perfect for children and complete with a small swimming pool. The price includes delicious home-cooked dinners for hotel guests only. **www.canfelicia.com**

BEUDA Mas Salvanera   €€

*Mas Salvanera s/n, 17850 (Girona) **Tel** 972 59 09 75 **Fax** 972 59 08 63 Rooms 9*

This handsome 17th-century Catalan farmhouse has been attractively converted into a small, family-run rural hotel. It is beautifully set in gardens, and offers delicious home-cooked food to its guests. Lots of opportunities for hiking, fishing and horseback riding in the local area. **www.salvanera.com**

BOLVIR DE CERDANYA Torre del Remei   €€€€

*Camí Reial s/n, 17539 (Girona) **Tel** 972 14 01 82 **Fax** 972 14 04 49 Rooms 20*

One of the most luxurious hotels in the region, this opulent Modernista mansion is set in magnificent gardens with a stunning mountain backdrop. The classically decorated rooms are perfectly equipped with up-to-the-minute gadgetry, and the extensive facilities include a new spa and gym. **www.torredelremei.com**

CADAQUÈS Misty   €€

*Carretera Nova Port Lligat, 17488 (Girona) **Tel** 972 25 89 62 **Fax** 972 15 90 90 Rooms 11*

Three houses and a swimming pool surrounded by shady gardens comprise this appealing hotel, one of the most unusual on the Costa Brava. It's a good spot for families, with a barbecue area, billiard room and a swimming pool. There's a snack bar in high season, but no restaurant. Closed from January to March **www.hotel-misty.com**

CARDONA Parador de Cardona   €€

*Carrer de Castell s/n, 08261 (Barcelona) **Tel** 93 869 12 75 **Fax** 93 869 16 36 Rooms 54*

One of the most striking paradors in Spain, this luxuriously converted medieval castle dominates Cardona and offers spectacular views of the countryside. Many of the elegant rooms boast four-poster beds, and it has a fine Catalan restaurant. **www.parador.es**

CASTELLDEFELS Gran Hotel Rey Don Jaime   €€€

*Avinguda del Hotel 22, 08860 (Barcelona) **Tel** 93 665 13 00 **Fax** 93 664 51 51 Rooms 220*

This huge Mediterreanean-style hotel has arches and whitewashed walls. Choose between modern rooms or more traditional decor in the rustic zone. There are excellent sports facilities, with everything from squash courts to a swimming pool. The hilltop setting offers wonderful views of the coast. **www.grup-soteras.com**

CASTELLÓ D'EMPURIES Allioli   €€

*Urbanització Castell Nou, 17486 (Girona) **Tel** 972 25 03 00 **Fax** 972 25 03 00 Rooms 42*

A 17th-century Catalan farmhouse, just off the main Roses-Figueres road, with simple rooms (some suitable for families). The restaurant is popular for Sunday lunch among locals. There's a pool in summer. The hotel is closed from mid-December until end-February. Restaurant open all year. **www.hotelallioli.com**

Key to Price Guide *see p134* **Key to Symbols** *see back cover flap*

CÓLL Casa Peyró €€

Carrer Unic s/n, 25527 (Lleida) **Tel** *973 29 70 02 Rooms 8*

A delightful, family-run little hostelry hidden away in a pretty mountain village. All the traditionally decorated rooms are en suite, and there's a sauna and facilities for massage. There is no restaurant, but the family prepares tasty home-cooked food for guests. Price includes half board.

FIGUERES Hotel Durán €€

Carrer de Lasauca 5, 17600 (Girona) **Tel** *972 50 12 50* **Fax** *972 50 26 09 Rooms 60*

This ochre-and-pink hotel is set above one of the finest restaurants in the region, established in 1855. It is still owned by the same family, who provide a friendly welcome. Rooms are attractively, if simply, furnished, and many have pretty wrought-iron balconies overlooking the street below. **www.hotelduran.com**

GIRONA Pensión Bellmirall €

Carrer de Bellmirall 3, 17004 (Girona) **Tel** *972 20 40 09 Rooms 7*

This is a rickety, old-fashioned charmer tucked away in the ancient heart of Girona. The ancient house has preserved its massive stone walls, and bedrooms are individually decorated with traditional furniture and original art. A huge breakfast is served in a pretty garden area. It's closed in February.

GOMBRÉN Fonda Xesc €

Plaça Roser 1, 17531 (Girona) **Tel** *972 73 04 04 Rooms 14*

Perfectly located in the heart of a traditional mountain village, this old-fashioned hotel offers modest, but immaculate rooms. The renowned restaurant serves fine Catalan specialities, including home-made *embutits*, which you can also pick up at their shop. **www.fondaxesc.com**

GRANOLLERS Fonda Europa €€

Carrer Anselm Clavé 1, 08400 (Barcelona) **Tel** *93 870 03 12* **Fax** *93 870 79 01 Rooms 7*

This small hotel has been an inn for travellers since 1714, and is still owned by the same family. The bedrooms, on the second floor, have been completely modernised, and are simply decorated. The restaurant is the big draw here, with its hearty Catalan specialities prepared to traditional recipes.

LA GARRIGA Gran Hotel Balneario Blancafort €€€€

Carrer Mina, 7, 08530 (Barcelona) **Tel** *93 860 56 00* **Fax** *93 861 23 90 Rooms 312*

This handsome 19th-century hotel is located in a relaxing spa town near Barcelona. It has recently emerged from major renovations which have added magnificent five-star luxuries. The rooms are classically decorated with prints and drapes, and excellent facilities include a beauty spa and gardens. **www.balnearioblancafort.com**

LA SEU D'URGELL Parador de La Seu d'Urgell €€

Carrer Sant Domènec 6, 25700 (Lleida) **Tel** *973 25 20 00* **Fax** *973 35 23 09 Rooms 80*

Only the Renaissance cloister, now used as the lounge, remains of a convent that occupied this site close to the 12th-century cathedral of La Seu. The modern parador has good facilities, including a covered pool, and there are excellent opportunities for hiking and skiing on the doorstep. **www.parador.es**

L'ESCALA El Roser €

Carrer L'Eglésia 7, 17130 (Girona) **Tel** *972 77 02 19* **Fax** *972 77 45 29 Rooms 22*

This charming, old-fashioned seaside hotel is right on the beach in the heart of the historic centre of L'Escala. The restaurant is one of the best in the area, and rooms are immaculate and brightly furnished. Closed in November. **www.elroserhostal.com**

L'ESPLUGA DEL FRANCOLÍ Hostal del Senglar €

Plaça de Montserrat Canals 1, 43440 (Tarragona) **Tel** *977 87 01 21* **Fax** *977 87 01 27 Rooms 38*

A three-storey, whitewashed hotel with simply furnished, traditional rooms including family rooms. There's a delightful shady garden where barbecues are held in summer. A menu of delicious dishes traditional to the area is served in the restaurant. **www.hostaldesenglar.com**

LLORET DE MAR Santa Marta €€€€

Platja Santa Cristina, 17310 (Girona) **Tel** *972 36 49 04* **Fax** *972 36 92 80 Rooms 78*

The low, white-painted modern Platja Santa Cristina overlooks a beautiful cove on the fringes of the frenetic resort of Lloret de Mar. Tranquil pine woods and gardens extend to the shore, and there are tennis courts and other sporting facilities. Closed from mid-December to January. **www.hstamarta.com**

MONTSENY Sant Bernat €€€

Finca El Clot, Ctra Sta Ma de Palautordera a Seva, km 20.7, 08460 (Barcelona) **Tel** *93 847 30 11 Rooms 23*

A gorgeous country house in the Serra de Montseny, the old stone walls are cloaked in greenery. The rooms and suites are stylishly decorated with traditional prints and rustic furniture. It's surrounded by extensive gardens with lawns and a pond, and all kinds of outdoor activities can be arranged. **www.santbernat.com**

MONTSERRAT Abat Cisneros €€

Plaça del Monestir, 08199 (Barcelona) **Tel** *93 877 77 01* **Fax** *93 87 77 24 Rooms 82*

Part of the celebrated monastery complex at Montserrat, this hotel is where Catalan newly-weds come to ensure that they have the blessing of La Moreneta, the miraculous figure of the Virgin, on their marriage. Rooms are modest but more comfortable than the ascetic setting would suggest.

PALS Lindos Huéspedes   P   €€€

Carretera de Torroella de Montgri a Pals km 10, 17256 (Girona) **Tel** *972 66 82 03* **Fax** *972 66 82 03 Rooms 6*

This is a chic little hotel, set in a former mill close to the pretty medieval town of Pals. It has been luxuriously converted to contain just a handful of coolly stylish rooms, decorated with pale fabrics and white-painted furniture. Children are not admitted. Closed in January and February. **www.lindoshuespedes.com**

PERAMOLA Can Boix de Peramola   €€

Carrer Afores s/n, 25790 (Lleida) **Tel** *973 47 02 66* **Fax** *973 47 02 81 Rooms 41*

This good-value, traditional mountain hotel has been in the same family for ten generations. It has charming rooms and apartments with breathtaking views, and is very convenient for walking in the Pyrenean foothills. Closed from mid-January to mid-February. **www.canboix.com**

REGENCÓS Hotel del Teatre   €€€

Plaça Major s/n, 17214 (Girona) **Tel** *972 30 62 70* **Fax** *972 30 62 73 Rooms 7*

In the heart of a rambling, medieval village, this boutique-style hotel is located in a pair of handsomely restored 18th-century mansions. Sleek minimalism and charming original features are stylishly combined in the bedrooms. There's a lovely semi-shaded pool in the garden. **www.hoteldelteatre.com**

SA TUNA (BEGUR) Hotel Sa Tuna   €

Platja Sa Tuna, 17255 (Girona) **Tel** *972 62 21 98* **Fax** *972 62 21 98 Rooms 5*

A simple, whitewashed small hotel on one of the Costa Brava's prettiest coves. Recent improvements by the grandson of the original owner have added to its charms. Rooms with own terrace overlooking the bay. The restaurant is well known in the area. Open from April to September only. **www.hostalsatuna.com**

SADURNI D'ANOIA Sol I Vi   €€

Ctra San Sadurni–Vilafranca km 4, Lavern, 08739 (Barcelona) **Tel** *938 99 32 04* **Fax** *938 99 33 26 Rooms 25*

A cheerful, traditional hotel set in a sea of vines, this is a good base for exploring the wine- and cava-producing region southwest of Barcelona. It offers comfortable, simple rooms and boasts a superb restaurant which specialises in traditional Catalan dishes. **www.solivi.com**

S'AGARÓ Hostal de la Gavina   €€€€€

Plaça de la Rosaleda, 17248 (Girona) **Tel** *972 32 11 00* **Fax** *972 32 15 73 Rooms 74*

This elegant Mediterranean-style beach mansion is set in its own exclusive estate with beautiful gardens and a sea water pool. Bedrooms are impressively decorated with silk-lined walls and burnished antiques, and the many facilities include a luxurious spa and a fine restaurant. Closed from mid-October to Easter. **www.lagavina.com**

SANT PERE DE RIBES Els Sumidors   €€

Carretera de Vilafranca km 2.4, 08810 (Barcelona) **Tel** *93 896 20 61* **Fax** *93 896 20 61 Rooms 9*

On the slope of a hill, with views of the Penèdes wine region, this rustic 18th-century house has plenty of atmosphere and charm but few luxuries. Half lost in greenery, it's a tranquil world away from the frenzied nightlife of nearby Sitges. **www.sumidors.com**

SANTA CRISTINA D'ARO Mas Torrellas   €€

Carretera Santa Cristina-Platja d'Aro, 17246 (Girona) **Tel** *972 83 75 26* **Fax** *972 83 75 27 Rooms 17*

An attractive 18th-century country house hotel, with ancient stone walls and flower-filled gardens. Its most comfortable bedroom is in the distinctive yellow tower, built at a later date. There's a pool and tennis courts and horseback riding can be arranged. The restaurant is excellent. Closed from October to March.

SANTA PAU Cal Sastre   €€

Carrer de les Cases Noves, 1, 17811 (Girona) **Tel** *972 68 01 32* **Fax** *972 68 04 81 Rooms 11*

A tastefully, modernised 18th-century rural house has been converted into a comfortable hotel. It is tucked into the ancient walls which circle medieval Santa Pau, and is surrounded by a shady garden. The area has excellent opportunities for hiking and volcano spotting. **www.calsastre.com**

SITGES Capri   €€

Avinguda de Sofia 13–15, 08870 (Barcelona) **Tel** *93 811 02 67* **Fax** *93 894 51 88 Rooms 26*

This hotel was built around 1900, and combines old-fashioned charm with up-to-the-minute facilities including a spa and a outdoor pool surrounded by gardens. It's just 50 metres from the beach and the town centre, and also offers luxurious suites. **www.grup-carbonell.com**

SITGES Romàntic   €€

Carrer Sant Isidre 33, 08870 (Barcelona) **Tel** *93 894 83 75* **Fax** *93 894 81 67 Rooms 58*

Well known in Sitges, this memorable hotel lives up to its name. Bedrooms are simple, but attractively decorated with antiques and paintings. A gloriously shady garden, with tinkling fountains, is perfect for breakfast and evening cocktails. **www.hotelromantic.com**

SOLDEU (ANDORRA) Sport Hotel Village   €€€

Ctra General s/n, **Tel** *376 87 05 00* **Fax** *376 87 05 33 Rooms 148*

This is the best-equipped hotel in the popular ski resort of Soldeu, and many of the comfortable rooms overlook the slopes. The four-star facilities include pool and Jacuzzi, and – best of all – the lift to the top of the slopes leaves directly from the hotel. **www.sporthotels.ad**

Key to Price Guide *see p134* **Key to Symbols** *see back cover flap*

TARRAGONA Lauria
Rambla Nova 20, 43004 (Tarragona) **Tel** *977 23 67 12* **Fax** *977 23 67 00 Rooms 72*

A modern, functional hotel in the town centre and close to the sea, with an elegant entrance under balustraded stone stairs. Rooms are large, although the decor is dated, but the hotel offers good amenities, including a pool and facilities for business travellers, for the price. **www.hlauria.es**

TARRAGONA Imperial Tarraco
Passeig Les Palmeres s/n, 43003 (Tarragona) **Tel** *977 23 30 40* **Fax** *977 21 65 66 Rooms 170*

The plushest option in Tarragona, this large, modern hotel has a panoramic location right on the Balconi del Mediterrani. Many of the spacious, elegant rooms and suites have large terraces and the hotel is conveniently close to the historic centre of the city. **www.husa.es**

TAVÉRNOLES El Banús
El Banús, 08519 (Barcelona) **Tel** *93 812 20 91* **Fax** *93 888 70 12 Rooms 12*

This small farmhouse is furnished with Banús family heirlooms. Two annexes are available for weekend of week-long stays, and are fully equipped with kitchens. The price here is for a weekend stay for four people (230 euros for a weekend, for 4 people, 260 euros for 6 people). Closed from November through March. **www.elbanus.com**

TAVERTET El Jufré
Tavertet, 08511 (Barcelona) **Tel** *93 856 51 67* **Fax** *93 856 51 67 Rooms 8*

This converted farmhouse is now a delightful casa rural with stunning mountain views, which has been in the same family for over 800 years. Warm, comfortable rooms have replaced the animal quarters. A perfect base for walking and exploring Osona. Price includes bed, breakfast and dinner.

TORRENT Mas de Torrent
Afueras, 17123 (Girona) **Tel** *972 30 32 92* **Fax** *972 30 32 93 Rooms 39*

A superbly converted 18th-century country house, this offers handsome accommodation in one of ten beautiful rooms in the main house, or in elegant bungalows scattered around the extensive gardens. There are also deluxe suites with private pools available. **www.mastorrent.com**

TORTOSA Parador Castillo de la Zuda
Castillo de la Zuda, 43500 (Tarragona) **Tel** *977 44 44 50* **Fax** *977 44 44 58 Rooms 72*

A medieval Moorish castle makes a superb hilltop parador with views of the town and valley of the Riu Ebre. The fine restaurant offers al fresco dining on the terrace, and there are plenty of luxurious extras including a swimming pool, in summer only. **www.parador.es**

TOSSA DE MAR Diana
Plaça d'Espanya 6, 17320 (Girona) **Tel** *972 34 11 16* **Fax** *972 34 18 86 Rooms 21*

A fine, Modernista mansion is the gorgeous setting for this delightful hotel. There are great views of the castle from the terrace and the best of the modest rooms have private balconies. The elegant lobby is full of original details and has been converted into a comfortable lounge area. **www.diana-hotel.com**

TREDÒS Hotel de Tredòs
Carretera a Baqueira-Beret km 177.5, 25598 (Lleida) **Tel** *973 64 40 14* **Fax** *973 64 43 00 Rooms 45*

Skiers and mountain-walkers find this hotel in the Val d'Aran good value. It is built of stone and slate in the local style, and offers attractive rooms with wooden beams. There's a cosy lounge with fireplace in winter, and a heart-shaped outdoor pool to cool off in summer. Closed in October, November, May and June. **www.hoteldetredos.com**

VIC Parador de Turismo de Vic
Paratge Bac de Sau, 08500 (Barcelona) **Tel** *93 812 23 23* **Fax** *93 812 23 68 Rooms 36*

This recently refurbished and comfortable stone-built parador, 14 km (9 miles) from Vic, has magnificent views of the Sau reservoir. It's a peaceful retreat amid pine forests and dramatic rock formations. Facilities include a tennis court and an outdoor pool in summers. **www.parador.es**

VIELHA (VIELLA) Parador Valle de Arán
Carretera de túnel, 25530 (Lleida) **Tel** *973 64 01 00* **Fax** *973 64 11 00 Rooms 118*

This modern parador has a panoramic circular lounge dominated by a large window from which there are magnificent mountain views. There's a wonderful spa and a fine restaurant, and the rooms are spacious and well appointed. **www.parador.es**

VILADRAU Hostal de la Glòria
Carrer Torreventosa 12, 17406 (Girona) **Tel** *938 84 90 34* **Fax** *938 84 94 65 Rooms 22*

A traditional hotel with a family atmosphere in a conventional Catalan house above the Serra de Montseny. The fine restaurant serves creative Catalan specialities and the outdoor pool is surrounded by gardens. You can rent bikes and horseback-riding can be arranged. **www.hostaldelagloria.com**

VILANOVA I LA GELTRÚ César
Carrer Isaac Peral 8, 08800 (Barcelona) **Tel** *93 815 11 25* **Fax** *93 815 67 19 Rooms 30*

This hotel, near the Ribes Roges beach, is located in a marvellous turn-of-the-19th-century mansion. It is owned by two sisters who pay great attention to detail, from the furniture and the fabrics in the bedrooms to the well-known restaurant. There are delightful gardens with a pool, which is covered in winter. **www.hotelcesar.net**

RESTAURANTS, CAFES AND BARS

Eating out remains both a common practice and one of the convivial joys of life in Catalonia. Catalans are proud of their regional cuisine and expect to eat well in restaurants, not only at celebratory dinners, but also at work-day meal breaks or at family Sunday lunches out. Country restaurants in particular are packed on Sundays. Barcelona has

Wall tile advertising a Barcelona restaurant

an unusually large number of restaurants. From the sophisticated feast to the simple tapa, fresh ingredients are usually in evidence as Catalans tend to despise convenience food. The restaurants and cafés listed on pages 146–53 have been selected for their food and atmosphere. Pages 30–1 and 144–5 illustrate some of Catalonia's best dishes.

Bodegues are bars that specialize in wines and do not serve food

RESTAURANTS AND BARS

Barcelona and Catalonia possess some of Spain's best restaurants, testifying to the quality of Catalan cooking, but the cheapest and quickest places to eat are the bars and cafés that serve *tapes* (tapas). Some bars, however, especially *pubs* (late-opening bars for socializing) do not serve food.

Family-run *bars i restaurants, hostals* and *fondes* – old Catalan words for the various types of inn – serve inexpensive, sit-down meals. *Xiringuitos* are beachside bars that are open only during the busy summer season.

Most restaurants close one day a week, some for lunch or dinner only, and most for an annual holiday. They also close on some public holidays. The main closing times of the restaurants on pages 146–51 are listed at the end of each entry. Always check the opening times, however, when phoning to book a table.

EATING HOURS

Catalans, in common with other Spaniards, often eat a light breakfast *(el esmorzar)* of biscuits or toast with butter and jam and *cafè amb llet* (milky coffee), then follow with a second breakfast or snack between 10 and 11am, perhaps in a café. This may consist of a croissant, or an *entrepà* (sandwich) with sausage, ham or cheese, or a slice of the ubiquitous *truita de patates* (potato omelette). Fruit juice, coffee or beer are the usual accompaniments.

From about 1pm onwards, people will stop in the bars for a beer or an *aperitivo* with tapas. By 2pm those who can will have arrived home from work for *dinar* (lunch), which is the main meal of the day. Others will choose to have lunch in a restaurant.

The cafés, *salons de te* (tea rooms) and *pastisseries* (pastry shops) fill up by about 5:30 or

Decoration, Barcelona bar

6pm for *el berenar* (tea) of sandwiches, pastries or cakes, with coffee, tea or fruit juice. Snacks such as *xurros* (fried, sugar-coated batter sticks) can also be bought from stalls.

By 7pm, bars are crowded with people having tapas with sherry, wine or beer. In Catalonia e*l sopar* (dinner or supper), begins at about 9pm. However, restaurants sometimes begin serving earlier for tourists. In summer, however, families and groups of friends often do not sit down to dinner until as late as 11pm. At weekend lunch times, especially in the summer, you will often find that restaurants are filled by large and noisy family gatherings.

HOW TO DRESS

A jacket and tie are rarely required, but Catalans dress smartly, especially for city restaurants. Day dress is casual in beach resorts, but shorts are frowned on in the evenings.

Eating out at Barcelona's Port Olímpic, a busy venue all year round

Outdoor tables at a *cafeteria* in Cadaqués on the Costa Brava

READING THE MENU

Aside from tapas, perhaps the cheapest eating options in Catalan restaurants are the fixed-price *plats combinats* and the *menú del dia*. A *plat combinat* (meat or fish with vegetables and, usually, fried potatoes) is offered only by cheaper establishments. Most restaurants – but not all – offer an inexpensive, fixed-price *menú del dia*, normally of three courses, but with little choice. Some gourmet restaurants offer a *menú de degustació* consisting of a choice of six or seven of the head chef's special dishes.

The Catalan word for menu is *la carta*. It starts with *sopes* (soups), *amanides* (salads), *entremesos* (hors d'oeuvres), *ous i truites* (eggs and omelettes) and *verdures i llegums* (vegetable dishes).

Main courses are *peix i marisc* (fish and shellfish) and *carns i aus* (meat and poultry). Daily specials are chalked on a board or clipped to menus. *Paella* and other rice dishes may be served as the first course. A useful rule is to follow rice with meat, or start with *fuet or secallona* (two popular types of sausage) or salad and follow with *paella*.

Desserts are called *postres*. All restaurants offer fresh fruit, but otherwise the range of *postres* is often limited – perhaps the famous *crema catalana (crème brûlée)*, or *flam* (crème caramel) and *natillas* (custard). Gourmet restaurants have more creative choices.

Vegetarians are rather poorly catered for. Some vegetable, salad and egg dishes will be vegetarian, but may contain pieces of ham or fish, so ask before you order.

All eating places welcome children and will serve small portions if requested.

Las Torres de Ávila *(see p163)*, a distinctive Barcelona bar

WINE CHOICES

Dry fino wines are perfect with shellfish, sausage, olives, soups and most first courses. Main dishes are often accompanied by wines from Penedès or Terra Alta *(see p32)* in Catalonia, or from Spain's other wine areas such as Rioja, Ribera del Duero and Navarra. Oloroso wines are often drunk as a *digestif. Cava (see pp32–3)* is popular for Sunday lunch.

SMOKING

In fine restaurants customers are offered cigars with their coffee and brandy. Many people in Spain smoke and very few restaurants have no-smoking areas or tables.

PRICES AND PAYING

If you order from *la carta* in a restaurant, your bill can soar way above the price of the *menú del dia*, especially if you order pricey items, such as fresh seafood, fish or *ibérico* ham. If there is an expensive fish such as sole or swordfish on the menu at a bargain price, it may be frozen. Sea bass and other popular fish and shellfish, such as large prawns, lobster and crab, are generally priced by weight.

El compte (the bill) does not usually include service charges, but may include a small cover charge. Menu prices do not include seven per cent VAT *(IVA)*, which is usually added when the bill is calculated. Clients rarely tip waiters more than five per cent, often just rounding up the bill.

Cheques are rarely used in restaurants. Traveller's cheques are usually accepted, but you might not be given change. The major credit cards and international direct debit cards are now accepted in most restaurants. However, do not expect to pay by credit card in smaller eating or drinking places like tapas bars, cafés, village *hostals* roadside *pubs or bodegues*.

WHEELCHAIR ACCESS

Since restaurants are rarely designed for wheelchairs, phone in advance (or ask the hotel staff to call) to check on access to tables and toilets.

Interior of Set Portes restaurant *(see p147)*, Port Vell, Barcelona

A Glossary of Typical Dishes

Olives

Catalan cuisine at its best, using fresh food, is known as *cuina de mercat* (market cuisine) and there is nowhere better to see produce laid out than at Barcelona's Boqueria market *(see p155)*. Peppers glisten, fish sparkle and no meat is wasted – even cock's combs are sold for the pot. Olives come in all sorts of varieties. Spring brings *calçot* onions and broad (fava) beans, while strawberries, from Easter onwards, are eaten with *cava*. In autumn 30 varieties of mushroom spill across the stalls.

TAPES (TAPAS – SNACKS)

Bar-hopping around Barcelona is a delightful way to spend an evening, and a good way to try the many local dishes laid out on the counters.

Anxoves: anchovies.
Escopinyes: cockles.
Bunyols de bacallà: salt cod fritters.
Calamars a la romana: fried squid rings.
Pa amb tomàquet: bread rubbed with tomato, garlic and olive oil – a good filler.
Panadons d'espinacs: small spinach pasties or pies.
Patatas bravas: potato chunks in spicy tomato sauce.
Pernil: ham – leg of pork seasoned and hung to dry.
Pescaditos: small fried fish.
Popets: baby octopus.
Truita: omelette.
Truita de patates: traditional potato and onion omelette.

Pa amb tomàquet (bread with tomato), often served with ham

ENTRANTS (STARTERS)

These are often unusual dishes and two may be enough for a meal. Some may appear as main courses.
Amanida catalana: Catalan mixed salad.
Arròs negre: black rice. Can be a main course.

Produce at La Boqueria, Barcelona's huge covered market on La Rambla

Cargols a la llauna: snails in a spicy sauce.
Empedrat: salad of salt cod and white beans.
Escalivada: char-grilled or roasted aubergines (eggplant) and peppers, all drizzled with olive oil.
Espinacs a la catalana: spinach with pine nuts, raisins and ham; sometimes made with chard *(bledes)*.
Esqueixada: raw salt cod salad.
Faves a la catalana: a broad (fava) bean stew of black pudding, bacon, onion and garlic.
Fideus: noodles, usually served with fish and meat.
Garotes: raw sea urchins, from the Costa Brava, eaten with bread, garlic or spring onions.
Musclos: mussels.
Ous remenats amb camasecs: scrambled eggs with wild mushrooms.
Pa de fetge: liver pâté.
Sardines escabetxades: pickled sardines.
Xató: salt cod and tuna salad with *romesco* sauce.

SOPES (SOUPS)

Caldereta de llagosta: spiny lobster soup.
Escudella i carn d'olla: the liquid from Catalonia's traditional hotpot; the meat and vegetables *(carn i olla)* are served as a main course.
Gaspatxo: a clear, cold soup with added raw vegetables.
Sopa de farigola: thyme soup.
Sopa de bolets: mushroom soup.

MAIN DISHES

Methods of cooking are: *a la brasa* (over open flames); *bullit* (boiled); *cremat* (crisp fried or caramelized); *estofat* (stewed); *farcit* (stuffed); *al forn* (in the oven); *a la graella/planxa* (cooked on a griddle, pan-fried or barbecued); *a la pedra* (on a hot stone).

PEIX I MARISCOS (FISH AND SHELLFISH)

Allipebre d'anguiles: spicy eel stew.
Anfós al forn: baked stuffed grouper.
Calamars farcits: squid stuffed with pork, tomatoes and onions.
Cassola de peix: fish casserole.
Congre amb pèsols: conger eel with peas.
Escamarlans bullits: boiled Dublin Bay prawns.
Gambes a la planxa: prawns cooked on a griddle.
Graellada de peix: mixed seafood grill.
Llagosta a la brasa: lobster cooked over open flames.
Llagostins amb maionesa: king prawns and mayonnaise.
Llobarro al forn a rodanxes: baked, sliced sea bass.
Lluç a la planxa: hake cooked on a griddle.
Molls a la brasa: red mullet cooked over open flames.
Orada a la sal: gilthead bream baked in salt, which is removed on serving.
Paella valenciana: paella with chicken and seafood.
Rap a l'all cremat: angler fish with crisped garlic.
Romesco de peix: seafood with the famous *romesco* sauce. Tarragona's master *romesco* makers compete each summer.
Sarsuela: fish, shellfish and spices, everything goes into

the pot that gives its name to a light Spanish opera.

Sèpia amb pèsols: cuttlefish with peas.

Suquet de peix: Catalonia's principal fish stew, made with various fish, tomatoes, peppers, potatoes and almonds.

Verats a la brasa: mackerel cooked over open flames.

CARN (MEAT)

Ànec amb naps: duck with turnips, ideally the "black" turnips of the Empordà region; also sometimes served with pears (*ànec amb peres*).

Boles de picolat: meatballs in tomato sauce. Meatballs with cuttlefish (*sèpia*) is classic *mar i muntanya* food.

Botifarra amb mongetes: sausage and beans.

Bou a l'adoba: beef casserole.

Costelles a la brasa amb allioli: flame-roast lamb cutlets with garlic mayonnaise.

Costelles de cabrit rostides: roast goat kid cutlets.

Cuixa de xai al forn: roast leg of lamb.

Estofat de bou: beef stew with sausages, potatoes, herbs and sometimes a little chocolate.

Estofat de quaresma: a filling Lenten vegetable stew.

Freginat: calf's liver with onions.

Fricandó: braised veal with wild mushrooms.

Llom de porc: pork chops.

Oca amb peres: goose with pears – traditional village festival fare.

Niu: a huge fish and meat stew from Palafrugell, Costa Brava, with pigeon, cuttlefish, cod tripe, pig's trotters, egg and garlic mayonnaise.

Peus de porc a la llauna: pig's trotters in a spicy sauce.

Pollastre amb samfaina: chicken with *samfaina*.

Pota i tripa: lamb's trotters and tripe.

Tripa a la catalana: tripe in *sofregit* and wine with pine nuts and almonds.

Xai amb pèsols: lamb with peas.

Barcelona's cheese and honey market *(see p155)* in the Plaça del Pi

CAÇA (GAME)

Although the hunting season is from October to February, some game is available all year round, especially rabbit.

Becada amb coc: woodcock in a bread roll.

Civet de llebre: jugged hare.

Conill a la brasa amb allioli: rabbit with garlic mayonnaise.

Conill amb cargols: rabbit with snails.

Conill amb xocolata: rabbit with garlic, liver, almonds, fried bread, chocolate and old wine.

Aubergines (eggplant) and peppers, used in abundance

Estofat de porc senglar amb bolets: wild boar casserole with wild mushrooms.

Guatlles amb salsa de magrana: quail in pomegranate sauce.

Perdiu: partridge.

Perdius amb farcellets de col: partridge with cabbage dumplings.

VERDURES (VEGETABLES)

Albergínies: aubergines (eggplant).

Bledes: chard.

Bolets: mushrooms.

Calçots: leek-sized green onions, roasted on an open fire and dipped in a spicy tomato sauce. A spring-time speciality of the Tarragona region.

Carbassó arrebossat: battered courgettes (zucchini).

Carxofes: artichokes.

Julivert: parsley.

Mongetes tendres i patates: French beans and potatoes.

Pastanagues: carrots.

Pebrots: red peppers.

POSTRES (DESSERTS)

Although *pastisseria* (pastries) and *dolços* (sweets) are very popular in Catalonia, desserts in restaurants are generally uneventful. The choice may be simply ice cream or fruit: apple (*poma*), peach (*préssec*), banana (*plàtan*), orange (*taronja*), grapes (*raïm*).

Crema catalana: rich egg custard.

Figues amb aniset: figs in anise.

Flam: crème caramel.

Formatge: cheese. There is little local cheese.

Gelat: ice cream.

Meli Mató: fresh goat's cheese, eaten with honey.

Menjar blanc: an almond blancmange.

Peres amb vi negre: pears in red wine.

Postre de músic: a bowl of mixed nuts and dried fruit, once given as a reward to itinerant musicians.

Recuit: curdled sheep's (or cow's) milk in a small pot.

Mel i mató – a traditional dessert of soft cheese served with honey

Choosing a Restaurant

The restaurants in this guide have been selected for their good value, food and location. The chart below lists restaurants in Barcelona by area, and the entries are alphabetical within each price category. Restaurants in the Further Afield section are listed by district and those in the rest of Catalonia are arranged by town.

PRICE CATEGORIES
For a three-course evening meal for one, including a half-bottle of house wine, tax and service.

€ under 20 euros
€€ 20–35 euros
€€€ 35–50 euros
€€€€ over 50 euros

OLD TOWN

Bar Pinotxo   🖾🏃   €

Mercat de la Boqueria (La Rambla 89), 08002   **Tel** *93 317 17 31*   **Map** *5 A1*

The most famous of all the bars in the Boqueria. Steel buckets hold chilled bottles of *cava*, and fresh ingredients from neighbouring market stalls are cooked and served hot on the spot. The bar is closed on Sundays and in the evenings after 8pm.

Can Culleretes   🏃📋♿   €

C/Quintana 5, 08002   **Tel** *93 317 30 22*   **Map** *5 A2*

The oldest restaurant in Barcelona dates from 1786 and oozes history from its many dining rooms, nooks and crannies. Original frescoes and tiles decorate the walls. Staff are brusque but efficient. Food is cheap, plentiful and satisfying. Try the goose with apples or duck with prunes. Closed Sunday dinner and Monday, and in July.

Dim Sum House   🏃   €

C/Bergara 7, 08007   **Tel** *93 270 12 93*   **Map** *5 A1*

Not the typical kitsch Chinese restaurant that you usually find in Spain. Clean and modern, this popular restaurant offers good value set-lunches and a decent range of dim sum. Try the shrimp and the four-station dumplings and the *chashao* stuffed bread. Closed on Sundays.

Elisabets   🖾🏃📋   €

C/Elisabets 2, 08001   **Tel** *93 317 58 26*   **Map** *2 F2*

A local institution, this homely bustling restaurant specialises in traditional Catalan cuisine. It is a favourite for diners in search of hearty, home-cooked midday meals, and Friday night tapas. Elisabets also has a lively bar where you can have a sandwich or drink at any time of the day. Good selection of beers. Closed three weeks in August.

Mosquito   🏃📋   €

C/Carders 46, 08003   **Tel** *93 268 75 69*   **Map** *5 C2*

A laidback bar peopled by a healthy mix of Catalans and resident expats. Groovy tunes on the stereo, friendly staff, cheap drinks and a solid array of Asian favourites like chicken tikka *brochetes*, Singapore noodles and *gyoza* dumplings make this a pleasant change from the usual tapas joints. Closed on Mondays.

Organic   🖾🏃📋♿🎵   €

C/Junta de Comerç 11, 08001   **Tel** *93 301 09 02*   **Map** *2 F3*

Spacious, clean and softly lit this good-value vegetarian restaurant offers an imaginative menu of Asian dishes, lasagnes, stews and an all-you-can-eat salad buffet. The home-made bread with nuts is a must. Occasionally, they have live music. They also have a small shop selling organic products.

El Salón   🏃📋   €€

C/Hostal d'en Sol 6–8, 08002   **Tel** *93 315 21 59*   **Map** *5 B3*

The Baroque-style interior, plump velvet chairs and grand chandeliers give this establishment the feel of an 18th-century boudoir. The menu changes constantly but promises sumptuous ingredients and inventive dishes, often featuring French and Catalan specialities. Closed on Sundays and two weeks in August.

Els Quatre Gats   🅿🏃📋🎵   €€

C/Montsió 3 bis, 08002   **Tel** *93 302 41 40*   **Map** *5 A1*

This emblematic Barcelona institution was the first place to ever show Picasso's work. It is decorated by original works of early 20th-century artists and oozes history. The opulent dining room verges on cheesy but is great fun, and the Mediterranean fare is good too.

Euskal Etxea   🏃📋♿   €€

Placeta Montcada 1–3, 08003   **Tel** *93 310 21 85*   **Map** *5 B3*

Home to the Basque Cultural Institute, the Euskal Etxea is one of the best places in town for Basque *pintxos* (small rounds of bread with a myriad toppings). It also serves exceptionally good *a la carte* meals. Closed on Sunday evenings and in August.

Key to Symbols *see back cover flap*

Mam i Teca
C/Lluna 4, 08001 **Tel** 93 441 33 35

Map 2 F2

Tiny, sunflower-yellow bar that plays well-known jazz, blues and rock tunes. The tapas is superb, and includes locally sourced cheeses, organic sausages, and country dishes such as ham and broad beans. They also have an excellent wine list, and a good range of Scottish single malts. Closed Tuesdays.

Pla de la Garsa
C/Assaonadors 13, 08003 **Tel** 93 315 24 13

Map 5 B2

Situated in the stables of a 17th-century palace, the cozy atmosphere of this pretty, split-level restaurant makes it a good place for romantic evenings. Lunch is excellent value and for cheese lovers the 40-strong list is a winner. There's also an interesting selection of red wines.

Taller de Tapas
C/Argenteria 51, 08003 **Tel** 93 268 85 59

Map 5 B2

Exposed brick and sleek steel fittings give this restaurant a contemporary urban feel. Staff are professional and friendly, and the extensive tapas dishes are all freshly made on the spot. You can also try regional dishes such as the Costa Brava's cherished Palamos prawns.

7 Portes
Passeig Isabel II, 14, 08003 **Tel** 93 319 30 33

Map 5 B3

A long-standing Barcelona institution since 1836 with a who's who of past guests, including Winston Churchill and Che Guevara. It is famed for its classic marble tiles and wood-panelled dining room, and most of all for *paella* which comes in ten different varieties.

Agua
Passeig Maritim de la Barceloneta 30, 08003 **Tel** 93 225 12 72

Map 6 D4

Classy seafront restaurant with floor-to-ceiling windows and abstract fish sculptures. It is popular with a young, up-beat crowd and serves excellent tapas, fish and rice dishes. Specials include steamed mussels, *butan* potatoes, Norway lobsters au gratin and grilled fish. There's an appealing terrace as well.

Biblioteca
C/Junta de Comerç 28, 08001 **Tel** 93 412 62 21

Map 2 F3

Elegant, cream-coloured restaurant-cum-cookbook shop with Modernista tiles and open kitchen. The high-class cooking focuses on seasonal ingredients and comforting flavours and textures. Specialities include rice with pigeon and black pudding; and black spaghetti with *calçots* (Catalan onions) and poached egg. Service can be careless.

Café de l'Academia
C/Lledó 1, 08002 **Tel** 93 319 82 53

Map 5 B3

An intimate, candle-lit restaurant with exposed brick walls and a pretty terrace in the lovely Plaça Sant, in the centre of Barri Gòti. The menu offers superb Catalan fare, interesting salads and home-made pasta. The desserts are top-notch. Closed on Saturdays and Sundays.

Cal Pep
Plaça de les Olles 8, 08003 **Tel** 93 310 79 61

Map 5 B3

Arguably the best bar in town for fresh fish and seafood, right off the boats. Cal Pep has an excellent selection of tapas. The long, narrow, standing bar means it gets crowded at peak times. Arrive early for one of five tables out back. Closed on Sundays and for Moday lunch.

Can Majó
C/Almirall Aixada 23, 08003 **Tel** 93 221 54 55

Map 5 B5

As places for *paella* go, this is one of the best especially when eaten on a warm summer's day on a terrace with sea views. If you start getting into the shellfish, prices hike right up, but it's worth it for freshness and quality of produce cooked to perfection. Closed for Sunday dinner and Mondays.

Comerç 24
C/Comerç 24, 08003 **Tel** 93 319 21 02

Map 5 C3

Designer tapas bar with charcoal grey walls and primary colour accents, serving some of the most inventive tapas in town. A "Festival" of tapas is served for groups of six or more. Try the *arròs a banda* (paella without the morsels) or the *tortilla de patatas* (potato omelet). Reservations necessary. Closed on Sunday and Mondays.

Taxidermista
Plaça Reial 8, 08002 **Tel** 93 412 45 36

Map 5 A3

Soft colour schemes and high ceilings give this trendy restaurant an edge over the touristy competition on the bustling Plaza Reial. Inventive market cooking offers a range of dishes from around the Mediterranean rim including *babaganush*, sardine tarts and duck *confit*. Closed on Monday.

Carballeira
C/Reina Cristina 3, 08003 **Tel** 93 310 10 06

Map 5 B3

The first Galician seafood restaurant in Barcelona. Carballeira is well known for its simply grilled fish and seafood, perfect *paellas* and the house special – Galician-style tender octopus sprinkled with paprika. Closed for Sunday dinner and on Mondays.

Hofmann
C/Argenteria 74–78, 08003 **Tel** 93 319 58 89

P 🏃 ▤   €€€€
Map 5 B2

The recent recipient of a Michelin star, this restaurant-cum-cooking school produces high-quality cuisine in a sophisticated locale and careful service. Daily specials are always a good bet. Hollywood stars such as Mel Gibson, Kevin Costner, John Travolta and Cindy Crawford have had dinner here. Closed on Saturdays and Sundays.

EIXAMPLE

Crêperie Bretonne
C/Balmes 274, 08006 **Tel** 93 217 30 48

P 🏃 ▤   €
Map 3 A1

This kitsch French pancake house has been around for more than 30 years. It serves 250 types of thin, light Brittany-style *crêpes*. They offer sweet or salted *crêpes* and with all kinds of French cheese fillings. Also try their herbal teas. Closed on Mondays.

Cata 1.81
C/València 181, 08011 **Tel** 93 323 68 18

P ▤   €€
Map 3 A4

Long, thin and blindingly white, this modern tapas bar was one of the pioneers of Post-Modernist tapas, turning classics like Russian salad into state-of-the-art taste explosions. The excellent wine list offers many by the glass. A top choice for those interested in the wonders of New Catalan cuisine. Closed daily for lunch and on Sundays.

Madrid-Barcelona
C/Aragó 282, 08007 **Tel** 93 215 70 27

P 🏃 ▤ &   €€
Map 3 A4

This smart, split-level restaurant with its cast-iron balustrades and polished wood looks more expensive than it is. It is hugely popular, often with long queues coming out the door, for Málaga-style *pescaditos fritos* (fried fish) and other good value tapas.

Thai Lounge
C/València 205, 08007 **Tel** 93 454 90 32

P 🏃 ▤   €€
Map 3 A4

Typical of a Thai restaurant with lots of Buddhas and teakwood furniture, Thai Lounge succeeds where others have failed in bringing the flavour of the country to Barcelona. The curries are the house specialty, but there are also a good range of less obvious dishes and the 24 euros evening menu is a bargain.

Cinc Sentits
C/Aribau 58, 08011 **Tel** 93 323 94 90

P ▤   €€€
Map 2 F1

This warm yet minimal restaurant offers impeccable service and a menu that is both unusual and accessible. Meticulously sourced products are cooked with flair and creativity. The *Omasake*, chef's choice, tasting menu is recommended. Kids are fine during the week and at lunchtime but not at other times.

Shibui
C/Comte d'Urgell 272–274, 08036 **Tel** 93 321 90 04

🏃 ▤ &   €€€
Map 2 E1

With its sleek blonde wood fittings, Japanese cardboard-brick walls and trim waiting staff this excellent sushi bar has Tokyo written all over it. The basement dining room also has custom-made tatami areas and sliding screens making them a brilliant choice for parties. Closed on Sundays.

Alkimia
C/Indústria 79, 08025 **Tel** 93 207 61 15

▤ &   €€€€
Map 3 C2

One of the rising stars of the Barcelona gastronomic scene, this small, designer restaurant revitalises traditional Catalan dishes with new techniques and foreign flavours. Signature dishes include creamy rice with crayfish and *nyora* peppers, sticky slow roasted bull tail and mandarin essence with *hortchata* (tiger-nut) foam.

Casa Calvet
C/Casp 48, 08010 **Tel** 93 412 40 12

🏃 ▤ &   €€€€
Map 3 B5

A beautiful restaurant that was originally designed by Gaudí as a private home and offices for a wealthy textile merchant. The cozy seating booths, formal table settings and old-school service harken back to another era, however the cooking is modern and executed with panache. Closed on Sundays.

El Prinicipal del Tragaluz
C/Provença 286–288, 08008 **Tel** 93 272 08 45

▤ & 🔲   €€€€
Map 3 A3

The smartest of the Tragaluz restaurants, the sleek, cream-toned interior with floor-to-ceiling windows and romantic plant-filled terrace is perfect for special occasions. The menu offers scallops, *foie gras*, truffles, lobster and other luxury goodies. Service however, can be a touch frosty. Live music from June to August.

Moo
C/Rosselló 265, 08008 **Tel** 93 445 40 00

P ▤ &   €€€€
Map 3 A3

In the short time that Moo has been open it has walked away with a string of accolades, thanks to the inspired cooking of the Roca brothers who manage the restaurant. The tasting menu with matching wines is magical: Dublin bay prawns with rose and licorice, sea bass with lemon thyme and desserts inspired by perfumes.

Key to Price Guide *see p146* **Key to Symbols** *see back cover flap*

FURTHER AFIELD

GRÀCIA Chido One
C/Torrijos 30, 08012 **Tel** *93 285 03 35*

Map *3 C2*

Lined floor to ceiling with Mexican Day of the Dead artifacts and trophies, as well as retro *jalapeño* chili cans this trendy eatery serves excellent regional fare including steaming bowls of heart warming *posole*, soft fat *enchiladas* slathered with chili sauce, tacos and lethal margaritas. Live music once a week.

GRÀCIA Envalira
Plaça del Sol 13, 08012 **Tel** *93 218 58 13*

Map *3 B1*

A real neighbourhood joint in the spirited Plaça del Sol in Barcelona, it's noisy, raucous and fun with a laidback anything-goes ambience. Intimate it is not, but it's a great place for hearty, no-nonsense fare with rice dishes topping the bill. Closed for Sunday dinner and on Mondays.

GRÀCIA La Rosa del Desierto
Plaça Narcís Oller 7, 08006 **Tel** *93 237 45 90*

Map *3 A2*

This was Barcelona's first ever Moroccan restaurant and is still widely regarded to be the best. With its atmospheric decor it's a fun place for *couscous* and delicious tagines. They have interesting meat dishes, soups and salads on their menu. Also try one of their typical Arab teas. Closed for Sunday dinner.

GRÀCIA Botafumeiro
C/Gran de Gràcia 81, 08012 **Tel** *93 218 42 30*

Map *3 A2*

A legendary seafood restaurant with ice-banks piled high with boat-fresh fish and seafood at the entrance. A-listers from Woody Allen to Madonna have all made this a favourite haunt whilst in town thanks to discreet management and luxury surroundings. Try the tender *pulpo Gallego* (Galician octopus). Reservations essential.

GRÀCIA Ot
C/Torres 25, 08012 **Tel** *93 284 77 52*

Map *3 B2*

Small, intimate and painted in sunset tones, this eatery arrived on the scene with a bang. It has just one tasting menu, boasting dishes such as wild garlic foam with smoked salt, wild boar and violet potatoes, or tuna stew with grape gratin, that changes daily depending on what's in season at the local Mercat de la Llibertat.

GRÀCIA Roig Robí
C/de Sèneca 20, 08006 **Tel** *93 218 92 22*

Map *3 A2*

Small and intimate with a pretty interior courtyard for summer dining, this restaurant is a classic for genuine Catalan cuisine. The menu boasts a good selection of *bacalao* (salt-cod) dishes as well as typical vegetable dishes of broad beans and artichokes. Closed for Saturday lunch and on Sundays.

HORTA Can Travi Nou
C/Jorge Manrique, 08035 **Tel** *93 428 03 01*

Few people venture so far from the centre for their supper, but this 14th-century farmhouse is well worth the trek to soak up the atmosphere of yesteryear, and the rolling terraces are wonderful for alfresco dining. Roast meats, rice dishes and fresh fish are on the menu. Closed for Sunday dinner.

POBLENOU Els Pescadors
Plaça Prim 1, 08005 **Tel** *93 225 20 18*

The multiple-spaced restaurant – terrace, formal dining room and old-fahioned, tiled cafeteria – is named after the fishermen that used to frequent it. It's an exellent place for a catch of the day special, zingy-fresh mussels and other fishy delights. Try the *anxoves* (anchovies). Closed on Sundays and for Monday lunch.

SANT GERVASI La Balsa
C/Infanta Isabel 4, 08060 **Tel** *93 211 50 48*

Much-loved by Barcelona's glitteratti: sportspersons, artists, actors and politicians are all in attendance at this uptown eatery. Service is discreet, the decor tasteful and the terraces among the best in town for enjoying Basque, Catalan and Mediterranean food at its finest.

TIBIDABO El Asador de Aranda
Avinguda del Tibidabo 31, 08022 **Tel** *93 417 01 15*

A meat-lovers paradise, this mansion-house restaurant at the top of the hill specialises in roasts, melt-in-the-mouth suckling pig and lamb; rich, juicy steaks, chops and ribs; and a fine line in *burgos morcillas* (black pudding). They also serve red wines from La Ribera.

TIBIDABO L'Orangerie
Carretera de Vallvidrera 83–93, 08035 **Tel** *93 259 30 00*

Perched high on the mountain above Barcelona and the sea, this beautiful restaurant has wonderful views and is well worth the 30-minute taxi ride, whether you're visiting for tea and cakes in the afternoon, the jazz brunch on a Sunday afternoon or the full gourmet experience. Live music on special days.

CATALONIA

ALTAFULLA Faristol

C/Sant Martí 5 (Tarragona), 43893 **Tel** 977 65 00 77

Experience traditional Catalan fare at this charming 18th-century farmhouse. The English-Catalan couple that run it are welcoming and it makes for a romantic getaway from the bustle of Barcelona. Rooms are also available. They usually have music on Friday and Saturday nights. From October to May Altafulla opens only from Friday to Sunday.

ANDORRA LA VELLA Borda Estevet

Carretera de la Comella 2, **Tel** 376 86 40 26

This old-country manor is still used for the traditional practice of drying tobacco that is grown nearby and oozes old-world atmosphere. Extensive menu of Andorran-Catalan and French fare. The meat dishes are exceptional, particularly *carns a la llosa* which arrive sizzling on a hot slate.

ARENYS DE MAR Hispania

C/Real 54, Carretera NII, 08350 **Tel** 93 791 04 57

A famous bistro that has earned numerous awards for the quality of its cooking. People travel from far and wide for its clam *suquet* (fish stew) and home-made *crema catalanas* (traditional vanilla custard with a burnt, caramel crust). Closed for Sunday dinner, on Tuesdays, Easter and in October.

BERGA Sala

Passeig de la Pau 27, 08600 **Tel** 93 821 11 85

A good choice for hearty winter dishes that feature freshly picked mushrooms from the nearby forests, Berga is mushroom country, and wild game is available in season. Very innovative cuisine. They also have a set tasting menu. Closed for Sunday dinner and on Mondays.

BOLVIR DE CERDANYA Torre del Remei

Camí Reial (Girona), 17539 **Tel** 972 14 01 82

One of the region's finest hotels and restaurants set in a summer palace and surrounded by verdant countryside. The chef de cuisine uses regional products to create meals such as melting veal cheeks with sweet and sour berry fruits, fresh scallops in Priorat sauce, desserts and local cheeses.

CAMBRILS Can Bosch

Rambla Jaume I, 19, 43850 **Tel** 977 36 00 19

A classic and highly-respected restaurant serving superb fish, seafood and rice dishes. Their *arroz negro* (rice cooked in squid ink) is justly famous. Patrons rave about their wine list almost as much as the food. Closed for Sunday dinner, on Mondays and one week in June.

FIGUERES Hotel Empordà

Hotel Empordà, Carretera NII, 17600 **Tel** 972 50 05 62

A legendary restaurant that played a great part in putting Catalan cuisine on the map for travelling gourmands. Established in 1961, folks still gather here to enjoy the legacy of chef Jaime Subirós' cuisine including classic dishes such as *mar y muntaña* (sea and mountain).

GIRONA El Celler de Can Roca

Carretera Taialá 40, 17007 **Tel** 972 22 21 57

Celler de Can Roca offers a fusion of Catalan and French "nouvelle cuisine" cooking. A must on the list of dedicated food enthusiasts, the brothers Roca turn out innovative, technically brilliant dishes at terrifying speed. A place to wow and be wowed. Closed on Sundays, Mondays, first two weeks in July and Christmas.

GRATALLOPS Cellers de Gratallops

Piró 32 (Priorat), 43737 **Tel** 977 83 90 36

This smart village restaurant is owned by the *bodega's* Clos l'Obac, one of the pioneers of new Priorat wines and serves their entire range, along with local olive oils and an excellent Moroccan influenced menu. Well worth seeking out during a trip to wine country.

LA SEU D'URGELL El Castell

Carretera N260 km 229 (Lleida), 25700 **Tel** 973 35 07 04

Situated at the foot of La Seu d'Urgell castle, surrounded by stunning scenery, lies this idyllic hotel-restaurant. El Castell serves top-flight modern Catalan cuisine and superlative wines. Many of the dishes include a variety of local wild mushrooms from the Pyrenees mountains and meat from the region. A different menu is served to outside tables.

LLEIDA Lo Punt del Gourmet

C/ Salmerón 10, 25004 **Tel** 973 23 45 10

Excellent regional cooking including chargrilled red peppers and aubergines (*escalivada*) and snails *a la llauna* (oven baked). Specialities include "Xatonada" with beans, ceps (mushrooms) and cod and *Esqueixada* with cod and elvers. It was formerly known as Forn del Nastasi. Closed for Sunday dinner and on Mondays.

Key to Price Guide see p146 **Key to Symbols** see back cover flap

LLORET DE MAR El Trull   🅿️🏃🍽️♿🎵🏧   €€

Ronda Europa 1, Cala Canyelles, 17310 **Tel** *972 36 49 28*

Should your travels take you through the hideous Lloret de Mar, this characterful rustic dining room is handy in a pinch. It serves good grilled lobster, fresh fish, *fideus* (Catalan noodles) and *paella*. They also have a wide range of wines and sparkling wines. Live music in summers only.

MANRESA Sibar   🏃🍽️♿🏧   €€€

C/Carrasco i Formiguera 18 (Barcelona), 08242 **Tel** *93 874 81 71*

This modern establishment has a cafeteria on the ground floor for coffee and cakes, and a sleek elegant restaurant in the basement for formal dining. The *chuleton* (T-bone steak for a minimum of two people) is superlative, as are the unlikely sounding fried eggs and potatoes. Regional wines are a must.

MARTINET Boix   🅿️🏃🍽️♿🏧   €€

Carretera N260 km 204,5 (Lleida), 25724 **Tel** *973 51 50 50*

A famous Catalan restaurant located on the banks of the Riu Segre. It serves slow-roasted leg of lamb so tender you could eat it with a spoon, complimented perfectly by a bottle of soft luscious local wine from the Costers del Segre. Closed for Sunday dinner and on Mondays.

MONT-RAS La Cuina de Can Pipes   🅿️🍽️♿🏧   €€€€€

Barri Canyelles (Girona), 17253 **Tel** *972 30 66 77*

This elegant, 18th-century farmhouse serves excellent regional dishes. Scallops with seaweed gratin, salmon caviar on roast red peppers, baby squid with velvety rich pigs trotters and turbot with wild mushroom rice are good. The desserts are heavenly, and the wine menu boasts more than 200 vintages. Bookings recommended.

PERALADA Castell de Peralada   🅿️🍽️   €€€€

Hotel Castell de Peralada, C/Sant Joan (Girona), 17491 **Tel** *972 53 81 25*

The setting of this medieval castle makes for a truly special lunch or dinner. It specialises in traditional Empordàn cuisine while the castle's own *bodegas* provide the wine. As the restaurant is inside a casino, under-18s are not allowed. Kids are allowed in Jul–Aug when a buffet is served on outside tables.

ROSES El Bulli   🅿️🏃🍽️🏧   €€€€

Cala Montjoi, Ap 30 (Girona), 17480 **Tel** *972 15 04 57*

Critics and foodies alike, widely believe this bistro to be, not only the best in Spain, but one of the best in the world. Super-chef Ferran Adrià is one of the most radical producing state-of-the-art dishes – more sci-fi than supper – in one of Spain's prettiest beachside settings. Reservations required. Closed from October to March.

SANT CELONI El Racó de Can Fabes   🅿️🍽️♿   €€€€

C/ de Sant Joan 6 (Barcelona), 08470 **Tel** *93 867 28 51*

Santi Santamaría is one of Spain's most emblematic chefs and this delightful country restaurant is in the house where he was born, and a gastronomic wonderland. The seasonal menu is full of delights including fennel cream with crab, sweetbreads with mashed potato, and wild duck in cocoa bean sauce. Reservations essential.

SANT POL DE MAR Sant Pau   🅿️🍽️♿🏧   €€€€

C/Nou 10 (Barcelona), 08395 **Tel** *93 760 06 62*

This beautiful restaurant is an hour-long train ride from Barcelona and makes a good lunch excursion. The bounty of earth and sea make for some wonderful dishes created from delicate courgette flowers, *espardenyes* (sea cucumbers) and wild boar. Only apéritif and coffee is served at the outside tables. Closed on Mondays.

SITGES El Velero   🏃🍽️♿🏧   €€

Passeig de la Ribera 38 (Barcelona), 08870 **Tel** *93 894 20 51*

A seaside restaurant whose imaginative creations are a cut above more standard offerings of *paella* and grilled fish. Here sole comes on a bed of wild mushrooms and is drizzled with unctuous crab sauce, lobster comes with chickpea cream and boat-fresh *navajas* (razor clams) are the king of the starters. Closed from 22 December to 22 January.

TARRAGONA El Merlot   🅿️🏃🍽️🏧   €€€

C/Cavallers 6, 43003 **Tel** *977 22 06 52*

Situated in the old part of town, this restaurant serves classical Mediterranean dishes. House specials include game in season, fresh fish and addictive home-made desserts. Specialities include flower salad with vinagrete of seeds and apples, tartar with *foie gras* and anise ice cream. They also serve good wines.

VALLS Masia Bou   🅿️🏃🏧   €€

Carretera Lleida km 21.5 (Tarragona), 43800 **Tel** *977 60 04 27*

The specialty here are *calcots* (a sort of cross between spring onions and leeks that are chargrilled over hot vines and served with a scrumptious almond, hazelnut and red pepper dipping sauce), which you eat by throwing your head back and slurping down. Lots of fun and very traditional.

VIC Floriac   🅿️🏃🏧   €€

Carretera Manresa-Vic N141 km 39.5, Collsuspina (Barcelona), **Tel** *93 743 02 25*

This 16th-century *masia* (farmhouse) serves huge platters of regional fare along with excellent game dishes in season. Home-made desserts are delicious and also try the cod gratin with *allioli* (garlic maionnaise). Closed for two weeks in February and two weeks in July.

Cafés and Bars

This section lists the best and most colourful cafés and bars in Barcelona, including both the traditional and the new and fashionable. Most cafés serve a small selection of alcoholic drinks as well as soft drinks, and most bars offer coffee, so customers will nearly always find something to their liking in any establishment.

PRICE CATEGORIES
For a three-course evening meal for one, including a half-bottle of house wine, tax and service.

€ under 20 euros
€€ 20–35 euros
€€€ 35–50 euros
€€€€ over 50 euros

OLD TOWN

Barcelona Rouge
€

C/Poeta Cabanyes 21, 08004 **Tel** 93 442 49 85

Map 2 D3

Few people know about this late-night bar, but, it is cherished by those that do. You have to ring a bell to get in, whereupon a small entrance way opens into a long, velvet-lined corridor guarded by angels to reveal a wide open space filled with sofas, and cocktail guzzling hipsters. Closed on Sundays and Mondays.

Boadas
€

C/dels Tallers 1, 08001 **Tel** 93 318 88 26

Map 2 F1

Sophia Loren and other celebrities liked to drink here, and the wall of black and white photographs is testament to their loyalty. The liveried bar-tenders mix the meanest martinis in town for a grown-up crowd of well-heeled Catalans and discerning tourists. Closed on Sundays.

Bodega La Palma
€

C/Palma de Sant Just 7, 08002 **Tel** 93 315 06 56

Map 5 B3

An old fashioned, rustic *bodega* (wine cellar) in the heart of the old city. In keeping with tradition wine is poured from weathered barrels, and is served in ceramic pitchers. The tapas are good as well. Closed on Sundays, Easter and in August.

Caelum
€

C/de la Palla 8, 08002 **Tel** 93 302 69 93

Map 5 A2

This elegant tearoom is housed in the former women's baths of the Jewish Quarter (El Call). The intimate, softly-lit dining room offers tea, infusions and cappuchinos as well as a good range of typical sweetmeats including *yemas* (sweet egg yolks), *roscoes* (ring shaped biscuits) and chocolate truffles. Closed on Monday mornings.

El Bosc de les Fades
€

Passatge de la Banca 72, 08002 **Tel** 93 317 26 49

Map 5 A3

Hollow tree trunks, twinkling fairy lights and trickling streams give this unusual bar a fairytale feel. More of a place for drinks than coffees, it is a must for bar flys. Relax and enjoy cocktails, wine and beer and delicious coffee concoctions.

El Café que pone Muebles Navarro
€

C/Riera Alta 4-6, 08001 **Tel** 93 442 39 66

Map 2 E2

The café where they send second-hand furniture to die, this elongated space is the popular haunt of Bohemian locals. No two pieces are alike, and the whole is a ramshackle mix of sofas, bubble chairs and formica coffee tables. It's a great place for groups and also offers imaginative snacks. Closed on Mondays.

El Xampanyet
€

C/Montcada 22, 08003 **Tel** 93 319 70 03

Map 5 B3

This tiny, tiled bar is beloved by Barcelona residents for cheap glasses of the Catalan champagne, excellent *montaditos* (little sandwiches) and tapas. Seating room is limited and the bar gets rammed, but no trip to Barcelona is complete without it. Closed on Sunday evenings and Mondays and in August.

Escribà
€

La Rambla 83, 08002 **Tel** 93 301 60 27

Map 5 A3

Situated in a whimsical, multi-coloured Modernista building on the southern edge of the Boqueria market, these famed coffee shops are a Barcelona institution. It's a great place for an atmospheric pick-me-up after a morning exploring the stalls.

Ginger
€

C/Palma de Sant Just 1, 08002 **Tel** 93 310 53 09

Map 5 B3

The folks at Ginger have hit on an inspired formula for their multi-levelled space. There's a wine bar at one end, cocktails at the other with banks of soft, squishy armchairs in between. Combined with low lighting, mellow jazz grooves and delectable tapas, it's easy to spend an entire evening here.

Key to Symbols *see back cover flap*

La Granja

C/Banys Nous 4, 08002 **Tel** *93 302 69 75* **Map** *5 A2*

A very bohemian place. Also called La Vaca Lechera (the milky cow), this is a gorgeously old-fashioned dairy with cream coloured walls, faded photographs and antique dairy equipment. Thick, custardy hot chocolate is the specialty here. Perfect for chilly winter mornings.

Luz de Gas – Port Vell

Moll del Dipòsit s/n, 08039 **Tel** *93 484 23 26* **Map** *5 B4*

This double-decked boat must be one of the most desireable summer haunts in all of Barcelona. Situated on the edge of the Port Vell harbour, alongside other gin palaces and luxury yachts, its fabulous for people-watching over a cool, iced *cava*. They also serve tapas.

Marsella

C/Sant Pau 65, 08001 **Tel** *93 442 72 63* **Map** *2 E3*

One of the oldest bars in the Barrio Chino, the lower part of the Raval, once notorious for its unsavoury characters and prostitutes, it retains a ravaged charm. Dusty chandeliers and ancient wine bottles lend to a convivial atmosphere where the drink of choice is the little green fairy (absinthe). They do not serve food here.

Sandwich & Friends

Passeig del Born 27, 08003 **Tel** *93 310 07 86* **Map** *5 B3*

Dominated by a giant mural of *Friends* painted by the well-known Catalan graphic designer Jordi Labanda (much of his work can be seen in *Wallpaper* magazine), the sandwiches here were invented by the people that frequent it, and you can still put in special requests among the myriad of fillings available.

Textil Café

C/Montcada 12, 08003 **Tel** *93 268 25 98* **Map** *5 B3*

This cozy café spills over into the courtyard of one of the Montcada's many palaces, and offers a retreat from the sun. The small kitchen does a good range of home-made cakes, quiches, salads and sandwiches. Good for a light lunch. Service however can be slow. Live music once a week, and DJs on Sundays. Closed on Mondays.

Va de Vi

C/Banys Vells 16, 08003 **Tel** *93 319 29 00* **Map** *5 B2*

With its stone archways, slate-tiled floors and beaten wooden dining tables, this place has buckets of atmosphere to add to a cellar that stocks more than 4,000 bottles of wine, *cava* and liqueurs. It's also a good place to try different Spanish cheeses and *charcuterie*. Perfect for a late-night supper. Opens daily at 6pm.

EIXAMPLE

Cacao Sampaka

C/Consell de Cent 292, 08007 **Tel** *93 272 08 33* **Map** *3 A4*

The chocolate emporium of Albert Adrià (master-chef Ferran Adrià's brother), this is a must stop for serious chocolate addicts. Choose from bonbons made from cocoa beans from different parts of South America, flower, fruit or spice concoctions, and more bizarre flavours such as anchovy and black olive. *(See p156)*.

Laie Librería Café

C/Pau Claris 85, 08010 **Tel** *93 302 73 10* **Map** *3 B3*

A stylish book shop-cum-café very close to the Plaça de Catalunya, this is a good spot to mull over your purchase with a cup of gourmet coffee. It also has a pretty interior terrace and offers light evening meals as well as occassional live music. Live jazz on Tuesdays in February. Closed on Sundays.

FURTHER AFIELD

GRÀCIA Café del Sol

Plaça del Sol 16, 08012 **Tel** *93 415 56 63* **Map** *3 B1*

One of Gràcia's most famous cafés it used to be run by Señor Ramón, a passionate pianist. He died some years ago but his piano still dominates one corner of the room though it is never played. Instead, the stereo plays an eclectic mix of rock, punk, reggae and blues for music lovers. They also serve tapas.

GRÀCIA Mirabé

C/Manuel Arnús 2, 08035 **Tel** *93 418 56 67*

An elegant lounge bar situated just where the funicular leaves for Tibidabo, the floor-to-ceiling windows offer fantastic views of the city, while the sprawling terraced gardens are idyllic for drinks in the spring and summer. They do not serve food.

SHOPPING IN BARCELONA

Barcelona is sophisticated, stylish and neatly divided into distinctive shopping districts – Passeig de Gràcia for chi-chi designer stores, the Barri Gòtic for more eclectic antiques and boutiques, El Born for serious fashion divas, and El Raval for markets and museum shops. Though these rules are by no means fixed, they do provide a useful rule of thumb and help define the city, when time is lim-

A Modernista shop window

ited. There are food markets as well – 44 in all – for every *barrio*, and a scattering of flea markets such as the Parisian-style Els Encants and the antiques fair in Sant Cugat, which has a more Provençal flavour. A convenient way to tour Barcelona's shops and markets is by taxi or public transport, which are both cheap and relaible. Even though there are many parking lots in the city, there's little point in hiring a car.

Some of the beautifully displayed confectionery at Escribà

FOOD AND DRINK

Barcelona's pastry shops are sights in themselves and, with its displays of chocolate sculptures, no *pastisseria* is more enticing or spectacular than **Escribà**. Other food stores also have a great deal of character, none more so than **Colmado Quílez** in the Eixample. This wonderful old place stocks a huge range of hams, cheeses and preserves, in addition to a comprehensive selection of Spanish and foreign wines and spirits.

DEPARTMENT STORES AND 'GALERIES'

The branch of **El Corte Inglés**, Spain's largest department store chain, on Plaça Catalunya is a Barcelona landmark and a handy place to find everything under one roof, including plug adaptors and services like key-cutting. Other branches are located around the city. Barcelona's hypermarkets also sell a wide

range of goods. As they are on the outskirts of the city – south along the Gran Via towards the airport, and on the Avingunda Meridiana to the north – a car is the best way to reach them.

The *galeries* (fashion malls), built mostly during the affluent 1980s, are hugely popular. **Bulevard Rosa** on the Passeig de Gràcia has hundreds of stores selling clothes and accessories. On the Avingunda Diagonal is **L'Illa**, a large, lively shopping mall containing chain stores as well as specialist retailers.

FASHION

International fashion labels are found alongside clothes by young designers on and around the Passeig de Gràcia. **Adolfo Domínguez** stocks classically styled clothes for men and women; **Armand Basi** sells quality leisure and sportswear; and discount designer fashion is available at

Contribuciones. Many stores offer traditional, fine-quality tailoring skills, and **Calzados E Solé**, which is situated in the Old Town, specializes in classic hand-made shoes and boots.

SPECIALITY STORES

A walk around Barcelona can reveal a wonderful choice of stores selling traditional craft items and handmade goods that in most places have now been largely replaced by the production line. **La Caixa de Fang** has a good variety of Catalan and Spanish ceramics, among them traditional Catalan cooking pots and colourful tiles. **L'Estanc** has everything for the smoker, including the best Havana cigars. **La Manual Alpargatera** is an old shoe store that specializes in Catalan-style espadrilles. These are handmade on the premises and come in all colours. The city's oldest store, **Cereria Subirà** (*see pp54–5*), sells candles in every imaginable form.

Menswear department in Adolfo Domínguez

DESIGN, ART AND ANTIQUES

If you are interested in modern design, or just looking for gifts, you should pay a visit to **Vinçon**, the city's famous design emporium. Situated on the Passeig de Gràcia, it has everything for the home, including beautiful fabrics and furniture. A must is **BD-Ediciones de Diseño**, which has the feel of an art gallery. Housed in a building designed by Domènech i Montaner, the store has furniture based on designs by Gaudí and Charles Rennie Mackintosh, and sells wonderful contemporary furniture and accessories.

Most of the commercial art and print galleries are found on Carrer Consell de Cent, in

Mouthwatering fruit stalls in La Boqueria market

the Eixample, while the Barri Gòtic – especially the Carrer de la Palla and Carrer del Pi – is the best place to browse around small but fascinating antiques shops. As well as fine furniture and old dolls, **L'Arca de l'Avia** sells antique silks and lace, all of which are set out in pretty displays.

BOOKS AND NEWSPAPERS

Most city-centre newsstands sell English-language newspapers, but the best stocks of foreign papers and magazines are at FNAC at **L'Illa** and at **Crisol**, which also sells books, videos, CDs and photographic equipment.

The stylishly sparse display of furniture at Vinçon

MARKETS

No-one should miss the chance to look around **La Boqueria** on La Rambla, one of the most spectacular food markets in Europe. Antiques are sold in the Plaça Nova on Thursdays, and cheese, honey and sweets in the Plaça del Pi on the first and third Friday, Saturday and Sunday of each month. On Sunday mornings coin and stamp stalls are set up in the Plaça Reial. The city's traditional flea market, **Encants Vells** *(see p99)*, takes place on Mondays, Wednesdays, Fridays and Saturdays just north of the Plaça de les Glòries Catalanes.

DIRECTORY

FOOD AND DRINK

Colmado Quílez
Rambla de Catalunya 63.
Map 3 A4.
Tel 93 215 23 56.

Escribà Pastisseries
La Rambla 83.
Map 2 F4.
Tel *93 301 60 27.*

Gran Via de les Corts
Catalanes 546.
Map 2 E1.
Tel *93 454 75 35.*

DEPARTMENT STORES AND 'GALERIES'

Bulevard Rosa
Passeig de Gràcia 55.
Map 3 A4.
Tel *93 378 91 91.*

El Corte Inglés
Avinguda Diagonal 617–19.
Tel 93 366 71 00.
One of several branches.

L'Illa
Avinguda Diagonal 545–57.
Tel 93 444 00 00.

FASHION

Adolfo Domínguez
P de Gràcia 89. **Map** 3 A3.
Tel *93 215 13 39.*

Armand Basi
Passeig de Gràcia 49.
Map 3 A3.
Tel *93 215 14 21.*

Calzados E Solé
Carrer Ample 7. **Map** 5 A3.
Tel *93 301 69 84*

Contribuciones
Riera de Sant Miquel 30.
Map 3 A2.
Tel *93 218 71 40.*

SPECIALITY STORES

La Caixa de Fang
C/ Freneria 1. **Map** 5 B2.
Tel 93 315 17 04.

Cereria Subirà
Bajada Llibreteria 7.
Map 5 B2. **Tel** *93 315 26 06.*

L'Estanc
Via Laietana 4. **Map** 5 B3.
Tel *93 310 10 34.*

La Manual Alpargatera
C/ d'Avinyó 7. **Map** 5 A3.
Tel *93 301 01 72.*

DESIGN, ART AND ANTIQUES

L'Arca de l'Avia
Carrer dels Banys Nous 20.
Map 5 A2.
Tel *93 302 15 98.*

BD-Ediciones de Diseño

Carrer de Mallorca 291.
Map 3 B4.
Tel *93 458 69 09.*

Vinçon
P de Gràcia 96. **Map** 3 B3.
Tel *93 215 60 50.*

BOOKS AND NEWSPAPERS

Crisol
Rambla de Catalunya 81.
Map 3 A4.
Tel *93 215 27 20.*

MARKETS

La Boqueria
La Rambla 101. **Map** 5 A2.

Encants Vells
C/ Dos de Maig, P de les
Glòries. **Map** 4 F5.

Food and Drink

Barcelonans are proud of their culinary heritage and rightly so. The land produces superlative fruit and vegetables, flavourful meats and an astonishing array of cheeses; the bounty of the sea offers daily fresh fish and seafood and the wine-growing regions of the Penedès and the Priorat make some of the best value vintages in the world. Less well known are the candy-makers, chocolate shops and *patisseries*, all of which add up to a complete and sophisticated cuisine that is fast becoming the envy of the world.

CHARCUTERIE, CHEESE AND DELICATESSENS

If you can't join them you can at least take some delicious treats home. Barcelona has several wonderful stores for stocking up on general goodies. The Boqueria, the city's most famous food market on La Rambla, is the obvious place to start, but if you prefer to shop without the hustle and bustle, head for one of the city's many specialist food shops.

Origins 99.9% in El Born specialises in strictly Catalan products – jars of small, dusky Arbequina olives, Sant Joan truffle-scented salt, oils and vinegars, home-made preserves and artisan *charcuterie*. Just around the corner, **La Botifarrería de Santa María** is great for artisan *charcuterie* and a lip-smacking array of home-made sausages in many intriguing flavours, such as pork and cuttlefish, beef and beetroot, lamb and wild mushroom. Then there's **Casa Gispert** for top-grade dried fruit and nuts as well as coffee, which is toasted in-house, and the fabulous **Formatgeria La Seu**. This is the only cheese shop in Spain that stocks exclusively Spanish and Catalan cheeses. Prowl around the walk-in dairy and choose from a great seasonal collection of cheeses made by small producers. These range from creamy Catalan goats cheese, six-month old Manchegos to beech-smoked San Simóns, that come in the shape of a dunce's cap. A tasting of three cheeses and a tumbler of

wine is available for the very reasonable price of €2.50. Formatgeria La Seu's owner, Katherine McLaughlin, also stocks a small range of artisan olive oils.

For more general food products and quintessentially Spanish canned goods (many of which come in wonderful packaging), **Colmado Quílez** is a fascinating old place that stocks just about everything from saffron to ham and sauerkraut. Another interesting store in the Eixample is **Mantequeria Ravell**, Barcelona's first proper delicatessen. Its merchandise isn't strictly Spanish – there are plenty of Italian and French goods as well – but it does boast the best and most expensive of everything from pink Himalayan salt to explosive pickled *guindilla* peppers from the Basque country. Its restaurant on the first floor, incidentally, is pricey but sublime.

The **Herboristeria del Rei** isn't actually a food store, but it does contain a formidable array of medicinal herbs, teas and honeys. When it opened in 1823, Queen Isabel II decreed that it be supplier to the royal household and the handsome marble fountain that contains a bust of Linneo, the botanist and famous herbalist, was where the leeches were kept.

CHOCOLATE AND CANDIES

Swanky chocolate and cake shops proliferate mainly in the Eixample with the exception of **Xocoa**, which has branches all over the city,

including one in El Born and one in the Barri Gòtic. This is the trendiest of the chocolate-makers in the city, with its retro packaging and fun shapes, including chocolate CDs and giant keys. **Escribà Pastisseries** is more extravagant, sculpting magnificent cakes, pastries and life-size chocolate models of famous person-alities. The most gourmet chocolate-makers however, are **Enric Rovira**. Although a little off the beaten path, it is worth the journey and effort to see his amazing chocolate re-creations of Gaudí's trademark *rajoles* paving stones and chocolate gift sets designed by well-known Catalan artists. **Cacao Sampaka** is the sweet shop owned by Albert Adrià (Ferran Adrià's brother) and offers amazing off-the-wall fillings of anchovy, black olive and blue cheese as well as the more traditional herb, spice and floral flavours.

Those looking to take home more traditionally Spanish sweets try **Antiga Casa Mauri** for thick bricks of *turrón* (Catalan nougat and almond pastes) and **Caelum** for convent-made sweetmeats such as *yemas* (sweetened egg yolks) and *mazapans* (marzipan treats). **Jauja** is a nostalgic experience, the nation's original candy store selling old-fashioned sweets and jewel-coloured candies.

A more recent incarnation is **Papabubble**, a gorgeous wood-panelled, marble-tiled shop where you can still occasionally observe the sweets being made.

BAKERIES AND PATISSERIES

Almost every street in the city features its very own *panadería*. Usually open all day, these shops are busiest early in the morning and at around 5pm, snack-time in Spain, when you will often find mothers indulging their kids with after-school treats.

Amongst the best of these shops is **Cusachs**, open since

1963 and still producing the traditional Catalan *coques*. These can either be sweet or savoury and are mostly eaten on 23 June, the San Joan festival *(see p35)* and the longest day of the year.

Another great *panadería* is **Foix de Sarriá** on Major de Sarriá, very well known for its excellent pastries and other baked goods. Amongst its specialities are "royal cake", *sachertorte panellets* (round marzipan cakes), *pasta de té* (fruit biscuits) and *saras* (sponge cake covered with butter cream and almonds).

For the best breads in town, visit **Bopan**, near Rambla de Catalunya. This smart café sells its own versions of many types of bread, randing from Continental favourites to African specialities.

WINE AND CIGARS

For sheer scope you can't beat **Lavinia**, the biggest wine shop in Spain, with branches in Madrid and more recently in Paris, which stocks thousands of labels from all over the world. Choice comes at a price, however, and you will get better deals downtown. In El Born, **Vila Viniteca** sells a formidable range of Spanish and Catalan wines ranging from cheap,

cheerful table wines for around €3 a bottle, to decadently expensive Priorats and Riojas that retail in the region of €300. Last, but by no means least, to leave Barcelona without a bottle of the nation's beloved Catalan champagne *(cava)* would be verging on the sacrilegious. You can buy it everywhere, but for something truly special head for **Xampany**, which specialises in artisan *cavas* from the Penedès wine-producing region. The ultimate place for cigar-lovers and pipe smokers is **Gimeno**. This legendary purveyor of all things tobacco-related also stocks a fine range of Cuban havanas.

DIRECTORY

CHARCUTERIE, CHEESE AND DELICATESSENS

La Botifarrería de Santa María
Carrer Santa María 4.
Tel 93 319 97 84.

Casa Gispert
C/Sombrerers 23, Born.
Map 5 B3.
Tel 93 319 75 35.

Colmado Quílez
Rambla de Catalunya 63, Eixample.
Map 3 A3.
Tel 93 215 23 56.

Formatgeria La Seu
C/Dagueria 16, Barri Gòtic.
Tel 93 412 65 48.

Herboristeria del Rei
C/ del Vidre 1, Barri Gòtic.
Tel 93 318 05 12.

Mantequeria Ravell
C/Arago 313.
Map 3 A4.
Tel 93 457 51 14.

Origins 99.9%
C/Vidrieria 6-8, Born.
Tel 93 310 75 31.

CHOCOLATE AND CANDIES

Antiga Casa Mauri
C/Flassanders 32.
Map 5 C2.
Tel 93 310 04 58.

Cacao Sampaka
C/Consell de Cent 292, Eixample.
Map 3 A4.
Tel 93 272 08 33.

Caelum
C/Palla 8, Barri Gòtic.
Map 5 A2.
Tel 93 301 69 93.
Marina Square, 6 Raffles Boulevard.
Tel 67 33 11 11.

Enric Rovira
Avinguda Jose Tarradellas 113, Eixample.
Tel 93 419 25 47.

Escribà Pastisseries
La Rambla 83, Barri Gòtic.
Map 5 A1.
Tel 93 301 60 27.

Jauja
C/Santa Anna 27, Barri Gòtic.
Map 5 A1.
Tel 93 318 13 45.

Papabubble
C/Ample 28, Barri Gòtic.
Map 5 A3.
Tel 93 268 86 25.

Xocoa
C/Vidreria 4, Born.
Map 5 B2.
Tel 93 319 63 71.
C/Princesa 10, Born.
Tel 93 319 66 40.
C/Petritxol 11-13.
Tel 93 301 11 97.

BAKERIES AND PATISSERIES

Bopan
Rambla de Catalunya, 119.
Map 3 A3.
Tel 93 237 35 23.

Cusachs
Bailén, 223.
Map 3 C2.
Tel 93 213 77 29.

Foix de Sarriá
Major de Sarriá, 57.
Tel 93 203 07 14.
Fax 93 280 65 56.

WINES AND CIGARS

Gimeno
La Rambla 100.
Map 5 A1.
Tel 93 318 49 47.

Lavinia
Av. Diagonal 605, Eixample.
Map 3 A2.
Tel 93 363 44 45.

Vila Viniteca
C/Agullers 7–9, Born.
Map 5 B3.
Tel 93 310 19 56.

Xampany
C/Valencia 200.
Map 3 A4.
Tel 93 453 93 38.

Clothes and Accessories

The streets of Barcelona are paved with clothing outlets and dedicated followers of fashion may be surprised to learn that the city can hold its own against any in New York, London or Paris. With cutting-edge, home-grown Catalan designers such as Antonio Miró and Custo, high-street fashion chains such as Mango and Zara, and literally thousands of unique boutiques, Spanish fashion is currently one of the most exciting in the world.

JEWELLERY, BAGS AND ACCESSORIES

Bags, jewellery, hats and other baubles are essential to serious style divas and Barcelona has plenty of tiny, Aladdin's Cave-type shops to help create the perfect outfit. **New Born** is little more than a hole-in-the-wall outlet, but it sells gorgeous hand-made jewellery fashioned from enamel flowers and butterflies in luscious rainbow colours. German designer Alexandra Steinforth also creates one-off evening dresses for special occasions. **Rafa Teja Atelier** makes exquisite embroidered jackets, patchwork scarves, appliqué handbags and hand-painted silk kerchiefs in sumptuous fabrics, textures and colours.

Take your own piece of Barcelona streetlife home – literally – with a **Demano** handbag from stockists all over town, including **Vinçon** (*see p154*) and **Casas**. These innovative designs have been produced in conjunction with designers Marcela Manrique, Liliana Andrade, Eleonora Parachini and the City Hall in an endeavour to recycle the waste material (polyester PVC) from banners and placards used to announce the cultural events in the city. **0,925** is housed in the stables of the 13th-century Palau Cerbello, which also comprises part of the Museu Picasso. It sells a good range of unusual, hand-made jewellery in silver, gold, titanium and palladium created by 20 or so different Spanish and Catalan designers. Another good bet for unique pieces is **Hipòtesi**. Started 17 years ago, today the store has around 650 different designers on their books and stocks mainly jewellery as well as scarves and bags in materials as diverse as buttons, zips and beads to white gold, wood and platinum. This is also a good place to check out the latest talent from the Massana School of Art.

SPANISH AND INTERNATIONAL DESIGNER LABELS

Independent designers **Giménez & Zuazo** offer truly unique skirts, dresses and long-pants for the discerning female customer and are well worth seeking out for affordable couture. El Born has plenty of stores selling a top range of designer labels, including **Black Jazz** for the boys with seasonal collections from Dolce & Gabbana, Bikkembergs and Vivienne Westwood among others. Avenida Diagonal and the Passeig de Gràcia, however, are the true homes of fashionistas, with all the big labels such as **Chanel, Carolina Herrera**, **Gucci** and **Hermès** as well as **Loewe** for luxury luggage and **Pelleteria La Sibèria** for prêt-a-porter and custom-made designers in suede, nappa and fur.

SECOND HAND AND VINTAGE FASHION

Diminutive Carrer Riera Baixa in El Raval is Barcelona's answer to London's Carnaby Street with its own Saturday market (opening times, however, can be erratic) and several wonderful shops. The theatre-turned vintage shop, **Lailo**, sells anything from collectable costumes from the Liceu opera house and vintage dresses to 1950s bathing suits. Across the road is **Mies & Felj** which specialises in more recent fashions dating from the 1960s and 70s as well as brightly-patterned curtains, fur-lined leather jackets, Chinese dresses and vintage sportswear.

HIGH STREET AND SPORTS FASHION

Ubiquitous Spanish fashion houses **Zara** and **Mango** have stores all over town. Both flagships are on the Passeig de Gràcia and they are great for good value basics, work-wear and fashionable party dresses. Both also offer a decent range of menswear. For slightly more upmarket tastes both **Massimo Dutti** and **Adolfo Domínguez** are reliable suppliers of more classical tailoring, smart casuals and practical items such as ties and belts.

More individual fashion is best sought out in the smaller, independent shops of El Born and the Barri Gòtic. Carrer d'Avinyo in the Old Town inspired the young Picasso to paint and today's hip young things to shop. A lively street with a market ambience, it is particularly good for independent clothing stores and essential sportswear – Adidas, Puma and Nike. **Overales & Bluyines** was one of the original fashion emporiums to open in El Born and continues to be one of the best for smart labels of all sorts of apparel. **Desigual** is good for urban casuals, while **Doshaburi** stocks the largest selection of vintage Levis in Spain as well as the more quirky Japanese labels. **Custo**, the most famous of Barcelona's local designers, has two shops in the old city, both are piled high with his trademark brightly printed T-shirts and mismatched coats and skirts.

Finally, football fans can head for FC Barcelona's official stores, the **Botiga del Barca**. They stock all kinds of merchandise related to the sport, including stripes, scarves, boots and balls.

HATS AND SHOES

Patterned leather shoes and decorative soles from the cult Mallorcan shoe-maker **Camper** can be purchased for around 25 per cent less in Barcelona than other places in Spain. **La Manual Apargatera** is another cult classic, beloved by *sardana* dancers (Catalonia's national dance) and celebrities alike for his exquisite hand-made, individually fitted espadrilles and straw hats. Another shop, **Casas Sabaters**, has several branches around town, all offering a top quality range of leading Spanish footwear brands. They are also good for last-minute sale items and last-season's knock-offs. **Le Shoe**, however, is the place for the discerning buyer in search of seriously classy and prohibitively expensive stilettos. The store has a wide collection of gorgeous Manolo Blahniks, Jimmy Choos and Miu Mius. Bargain hunters can head for nearby **I12** where last season's Marc Jacobs, Emma Hoes and Sonia Rykiels are sold off at rock-bottom prices. The old-fashioned hat shop **Sombrereria Obach** sells all the classics ranging from Basque berets to stetsons, trilbys and hand-woven Montechristi Panamas.

DIRECTORY

JEWELLERY, BAGS AND ACCESSORIES

0,925
C/ Montcada 25,
Born.
Map 5 B3.
Tel 93 319 43 18.

Demano
Pallars 94, 7, 1a.
Map 6 E2.
Tel 93 300 4807.

Hipòtesi
Rambla de
Catalunya 105,
Eixample.
Map 3 A3.
Tel 93 215 02 98.

New Born
C/Princesa 24,
Born.
Map 5 B2.
Tel 93 511 31 25.

Rafa Teja Atelier
C/Sta. Maria 18,
Born.
Tel 93 310 27 85.
Fax 93 289 28 05.

SPANISH AND INTERNATIONAL DESIGNER LABELS

Black Jazz
C/Rec 28.
Map 5 C3.
Tel 93 310 42 36.

Carolina Herrera
Passeig de Gràcia 87,
Eixample.
Map 3 A2–A5.
Tel 93 272 15 84.

Chanel
Passeig de Gràcia,
Eixample.
Map 3 A2–A5.
Tel 93 488 29 23.

Giménez & Zuazo
C/Elisabets 20,
El Raval.
Map 2 F2.
Tel 93 412 33 81.

Gucci
Avenida Diagonal 415,
Eixample.
Map 3 A2.
Tel 93 416 06 20.

Hermès
Passeig de Gràcia 33.
Map 3 A2–A5.
Tel 93 272 15 27.

Loewe
Passeig de Gràcia.
Map 3 A2–A5.
Tel 93 216 04 00.

Pelleteria La Sibèria
Rambla de Catalunya 15,
Eixample.
Map 3 A3.
Tel 93 317 05 83.

SECOND HAND AND VINTAGE FASHION

Lailo
C/Riera Baixa 20,
El Raval.
Map 2 F2.
Tel 93 441 37 49.

Mies & Felj
C/Riera Baixa 4,
El Raval.
Map 2 F2.
Tel 93 442 07 55.

HIGH STREET AND SPORTS FASHION

Adolfo Dominguez
Passeg de Gràcia 89,
Eixample.
Map 3 A2–A5.
Tel 93 215 13 39.

Botiga del Barca
Maremàgnum
(Moll d'Espanya).
Map 5 A4.
Tel 93 225 80 45.

Custo
Plaça de les Olles 7.
Map 5 B3.
Tel 93 268 78 93.

Desigual
C/Argenteria 65,
Born.
Map 5 B2.
Tel 93 310 30 15.

Doshaburi
C/Lledó 4-6,
Barri Gòtic.
Map 2 F2.
Tel 93 319 96 29.
www.doshaburi.com

Mango
Passeig de Gràcia.
Map 3 A2–A5.
Tel 93 215 75 30.

Massimo Dutti
C/Argenteria 65,
Born.
Map 5 B2.
Tel 93 310 30 15.

Overales & Bluyines
Rec 65,
Born.
Map 5 C3.
Tel 93 319 29 76.

Zara
Passeig de Gràcia 16,
Eixample.
Map 3 A2–A5.
Tel 93 318 76 75.

HATS AND SHOES

Camper
Plaça Àngels con
C/Elizabets,
El Raval.
Map 2 F2.
Tel 93 342 41 41.

Casas Sabaters
C/Portaferrissa 25.
Map 5 A2.
Tel 93 302 11 32.

I12
C/Laforja 105,
Gràcia.
Map 3 A1.
Tel 93 414 55 13.

La Manual Apargatera
C/D'Avinyó 7,
Barri Gòtic.
Map 5 A3.
Tel 93 301 01 72.

Le Shoe
C/Viñas 6,
Eixample.
Tel 93 241 10 22.

Sombrereria Obach
Carrer del Call 2,
Barri Gòtic.
Map 5 A2.
Tel 93 318 40 94.

Speciality Stores

Part of the fun of getting to know Barcelona is to meander through the Old Town's rabbit-warren-like streets, or to explore the wide boulevards of the Eixample. Both the areas have a wonderful choice of stores selling traditional crafts and hand-made goods that in many places have been replaced by the production line. The endless array of shops are a dazzling sight in themselves and even if you are just window-shopping, it's well worth taking a proper look around to see the merchandise on offer.

ART AND ANTIQUES

Antiques aficionados and collectors will be richly rewarded by what Barcelona has to offer. The equivalent of an antiques shopping mall, **Bulevard dels Antiquaris** is home to over 70 shops brimming over with relics from the past. These can range from ancient coins and alabaster statues to tin drums, Regency-period candelabras and assorted bric-a-brac. Carrer del Call, the old Jewish quarter in the Barri Gòtic, is another hub for collectors with plush shops, such as **L'Arca de l'Àvia**, which sells antique lace and linens, old dolls and fine furniture, **Heritage**, a purveyor of semi-precious stone jewellery, antique silks and textiles and the odd mink stole, and **Gemma Povo** for decorative antique iron-work. Also check out several shops belonging to **Artur Ramon** on Carrer de la Palla (all bear his name) for 18th- and 19th-century glassware and ceramics and paintings dating back to the 14th century. **Tandem** specialises in a wonderful range of tawny, old globes.

Barcelona's oldest and most prestigious art gallery is **Sala Parés**, which exhibits serious Catalan artists, both past and present. For keepsake wall hangings that won't break the bank, try the **Boutique Galería Picasso** for prints, lithographs, posters and postcards by the great Spanish masters, Miró, Picasso and Dalí. **Metrònom** is more contemporary and is a showcase for multimedia exhibitions and other 21st-century artistic interpretations of life through performance, video and installation.

BOOKS, MUSIC, DVDS AND STATIONERY

Barcelona is a wonderful city for unearthing intriguing knick-knacks and unique, one-of-a-kind gifts that people will treasure forever. **Papirvm** is an old fashioned stationary store, piled high with beautiful fountain pens, leather-bound and William Morris print notepads, and even feather quills as well as retro Boqueria waiters pads. **Altaïr** is arguably Spain's finest specialist travel bookshop stocking a stupendous range of armchair reads, maps, travel guides and coffee-table books for anyone who lives and loves to move. But if you're just looking for some holiday reading try the **Casa del Llibre**, Barcelona's biggest bookstore for English language novels, magazines, travel guides, maps and glossy coffee-table books.

Thanks to the wide influence of Barcelona's annual electronic music festival, Sonár (see p163), the city has become a hot spot for music collectors. **Cable Records** and El Raval in general are good for stocking up on the latest club tunes and old vinyl, while **Herrera Guitars** is a safe bet for anyone in the market for a hand-made classical Spanish guitar. Commissions are accepted.

UNUSUAL GIFTS AND KNICK-KNACKS

El Born and the Barri Gòtic are treasure troves, at once delightful and inspiring. **Brasil Style** stocks a wide and unusual range of objects for the home including amusing ceramic chickens and wonderful hand-made dinner sets. **Natural** is ideal for cheap and chic presents such as groovy candy-striped socks, duvet slippers, Chinese-style notepads and other Oriental toys and trinkets. For the Don Quixote in your life, **La Condonería** (the condom emporium) stocks all manner of rubber delights in every shape, size, colour and flavour imaginable. **Cereria Subirà** is a gorgeous shop and the city's oldest dating back to 1761. Today, it sells a phenomenal array of decorative and votive candles in numerous shapes and sizes, including some several feet tall for dramatic effect. **El Rei de la Màgica** is another golden-oldie, founded in 1881. It reveals a world of fairytale magic for budding magicians. Nearby, **Arlequí Màscares** creates traditional hand-painted folk masks out of papier-mâché, including Italian Commedia dell'arte masks, glossy French party masks, grotesque Catalan *gigantes* (giant heads used in local festivals), Greek tragedy and Japanese Noh masks.

LINGERIE AND PERFUMES

The French chain **Sephora** stocks a wide selection of brand-name perfumes and cosmetics often cheaper than those at the airport. But, for the perfect aromatic memento check out Ricardo Ramos' perfume; Agua de Barcelona No 7 *para ella* (for her), No 21 *para el* (for him), and No 69 unisex, from **R Que R Rec**. **Regia** is reputed to be one of the best perfume stores in the city, with a large selection of designer classics, local favourites and the most up-to-date trendy fragrances from around the world.

Le Boudoir is decked out like an 18th-century love nest complete with brass bed, gilded mirrors, velvet drapery and love poetry inscribed on the walls. It is also the sexiest shop in Barcelona for lace and silk lingerie, nightgowns, fluffy mules and furry handcuffs as well as tasteful sex toys and aphrodisiacs. For more conventional underwear, the quality Spanish chain **Women's Secret** goes in for a funky line of candy-coloured bra and pants sets, swimwear and hip pyjamas.

INTERIORS

Strictly speaking, **Pile 43** is more of a café-bar than a shop, but it sells everything from the ashtrays to the battered

leather armchairs. **Ici et Là** is good for one-off pieces for the home and design classics at unbeatable prices. **Dom**, on the other hand, is more trendy and quirky, stocking neon-coloured inflatable sofas, metallic bead curtains and "PUSH" bins. It has several branches in the city. Fans of gizmos and gadgets will enjoy **Vinçon**. This is the mecca of Barcelona's design stores. Housed in a 1900

upper-class apartment, its vast space is filled with everything from French Le Creuset cookware to Basque *chiquito* straight-edged tumblers, silk bean bags and futons. The old-fashioned clientele is more inclined towards **Coses de Casa**. This is a superb place for hand-made patchwork quilts, feminine rosebud prints and Laura Ashley style floral designs for lovers of chintz.

DIRECTORY

ART AND ANTIQUES

L'Arca de L'Avia
C/Banys Nous 20,
Barri Gòtic.
Map 5 A2.
Tel 93 302 15 98.

Artur Ramon
Col.leccionisme C/Palla 23,
Barri Gòtic.
Map 5 A2.
Tel 93 302 59 70.

Artur Ramon Antiquari
C/Palla 25,
Barri Gòtic.
Map 5 A2.
Tel 93 302 59 70.

Artur Ramon Mestres Antics
C/Palla 10,
Barri Gòtic.
Map 5 A2.
Tel 93 301 16 48.
www.altair.es

Boutique Galería Picasso
C/Barra de Ferro 7.
Tel 93 268 44 50.

Bulevard dels Antiquaris
Passeig de Gràcia.
Map 3 A2–A5.
*Tel 93 310 30 15/
93 215 44 99.*

Gemma Povo
C/Banys Nous 5,
Barri Gòtic.
Map 5 A2.
Tel 93 301 34 76.

Heritage
C/Banys Nous 14,
Barri Gòtic.
Map 5 A2.
Tel 93 317 85 15.

Metrònom
C/Fusina 9, Born.
Map 5 C2.
Tel 93 268 42 98.

Sala Parés
C/Petritxol 5,
Barri Gòtic.
Map 5 A2.
Tel 93 318 70 08.

Tandem
C/Banys Nous 19,
Barri Gòtic.
Map 5 A2.
Tel 93 317 44 91.

BOOKS, MUSIC, DVDS AND STATIONERY

Altaïr
Gran Via 616,
Eixample.
Tel 93 342 71 71.
Fax 93 342 71 78.

Cable Records
C/Joaquín Costa 46,
El Raval.
Map 2 F2.
Tel 93 317 20 59.

Casa del Llibre
Passeig de Gràcia.
Map 3 A2–A5.
Tel 93 272 34 80.

Herrera Guitars
C/Marlet 6,
Barri Gòtic.
Tel 93 302 66 66.
www.herreraguitars.
com

Papirvm
C/Baixada de la
Llibreteria 2,
Barri Gòtic.
Map 5 A2.
Tel 93 310 52 42.
www.papirum-bcn.com

UNUSUAL GIFTS AND KNICK-KNACKS

Arlequí Màscares
C/ Princesa 7.
Map 5 B2.
Tel 93 268 27 52.
www.arlequimask.
com

Brasil Style
Pl. Comercial 3,
Born.
Map 5 C3.
Tel 93 268 86 30.
Fax 93 268 86 31.
www.brasilstyle.com

Cereria Subirà
Baixada Llibreteria 7.
Map 5 A2.
Tel 93 315 26 06.

La Condoneria
Placa Sant Josep
Oriol 7,
Barri Gòtic.
Map 2 F2.
Tel 93 302 77 21.

Natural
C/Argenteria 78,
Born.
Map 5 B2.
Tel 93 268 25 25.

El Rei de la Màgica
Carrer de la Princessa 11.
Map 5 B2.
Tel 93 319 73 93.

LINGERIE AND PERFUMES

Le Boudoir
C/Canuda 21.
Map 5 A1.
Tel 93 302 52 81.
www.leboudoir.net

R Que R Rec
C/Rec 75,
Born.
Map 5 C3.
Tel 651 616 962.

Regia
Passeig de Gracia 39.
Map 3 A2–A5.
Tel 93 216 01 21.

Women's Secret
C/Portaferrissa 7,
Barri Gòtic.
Map 5 A2.
Tel 93 318 13 66.

INTERIORS

Coses de Casa
Plaça Sant Josep Oriol 5,
Barri Gòtic.
Map 2 F2.
Tel 93 315 26 06.

Dom
Passeig de Gràcia 76,
Eixample.
Map 3 A2–A5.
Tel 93 487 11 81.

Ici et Là
Plaça de Santa María
del Mar 2.
Tel 93 268 11 67.

Pilé 43
C/Agla 43.
Tel 93 301 30 54.

Vinçon
Passeig de Gràcia 96.
Map 3 A2–A5.
Tel 93 215 60 50.

ENTERTAINMENT IN BARCELONA

arcelona has one of the most colourful and alternative live arts scenes in Europe, offering a smörgasbord of entertainment from the gilded Liceu opera house and the spectacular Modernista masterpiece Palau de la Música, to small independent theatres hosting obscure Catalan comedies and dark Spanish dramas. But there's also much to

Busker in the Barri Gòtic

see simply by walking around. Street performance ranges from the human statues on La Rambla to excellent classical, ragtime and jazz buskers in the plazas. In addition, there are a series of weekend-long musical and arts fiestas that run throughout the year, many of which now attract an international audience of people from all over Europe and beyond.

The magnificent interior of the Palau de la Música Catalana

ENTERTAINMENT GUIDES

The most complete guide to what's going on each week in Barcelona is the *Guía del Ocio*, out every Thursday. It includes a cinema listings section. The Friday *El País* and *La Vanguardia* also have entertainments supplements.

SEASONS AND TICKETS

Theatre and concert seasons for the main venues run from September to June, with limited programmes at other times. The city's varied menu of entertainment reflects its rich multi-cultural artistic heritage. In summer the city hosts the Festival del Grec *(see p35)*, a showcase of international music, theatre and dance, held at open-air venues. There is also a wide variety of concerts to choose from during September's Festa de la Mercè *(see p36)*. The simplest way to get theatre and concert tickets is to buy them at the box office,

although tickets for many theatres can also be bought from branches of the Caixa de Catalunya and La Caixa savings banks, or from Servi Caixa machines *(see p178)*. Tickets for the Grec festival are sold at tourist offices.

FILM AND THEATRE

The **Mercat de les Flors** *(see p165)* is an exciting theatre presenting high-quality productions of classic and modern plays in Catalan. The new **Teatre Nacional de Catalunya** *(see p99)*, next to the Auditori de Barcelona, is another fine showcase for Catalan drama. The main venue for classical ballet is the **Liceu** opera house. There are also many contemporary dance companies and regular performances are staged at the Mercat de les Flors in Montjuïc.

MUSIC

Barcelona's Modernista **Palau de la Música Catalana** *(see p62)* is one of the world's

most beautiful concert halls, with its stunning interior decor and world-renowned acoustic. Also inspiring is the **Auditori de Barcelona** *(see p167)*, opened in 1999 to give the city two modern halls for large-scale and chamber concerts. Its reputation was considerably bolstered when it became the home of the Orquestra Simfònica de Barcelona.

Musical life suffered a setback when the Liceu opera house burned down in 1994. Fortunately, the city had enough credit in the bank of operatic excellence to ensure that its reputation remained undiminished. Restoration was completed in 1999, and the Liceu is now back in operation at full-octave level.

Big names like David Byrne and Paul McCartney have performed at **Razzmatazz** *(see p167)*. Jazz venues include the **Harlem Jazz Club** *(see p167)* and **Jamboree** *(see p167)*, and salsa fans will enjoy a quick slink down to **Antilla Barcelona**.

Outrageous stage show at one of Barcelona's many clubs

Auditorium of the Teatre Nacional de Catalunya

NIGHTLIFE

Among Barcelona's most famous modern sights are the hi-tech designer bars built in the prosperous 1980s, for example the **Mirablau**, which looks over the city. The **Torres de Ávila**, in the Poble Espanyol *(see p89)*, is the height of post-Modernism. **Otto Zutz** has regular DJs and the less chic but still fun **Apolo** has live music. **La Paloma** is a dance hall complete with a 1904 interior and its own orchestra.

Two of the best-known bars are in the old city: **Boadas** for cocktails and **El Xampanyet** *(see p152)* for sparkling wine and tapas. **El Bosc de les Fades** is the café of the wax museum and is imaginatively decorated like a fairy's woodland grotto.

FESTIVALS

During the summer, the streets are alive with outdoor festivals, performances and music. The **Festival del Sónar**, in June, began in an experimental manner as a place to showcase the latest musical talents of Southern European youth using new technologies. The **Clàssica als Parcs**, in June-July, is a good bet for a more serene entertainment.

AMUSEMENT PARK

In Summer, Barcelona's giant amusement park on the summit of **Tibidabo** *(see p98)* is usually open till the early hours at weekends, but also busy on other days. It is even more fun if you travel there by tram, funicular or cable car.

SPORTS

The undoubted kings of sport in Catalonia are **FC Barcelona,** known as Barça. They have the largest football stadium in Europe, Camp Nou, and a fanatical following *(see p95)*. Barcelona also has a high-ranking basketball team.

Packed house at the gigantic Camp Nou stadium

DIRECTORY

FILM AND THEATRE

Liceu
La Rambla 51–59.
Map 2 F3.
Tel *93 485 99 00.*

Teatre Nacional de Catalunya
Plaça de les Arts 1.
Map 4 F5.
Tel *93 306 57 00.*

MUSIC

Auditori de Barcelona
Carrer de Lepant 150.
Map 6 E1.
Tel *93 247 93 00.*

Antilla Barcelona
Carrer de Aragó 141–143.
Tel *93 451 45 64.*

Palau de la Música Catalana
Carrer de Sant Francesc de Paula 2. **Map** 5 B1.
Tel *90 244 28 82.*

NIGHTLIFE

Apolo
Carrer Nou de la Rambla 113. **Map** 2 E3.
Tel *93 441 40 01.*

Boadas
Carrer dels Tallers 1.
Map 5 A1.
Tel *93 318 88 26.*

El Bosc de les Fades
Pasatge de la Banca.
Tel *93 317 26 49.*

Mirablau
Plaça Doctor Andreu.
Tel *93 418 58 79.*

Otto Zutz
Carrer de Lincoln 15.
Map 3 A1.
Tel *93 238 07 22.*

La Paloma
Carrer del Tigre 27.
Map 2 F1.
Tel *93 301 68 97.*

Torres de Ávila
Poble Espanyol, Avinguda del Marqués de Comillas.
Map 1 A1.
Tel *93 424 93 09.*

El Xampanyet
Carrer Montcada 22.
Map 5 B2.
Tel *93 319 70 03.*

FESTIVALS

Classics als Parcs
Information Parcs i Jardins
Tel *93 413 24 00.*
www.bcn.es/parcsijardins

Festival del Sónar
Palau de la Virreina.
Tel *90 288 89 02.*
www.sonar.es

Tickets
Tel *90 210 12 12.*
www.telentrada.com

Tel Entrada
www.telentrada.com

Barcelona Metropolitan
www.barcelona-metropolitan

AMUSEMENT PARK

Tibidabo
Tel *93 211 79 42.*

SPORTS

FC Barcelona
Camp Nou, Avinguda Aristides Maillol.
Tel *93 496 36 00.*

Film and Theatre

Large, multiscreen complexes as well as smaller, more intimate venues today screen a variety of films, catering to all tastes. As a result, Barcelona now hosts several film festivals through the year. Theatre, on the other hand, dates back to medieval times and the city's productions have evolved to become the most cutting-edge in Spain. Although language may be a problem, it's well-worth seeing a theatrical production. If not, there are always many dinner-shows to interest non-purists.

FILM

In recent years, directors such as Alejandro Amenábar (*The Others*), Catalan writer and director Isabel Coixet (*My Life Without You*) and, of course, Spain's bad boy of film, Pedro Almodóvar (*All About My Mother, Bad Education*) have revitalised Spanish cinema. Today, Barcelona itself has become the venue for independent film festivals and the biggest event of the year is the **International Film Festival in Sitges**, held in December.

Most Spanish cinemas dub films into Spanish or Catalan, but there are an increasing number of VO (original version) venues that screen not only Hollywood block-busters, but also film *noir* and independent art house movies. The **Centre de Cultura Contemporània (CCCB)** has provided a focal point for modern Barcelona since its opening in 1995, and, has played an integral part in the rejuvenation of El Ravel. The CCCB serves as a crossroads of contemporary culture with cutting-edge art exhibits, lectures and film screenings.

Icària Yelmo Cineplex is the town's biggest multiscreen VO complex, built around an American-style mall with a number of fast food eateries on the ground floor and shops on the first. Barcelona's biggest cinema, with a capacity of 1,832, is **Urgel**. Featuring one of Europe's largest screens at over 200 sq m (518 sq km), this is a great place to watch the latest releases. For something a bit more risqué, try the **Renoir Floridablanca**, a relatively

new cinema on the edge of El Raval and the Eixample. It screens a range of European and international movies (subtitles are usually in Spanish or Catalan). In Gràcia, **Verdi's I** and **II** are also good for more independent movie-making as well as an interesting selection of foreign films. They also occasionally have small, themed film festivals that include shorts by new local talent. During the summer, both the **Castell de Montjuïc** and the **Picina Bernat Picornell**, the Olympic swimming pool in Montjuïc, host a number of open-air cinema screenings.

The Catalan government's repertory cinema, the **Filmoteca de la Generalitat de Catalunya**, screens an excellent range of films over a period of two or three weeks before the schedule changes. The line-up encompasses anything from obscure, bleak Eastern European epics to up-beat modern musicals such as Baz Luhrmann's *Moulin Rouge*. The two-screen **Méliès** is a gem offering art-house movies, Hollywood classics, B&W horrors and anything by Fellinni or Alfred Hitchcock. **Alexis** is small arty cinema on Rambla de Catalunya, and was originally a theatre. Showing new independent films from around the world in the original language, this is a favourite amongst local buffs.

There are also an increasing number of small "bar-cinemas," where for the price of a beer you can watch a film on a small screen on a hardbacked school playground chair. **Void** may not

be the most comfortable, but it's the best place to meet local film buffs. The programme is usually more obscure than what main-stream cinemas would allow. For children, there is the **IMAX Port Vell**, which shows the usual 3-D roller-coaster knuckle-biters, Everest expeditions and squid entangled journeys to the bottom of the sea.

It's worth knowing that Monday night and weekend matinées sell cheaper seats. Many cinemas offer midnight and early hours screenings.

THEATRE AND DANCE

Although English language productions are still in short supply, there are some rather good independent groups that perform at the **Llantiol Teatre** in El Raval. However, many Catalan and Spanish productions are well worth seeing, regardless of the language constraints. Theatre groups **Els Comdiants and La Cubana**, in particular, offer a thrilling mélange of theatre, music, mime and elements from traditional Mediter-ranean fiestas. The tiny Llantiol stages a repertoire, that changes weekly, of alternative shows, comedy, magic and other off-the-cuff performances designed to attract a mixed crowd from the city's growing expatriate community to local arts lovers. Similarly, the **L'Antic Teatre**, on the other side of town, is a cultural centre and bar with a scruffy but pleasant summer roof-terrace and small vegetarian restau-rant that hosts a number of alternative production companies, such as the Argentinean Company 4D Òptic. Also good for avant-garde performances and music is the **Mercat de les Flors**, a converted flower market in the Montjuïc. It is also host to a handful of different themed film festivals including a celebration of Asian film in the autumn.

La Ramblas and Paral.lel are the main hubs of the city's

bigger, more mainstream theatres. The **Teatre Tivoli** is a gargantuan theatre where high quality productions, dance and musical recitals by Catalan, Spanish and international stars are held. The **Teatre Poliorama** on La Rambla meanwhile goes more for musicals, occasional operas and contemporary flamenco performances. For serious theatre-lovers however, the **Teatre Nacional de Catalunya (TNC)** is an imposing columned affair designed by the Catalan architect Ricard Bofill, with state-of-the-art facilities and a weighty line-up of Spanish and Catalan directors. The **Teatre Apolo** is good for big-bang musicals such as Queen's *We Will Rock You* and ABBA's *Mama Mia*.

Modern dance is much loved in Barcelona and there's no shortage of productions, often staged at the city's main theatres. The **Teatre Victòria** on Avinguda del Paral.lel is a reasonable bet for ballet and more classical dance productions, as is the Liceu opera house *(see p166)*.

Visitors who want to see flamenco *(see p167)* while in Barcelona can experience reasonably authentic renditions of the sexy, foot-stomping excitement of the *peñas* (folk bars) of Andalusia. However, if you do get a chance to see the Catalan flamenco singer Mayte Martín, it's well worth snapping up tickets.

There are also a handful of places that put on a reasonable dinner and show for

non-purists including **El Tablao de Carmen** *(see p167)*. For something grungier and more off-the-cuff, **Soniquete** in the Barri Gòtic is the most authentic bar in town for genuine flamenco. Performers here more often than not are locals out for a party. There's no fixed schedule, visitors just have to wait and see what happens.

Salsa, merengue and other sizzling Caribbean moves have a solid following with various clubs playing host to big name bands from New York, Puerto Rico and Cuba. Join the party (and take part in regular, free dance lessons) at **Antilla BCN Latin Club**, or, the **Buenavista Salsa Club** in Exiample.

DIRECTORY

FILM

Alexis
Rambla de Catalunya 90.
Map 3 A3.
Tel 93 215 05 06.

CCCB
C/Montalegre 5.
Map 2 F2.
Tel 93 306 41 00.
www.cccb.org

Festival Internacional de Cinema de Catalunya
Sitges.
Tel 93 419 36 35.
www.sitges.com/cinema

Filmoteca de la Generalitat de Catalunya
Avda Sarrià 31–3, Eixample.
Tel 93 410 75 90.

Icària Yelmo Cineplex
C/Salvador Espriu 61, vila Olímpica.
Map 6 E4.
Tel 93 221 75 85.
www.yelmocineplex.es

IMAX Port Vell
Moll d'Espanya, Port Vell.
Map 5 A4.
Tel 93 225 11 11.

Méliès
C/Villarroel 102, Eixample.
Map 2 E1.
Tel 93 451 00 51.

Renoir Floridablanca
C/Floridablanca 135, Eixample.
Map 1 C1.
Tel 93 228 93 93.
www.cinesrenoir.es

Urgel
Comte d'Urgell 29.
Map 2 E1.
Tel 90 242 42 43.

Verdi I
C/Verdi 32, Gràcia.
Map 3 B1.
Tel 93 238 79 90.
www.cines-verdi.com

Verdi II
C/Torrijos 49, Gràcia.
Map 3 C2.
Tel 93 238 79 90.

Void
C/Ferlandina 51.
Map 2 E1.
Tel 93 443 42 03.
www.void-bcn.com

THEATRE AND DANCE

L'Antic Teatre
C/Verdaguer i Callís 12, La Ribera.
Map 5 A1.
Tel 93 315 23 54.

Antilla BCN Latin Club
C/Aragó 141, Eixample.
Map 3 A4.
Tel 93 451 45 64.
www.antillasalsa.com

Buenavista Salsa Club
C/Roselló 217, Eixample.
Map 3 A3.
Tel 93 237 65 28.
www.salsabuenavista.com

Gran Teatre del Liceu (Opera House)
La Rambla 51–59.
Map 5 A1.
Tel 93 485 99 00.
www.liceubarcelona.com

Llantiol
C/Riereta 7, El Raval.
Map 2 E2.
Tel 93 329 90 09.

Los Tarantos
Plaça Reial 17.
Map 5 A3.
Tel 93 318 30 67.

Mercat de les Flors
C/de Lleida 59.
Map 1 B2.
Tel 93 426 18 75.

Soniquete
C/Milans 5, Barri Gòtic.
Map 5 A3.

Teatre Apolo
Av del Paral.lel 57.
Map 1 B1.
Tel 93 441 90 07.

Teatre Nacional de Catalunya (TNC)
Plaça de les Arts 1.
Tel 93 306 57 06.

Teatre Poliorama
La Rambla 115, Barri Gòtic.
Map 5 A1.
Tel 93 317 75 99.
www.teatrepoliorama.com

Teatre Tívoli
C/Casp 10–12, Eixample.
Map 3 B5.
Tel 93 412 20 63.

Teatre Victòria
Av del Paral.lel 67–69.
Map 1 B1.
Tel 93 443 29 29.

Music

Few cities in the world can match the eclectic range of Barcelona's music scene. Stunning world-class venues such as Palau de la Música and L'Auditori de Barcelona play host to mega-stars, while smaller jazz rooms attract smouldering songsters. Then there are also the underground dives for the best in experimental electronica as well as the dusty, dimly-lit flamenco folk clubs, which attract crowds of wandering gypsies for nights of impromptu cheer.

OPERA AND CLASSICAL MUSIC

Opera and classical music are beloved by Catalans who lap it up with near religious reverence. Indeed, many of the great artists of the 20th century were locals, including the cellist Pablo Casals and opera singers José Carreras and Montserrat Caballé, who performed *Barcelona*, the dramatic operatic duet with the late Freddy Mercury.

The city is also home to some of the most spectacular venues in the world including the glamorous, gilded **Gran Teatre del Liceu**, which first opened its doors in 1847. The opera house has been a continuing beacon of Catalan arts for more than a century and a half, with a rich and dramatic history of fire and bomb attacks. It burned down for the third time in 1994, but careful renovations have restored it to its former glory. Despite its misfortunes, it has sustained a stellar line-up of the greatest composers in the world, among them Puccini, Tchaikovsky and Diaghilev's Russion Ballets, as well as Catalan composers such as Pedrell, Vives and Enric Granados.

The whimsical fancy of the **Palau de la Música** is another of Barcelona's architectural triumphs. A jewel-bright vision by the Modernista master Lluís Domènech i Montaner, this sublime concert hall has a dedicated public, and performers who vie to play here. The Palau is the main venue for the city's jazz and guitar festivals and national and international symphony orchestras perform here regularly. Both of these venues can be visited on daytime guided tours, but booking tickets for a production is the best way to experience the atmosphere.

Modern, but no less important as a shrine to the Catalan arts scene, **L'Auditori de Barcelona** was built to accommodate growing demand for better facilities and to attract ever greater numbers of world class musicians. It began primarily as a place for classical concerts and orchestral recitals, but has since begun to embrace giants of jazz, pop and rock. It is also worth keeping your eyes peeled for regular choral music being performed at the city's churches and cathedrals, most notably the Iglesia Santa Maria del Pi, the main cathedral on Plaça del Pi, and the Iglesia Santa Maria del Mar particularly around Christmas time.

LIVE MUSIC: ROCK, JAZZ AND BLUES

In terms of popular music Barcelona may not have the endless clubs, pubs, stadiums and music emporiums that make London the best place on the planet for live music, but it doesn't do too badly considering its size. The city attracts a star-studded cast that range from pop stars such as Kylie Minogue and Madonna to contemporary jazz prodigies such as the Brad Mehldau Quartet, hip-hoppers, rappers and world groove mixers, country and good old-fashioned rock and roll.

In 2004, two of the city's most iconic jazz venues – La Boite and La Cova del Drac – closed down much to the disbelief of residents. What will fill the gap remains to be seen, but for now Barcelona still has a clutch of tiny, intimate venues. **Jamboree**, a cellar-like venue on Plaça Reial, attracts a number of jazz heavyweights as well as more experimental outfits and solo artists such as the saxophonist Billy McHenry. Another good bet is the **Jazz Sí Club**, a more obscure destination but much beloved by aficionados of the genre. It doubles up as a jam session space for students from the nearby music school.

Concerts are generally free, or very cheap. The **Harlem Jazz Club** is narrow, crowded and smoky but it's one of the city's longest surviving clubs for alternative and lesser-known jazz troupes. **Little Italy** is a boon for those who like the tinkle of the piano keyboard and the soft pluck of the double base over dinner. Similarly, **Nao Colón** is another restaurant that morphs into a music venue once the plates are cleared away. It offers an eclectic mix of bossa nova, soul and funk. The most formal of the jazz venues however is Barcelona's "free" theatre – the **Teatre Lliure** in Montjuïc is an excellent source for contemporary jazz masters, modern orchestras and experimental grooves playing host to a diverse number of musicians from Eric Mingus to The Sun Ra Arkestra directed by Marshall Allen. For lovers of the genre, this is the best of the lot.

One of the two major players for pop and rock maestros is **Bikini**, Barcelona's very own Studio 54 – in fact, it opened in 1953, preceding the New York icon by a year. This veteran of the scene, which opens from midnight onwards, is still going strong with a robust line-up of big name bands and a cocktail of different club nights. The other, **Razzmatazz**, arguably the city's most important live music venue, plays host to the likes of the 1990s Indie rivals Blur and Pulp, and

2004's answer to the Beastie Boys, Welsh rappers the Goldie Looking Chain. Club sessions go until dawn in Razz Club and The Loft, next door. This trendy club also holds rock and jazz concerts several nights a week.

For a touch of unbeatable glam **Luz de Gas** is a glitzy ballroom that oozes old-fashioned atmosphere with its lamp-lit tables, chandeliers and a list of bands and shows that enjoyed their heyday in the 1970s and 80s. It's not quite cabaret but gets close, though not as close however, as the infamous **El Cangrejo**; drag cabaret at its outrageous best, with shockingly attired queens in full make-up and sequins miming along to Sara Montiel

(the Spanish sex symbol) numbers and back-chatting with the crowd. If your taste is for the small and subtle, the **Bar Pastis** is a miniscule bar, decorated with dusty bottles and yellowing posters from French musicals. Live French love ballads can be heard here most nights of the week.

FLAMENCO

Although flamenco is traditionally an Andalucian artform, originally created by the gypsies of Southern Spain to depict their sufferings and hardship, it has for many years been a popular form of entertainment in Barcelona and throughout Spain. One of the best places to see a live show is **El Tablao**

de Carmen, a stylish restaurant serving both Catalan and Andalucian dishes in the Poble Espanyol. The venue is named after Carmen Amaya, a famous dancer who performed for King Alfonso XIII in 1929, in the very spot where it now stands. Various dinner/show packages are available.

For a less formal ambience, **Los Tarantos**, situated in the Plaça Reial, is a lively atmospheric nightspot with live flamenco and Latin music every night of the week.

For those who like to try their hand at this sultry, passionate dance, go to **La Paloma** (see p168–9), a beautiful and popular dancehall from the turn-of-the-19th century. The younger crowd arrives after midnight.

DIRECTORY

OPERA AND CLASSICAL MUSIC

L'Auditori de Barcelona
C/de Lepant 150,
Eixample.
Map 4 E1.
Tel 93 247 93 00.
www.auditori.org

Gran Teatre del Liceu
La Rambla 51–9,
Barri Gòtic.
Map 5 A1.
Tel 93 485 99 13.
www.liceubarcelona.com

Palau de la Música Catalana
C/Sant Francesc de Paula 2, La Ribera.
Map 5 B1.
Tel 93 295 72 00.
www.palaumusica.org

LIVE MUSIC: ROCK, JAZZ AND BLUES

Bar Pastis
C/Santa Mònica 4,
El Raval. **Map** 2 F4.
Tel 93 318 79 80.

Bikini
Deu I Mata 105,
Les Corts.
Tel 93 322 08 00.
www.bikinibcn.com

El Cangrejo
C/Montserrat 9,
El Raval.
Map 2 F4.
Tel 93 301 29 78.

Harlem Jazz Club
C/Comtessa de Sobradiel 8,
Barri Gòtic.
Tel 93 310 07 55.

Jamboree
Plaça Reial 17,
Barri Gòtic.
Map 5 A3.
Tel 93 301 75 64.
www.masimas.com

Jazz Sí Club
C/Requesens 2,
El Raval.
Tel 93 329 00 20.
www.tallerdemusics.com

Little Italy
C/Rec 30,
Born.
Map 5 C3.
Tel 93 319 79 73.

Luz de Gas
C/Muntaner 246,
Eixample.
Map 2 F1.
Tel 93 209 77 11.
www.luzdegas.com

Nao Colón
Av. Marquès de l'Argentera 19,
Born.
Map 5 B3.
Tel 93 268 76 33.

Razzmatazz
C/Pamplona 88,
Poblenou.
Map 4 F5.
Tel 93 272 09 10.
www.theloftclub.com

Teatre Lliure
Tel 93 228 97 48.
www.teatrelliure.com

FLAMENCO

El Tablao de Carmen
Arcs, 9.
Poble Espanyol.
Map 1 B1.
Tel 933 25 68 95.
www.tablaodecarmen.com

Los Tarantos
Plaça Reial 17.
Map 5 A3.
Tel 933 18 30 67.

CONCERT VENUES

L'Auditori
C/Lepant 150.
Tel 93 247 93 00.
www.auditori.com

Espai Lliure
Plaça Margarida Xirgu 1,
Montjuïc.
Tel 93 228 97 47.

Sala Fabià Puigserver
Passeig Santa Madrona 40-46, Montjuïc.
Map 1 B3.
Tel 93 228 97 47.

Nightlife

If New York is the city that never sleeps, then Barcelona is the one that never goes to bed and those with energy can party around the clock, all week. It has one of the most varied scenes, with something for everybody. Old-fashioned dance halls rub shoulders with underground brass clubs and trashy techno discos, and club-goers are either glammed-up or grunged-out. Each *barrio* (neighbourhood) offers a different flavour.

NIGHTLIFE

In the summer the beaches become party havens when the *chiringuitos* (beach bars) spring back into life. Wander from Platja de Sant Sebastià in Barceloneta, all the way to Bogatell (a few kilometres beyond the Hotel Arts) and you'll find people dancing barefoot on the sand to the tune of Barcelona's innumerable DJs. Way uptown (above the Diagonal), the city's most glamorous terraces morph into social hubs while the Barri Gòtic – lively at the best of times – becomes one massive street party throughout the summer. If you want to hang with the locals, the demolition of some of El Raval's less salubrious streets has meant that the neighbourhood has become much safer and easier to move about. The underground vibe, however, remains steadfastly intact with tiny hole-in-the-wall-style bars where folks drink and boogie till the early hours. Similarly Gràcia has a bohemian, studenty ambience. If it's an alternative scene you seek Poble Sec has a handful of "ring-to-enter" joints and the city's only serious drum and bass club, **Plataforma**. The city also has a thriving and friendly gay scene, most notably within the Eixample Esquerra, also known as the Gay Eixample, boasting numerous late-night drinking holes, discothèques, saunas and cabarets.

BARRI GÒTIC

The Plaça Reial is overrun with tourists banging on tin drums and whooping it up, but if you're looking for more grown-up fun, check out

Café Royal, just off the square. Here you'll find Barcelona's beautiful people draped over battered leather sofas, sipping cocktails or grooving to the mellow beats of funk, soul and acid jazz.

For the more adventurous, **Moog** is more extreme with blaring, heart-pumping techno for aficionados of the genre. The stark industrial interior gives it the character of a New York nightclub in the mid-1990s. Likewise, the state-of-the-art sound system ensures a thumping, ear-bleedingly good night out. The nightclub **New York**, in contrast, has come over all loungey in a recent revamp and these days is inclined towards more commercially gratifying tunes. The vibe here is more disco.

EL RAVAL

Designer clubs proliferate in Barcelona these days, but check out the original at **Club Salsitas**, an achingly cool space decked with giant white pineapples and palm trees. Amazingly, after several years at the top it's still looking good and resident DJ Toni Bass continues to whip the crowd into a frenzy every Thursday, Friday and Saturday night. Next-door, pint-sized **Milk** offers a 1970s style chill-out space for those exhausted from strutting on the dance floor. Going back in time **La Paloma** is the city's most brilliantly gilded ballroom dating back to 1904. It's still going strong offering dance hall classics, including cha-cha-cha, tango, salsa and the waltz, accompanied by a brass band until midnight. Thereafter, DJs and house take over, catering to a younger set.

PORT VELL AND PORT OLÌMPIC

Beach parties aside, this area continues to be a hub for creatures of the night. The Port Olímpic itself is nothing but bars and boats, while **Maremagnum** has a clutch of *salsatecas* and a rooftop pub. The **Sugar Club** (another *salsitas* offspring) is the newest kid on the block, which offers a splash of sophistication, not to mention society, to the downtown scene. **C.D.L.C.** in front of the Hotel Arts, however, still manages to draw the celebrities staying nearby.

EIXAMPLE

One of the city's best loved discos **City Hall** is a multiple space and terrace, where you can pick and choose your groove according to your mood. It has different themes every night from Saturday night-fever discos to Sunday chill-outs. **Buda Barcelona** is quite literally oozing with glitz and glamour, beloved by models and their entourages. It is a place where anything goes from dancing on the bar tops to dancing with your top off. For a more understated type of glamour, **Astoria** is housed in a converted cinema and therefore bags the title for the best projections in town. Finally, there's **L'Arquer**. Only in Barcelona would you find a bar that dared combine archery lessons with mammoth shots of vodka.

POBLE SEC

The most alternative nightlife has come to roost in the "dry village," though in name only. The bars are wet and the music is happening. **Apolo** is another old-fashioned music hall, similar to La Paloma, though it attracts a more independent breed of DJ and performer. Expect anything from soulful gypsy folk singers from Marseille, to the legendary purveyor of deep funk, Keb Darge.

Further into the village, **Mau Mau** is an alternative club and cultural centre with a firm eye on what's new and happening. This could mean local DJs, Japanese musicians such as the cultish Cinema Dub Monks, alternative cinema, and multimedia art installations. If it's of the here and now, chances are Mau Mau's on it. For the seriously hardcore and lovers of high-speed garage, **Plataforma** is Barcelona's only serious drum and base club hosting DJs from far and wide in a huge concrete warehouse.

GRÀCIA AND TIBIDABO

Tiny and always packed the **Mond Bar** attracts music-lovers from all over wishing to dip into tunes from the past. Resident DJ Mr Stream

delights a 30-something crowd with his swing-back to the 1970s sessions of northern soul and Motown. And high up above the rest, **Danzatoria** offers the best in mansion house clubbing experiences with chill-out lounges and several dance floors, vodka bars and sprawling terraces, and prices to suit the altitude.

OUT OF TOWN

The mega-clubs are located away from the city centre and from anyone trying to sleep. The big boys are based in Poble Espanyol where folks can party until the sunrise. **Discothèque**, a sleek elegant club has it all – disco lights, strobes and top-name DJs from the international circuit. **La Terrazza** is its summer sidekick for rave-like parties

under the stars. It takes its name from the giant terrace it occupies. Nearby on Plaça Espanya, after much bated breath, the Ibiza-style **Space** finally opened in 2004. Don't even think about getting in without an appropriately glamorous outfit, and remember, less is most definitely more.

Further out of town you will find the world's most famous nightclub, **Pacha**. What most people don't realize, however, is that it was born in Barcelona and continues to stage the most sensational nights out. Alternatively, **Liquid** is the only club with a swimming pool in the city. The only drawback is that should you wish to leave before the party's over, finding a taxi can be a big problem.

DIRECTORY

BARRI GÒTIC

Café Royale
C/Nou de Zurbano 3,
Barri Gòtic.
Tel 93 412 14 33.

Moog
C/Arc del Teatre 3,
El Raval.
Map 2 F4.
Tel 93 301 72 82.
www.masimas.com

New York
C/Escudellers 5,
Barri Gòtic.
Map 5 A3.
Tel 93 318 87 30.

EL RAVAL

Club Salsitas
C/Nou de la Rambla 22.
Map 2 D4.
Tel 93 318 08 40.
www.salsitas.
gruposalsitas.com

Milk
C/Nou de la Rambla 24,
El Raval.
Map 2 D4.
Tel 93 301 02 67.

La Paloma
C/Tigre 27,
El Raval.
Map 2 E1.
Tel 93 301 68 97.
www.lapaloma-bcn.com

PORT VELL AND PORT OLÍMPIC

C.D.L.C.
Passeig Marítim 32,
Port Olímpic.
Map 6 E4.
Tel 93 224 04 70.
www.cdlcbarcelona.com

Sugar Club
Moll de Barcelona s/n,
Port Vell.
Tel 93 508 83 25.

EIXAMPLE

Astoria
C/Paris 193,
Eixample.
Tel 93 414 63 62.
www.costaeste.com

L'Arquer
Gran Via de les Corts
Catalanes 454,
Eixample.
Map 1 A1.
Tel 93 423 99 08.

Buda Barcelona
C/Pau Claris 92,
Eixample.
Map 3 B3.
Tel 93 318 42 52.
www.budabarcelona.com

City Hall
Rambla Catalunya 2–4,
Eixample.
Map 3 A3.
Tel 93 317 21 77.
www.ottozutz.com

POBLE SEC

Apolo
C/Nou de la Rambla 113,
Poble Sec.
Map 2 D4.
Tel 93 441 40 01.
www.salaapolo.com

Mau Mau
C/Fontrodona 33,
Poble Sec.
Map 2 D3.
Tel 60 686 06 17.
www.
maumauunderground.com

Plataforma
C/Nou de la Rambla 145,
Poble Sec.
Map 2 D4.
Tel 93 329 00 29.

GRÀCIA AND TIBIDABO

Danzatoria
Av Tibidabo 61,
Tibidabo.
Tel 93 211 62 61.
www.danzatoria.
gruposalsitas.com

Mond Bar
Plaza del Sol 21, Gràcia.
Map 3 B1.

OUT OF TOWN

**Discothèque/
La Terrazza**
Poble Espanyol, Avda
Marquès de Comillas.
Map 1 B1.
Tel 93 423 12 85
www.nightsungroup.com

Liquid
Complex Esportiu
Hospitalet Nord,
C/Manuel Azaña.
Tel 65 009 14 79.
www.liquidbcn.com

Pacha
Avda. Gregorio
Marañon 17.
Tel 93 334 32 33.
www.clubpachabcn.com

Space
C/Tarragona 141–147.
Tel 93 426 84 44.

Sports and Outdoor Activities

From the mountains to the sea, Catalonia provides all manner of terrain for enjoying the outdoor life. The hot summer months can be filled with water activities, from fishing to white-water rafting, while skiers head for the hills with the first snowfalls of winter. Nature lovers will find spectacular wildlife habitats, while Barcelona city offers beaches and numerous sports facilities.

CITY FACILITIES

Barcelona has around 30 municipal pools *(piscines municipales)*, including the **Piscines Bernat Picornell** next to the **Estadi Olímpic** and **Palau Sant Jordi** sports stadia on Montjuïc. The pools were the venue for the 1992 Olympic swimming events. The Estadi Olímpic is an athletics stadium and is often used for concerts. The Palau Sant Jordi is used for indoor sports, as well as musical and recreational activities. Tennis fans are well provided for and the **Centre Municipal de Tennis Vall d'Hebron** caters for younger players too. Ice-skating can be fun and the **Pista de Gel del FC Barcelona** offers skate rental and runs an ice hockey school. Golf courses within easy reach of Barcelona are **Golf Sant Cugat** and **Golf El Prat**. There are several riding stables, and the **Escola Hípica** at Sant Cugat allows day outings over the Collserola hills. Cycle shops hire by the hour, half day and full day. **Un Cotxe Menys** organizes cycle tours around Barcelona.

AIRBORNE ACTIVITIES

Catalonia has several small airports where planes can be hired and parachute jumps made. One of the best known flying clubs is **Aeroclub** in Sabadell. Paragliding is popular from any high spot and **Free Evolució** offers all kinds of adventure sports for groups of 10–12 people, including bungee jumping and ballooning, as an exciting alternative way to see the sights.

BIRD-WATCHING

Bird life in Catalonia is a huge attraction for dedicated bird-watchers. Northern European visitors in particular will be thrilled by the sight of hoopoes, bee-eaters, golden orioles and pratincoles. Two major wetland areas, where migratory birds include flamingoes, are **Delta de l'Ebre** *(see p129)*, south of Tarragona, with a visitor centre in Deltebre, and **Aiguamolls de l'Empordà** around Sant Pere Pescador in the Bay of Roses. Both are easy to get to, and their visitor centres supply binoculars and guide services.

Griffon vulture

The best times to visit are early morning and evening. The Pyrenees are home to many raptors, including short-toed, golden and Bonelli eagles, and Egyptian, griffon and bearded vultures. The **Parc Natural del Cadí-Moixeró** *(see p114)*, in the foothills of the Pyrenees, has a visitor centre in Bagà. Look out for alpine choughs, wallcreepers and peregrine falcons, as well as black woodpeckers in the wooded areas.

An angler's paradise – fishing for trout amid spectacular scenery

FIELD SPORTS

Sea fishing is free, but a permit *(un permís)* is required for river fishing. Permits can usually be obtained through local tourist offices.

The Noguera Pallaresa and Segre are fine trout fishing rivers and the season runs from mid-March to the end of August. The game-hunting season is generally from October to March. Short leases and permits can be obtained from the **Patrimonio Natural** in Barcelona or from a local hunting association *(associació de caça)*. Travel agents specializing in hunting and fishing breaks will also readily organize licences.

HIKING

All the national parks and reserves publish maps and walking suggestions. Good areas close to Barcelona are the Collserola hills and the chestnut woods of Montseny. Long-distance GR *(Gran Recorrido)* footpaths criss-cross Catalonia and the walking

Paragliding above the Vall d'Aran in the eastern Pyrenees

Shooting the rapids on the white waters of the Noguera Pallaresa

Aeroclub de Sabadell
Tel 93 710 19 52.

Aiguamolls de l'Empordà
Tel 972 45 42 22.

ACEM (Associació Catalana d'Estacions d'Esquí i Activitats de Muntanya)
Tel 93 416 01 94.

Centre Excursionista de Catalunya
Tel 93 315 23 11.

Centre Municipal de Tennis Vall d'Hebron
Tel 93 427 65 00.

Centre Municipal de Vela Port Olímpic
Tel 93 225 79 40.

Un Cotxe Menys
Tel 93 268 21 05.

Delta de l'Ebre
Tel 977 48 96 79.

Escola Hípica
Tel 93 589 89 89.

Espot Esquí Parc
Tel 97 362 4058.

Estadi Olímpic/ Palau Sant Jordi
Tel 93 426 20 89.

Free Evolució
Tel 93 454 91 41.

Golf El Prat
Tel 93 728 1000.

Golf Sant Cugat
Tel 93 674 39 08.

Llibreria Quera
Tel 93 318 07 43.

Parc Nacional d'Aigüestortes
Tel 973 62 40 36.

Parc Natural del Cadí-Moixeró
Tel 93 824 41 51.

Patrimonio Natural
Tel 93 567 42 00.

Piscines Bernat Picornell
Tel 93 423 40 41.

Pista de Gel del FC Barcelona
Tel 93 496 36 30.

Teletiempo
Tel 807 17 03 08 (Barcelona); 807 17 03 65 (Spain).

Yetiemotions
Tel 97 362 22 01 (office); or 63 082 75 36.

possibilities in the **Parc Nacional d'Aigüestortes** *(see p113)* and the Pyrenees are particularly good, with mountain refuges *(see p133)* for serious hikers. Walkers can obtain information from the **Centre Excursionista de Catalunya** *(see p133)*. The **Llibreria Quera**, in Carrer de Petritxol (No. 2) in Barcelona's Barri Gòtic, is the best bookshop for maps and guide books.

All the usual rules apply to those setting off to explore the wilderness – check weather forecasts, wear appropriate clothing, take adequate provisions and let someone know where you are going.

WATER SPORTS

There are around 40 marinas along Catalonia's 580 km (360 miles) of coast, and a very wide range of watersports and activities is available. In Barcelona itself, the **Centre Municipal de Vela Port Olímpic** gives sailing lessons and has a variety of craft. The Costa Brava has long been a good spot for scuba diving. The best place is around the protected Illes Medes *(see p121)*, from the resort of L'Estartit. There are also diving schools around Cadaqués and Cap Begur, notably at Calella de Palafrugell, launching point for the Illes Ullastres.

The town of Sort on the Riu Noguera Pallaresa is a centre for exciting water sports such as white-water rafting, canoeing, kayaking and cave diving. Bookings for these and other adventure activities can be made through **Yetiemotions or Espot Esquí Parc**.

WINTER SPORTS

The Pyrenees offer great winter skiing just two or three hours' drive from Barcelona and at weekends the resorts fill up with city crowds. There are some 20 ski areas. La Molina is good for beginners and Baqueira-Beret *(see p113)* is where Spain's royal family skis. Puigcerdà *(see p114)* in the Cerdanya is a good base for downhill and nordic skiing within reach of 15 ski stations in Catalonia, Andorra and France. The **Associació Catalana d'Estacions d'Esquí i Activitats de Muntanya (ACEM)** supplies resort details, while **Teletiempo**, a weather hotline, provides information on current weather conditions. In Barcelona, a dry ski slope has been installed beside the Piscines Bernat Picornell on Montjuïc.

Skiing at one of the many ski stations in the Pyrenees within easy reach of Barcelona

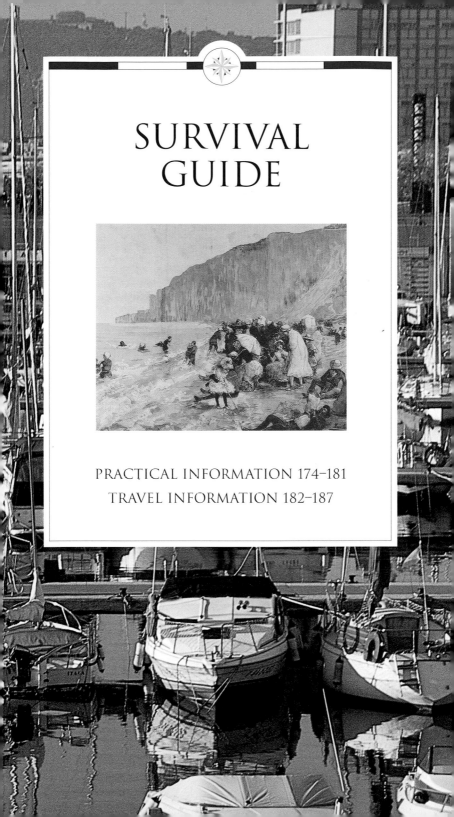

SURVIVAL
GUIDE

PRACTICAL INFORMATION

Catalonia has an excellent tourist infrastructure and Barcelona is particularly well organized for visitors. There are tourist offices in every town and all offer help in finding accommodation, restaurants and activities in their area. Larger offices usually have a wealth of leaflets in several languages. August is Spain's main vacation month.

Sign for a tourist office

Many businesses close for the whole month and roads are very busy at the beginning and end of this period. At any time of year, try to find out in advance if your visit will coincide with local *festes* (fiestas). Although these are attractions, they often entail widespread closures. It is a good idea to plan leisurely lunches, as most of Catalonia stops from 2pm to 4pm.

Ajuntament →

Sign to a town hall

A "closed" sign

LANGUAGE

Though Catalan is the language spoken by native Catalans, Catalonia is a bilingual country where people also speak *castellano* (Spanish). If you respond in Spanish to a question or greeting made in Catalan, the speaker will automatically switch to Spanish. All official signs and documents are in both languages. However, as Barcelona in particular regards itself as truly cosmopolitan, most tourist literature is also in English and French.

MANNERS

Catalans greet and say goodbye to strangers at bus stops, in lifts, in shops and in other public places. They shake hands when introduced and whenever they meet. Women usually kiss on both cheeks when they meet, and friends and family members of both sexes may kiss or embrace briefly.

VISAS AND PASSPORTS

Visas are not required for tourists who are citizens of specified countries including the EU, Iceland, Liechtenstein, Norway, the USA, Canada, Australia and New Zealand.

However it is always best to check visa requirements before travelling.

Spanish embassies supply a list of the other countries in the non-visa category. Tourists from these countries may stay 90 days within a continuous 180-day period. The *Oficina d'estrangers de Barcelona* (a local government office) deals with visa extensions. Proof of employment, study schedules, or sufficient funds for living are needed for a long stay.

No parking sign

TAX-FREE GOODS AND CUSTOMS INFORMATION

Non-Eu residents can reclaim *IVA* (VAT) on single items worth over 90 euros bought in shops displaying a "Tax-free for Tourists" sign. (Food, drink, cars, motorbikes, tobacco and medicines are exempt.) You pay the full price and ask the sales assistant for a *formulari* (tax exemption form), which you ask customs to stamp as you leave Spain (this must be within six months of the purchase). You receive the refund by mail or on your credit card account. Banco Exterior branches at Barcelona airport will give refunds on completed *formularis*.

TOURIST INFORMATION

Barcelona has three main *oficines de turisme* providing information on the city, its attractions, transport and

places to stay and eat, all run by **Turisme de Barcelona**.

A fourth office, in the Passeig de Gràcia, run by **Turisme de Catalunya**, a department of the Generalitat (Catalonia's government), provides information on the rest of the region. Other major towns have tourist offices providing information published by the Generalitat and the province's local administration *(patronat)*.

There is a Spanish National Tourist Office in the following English-speaking cities: New York, Chicago, Miami, Los Angeles, London and Toronto.

In Barcelona during the summer, pairs of young information officers, known as Red Jackets and generally English-speaking, provide tourist information in the streets of the Barri Gòtic, La Rambla and the Passeig de Gràcia.

Turisme de Catalunya's Barcelona office

OPENING HOURS

Most museums and monuments close on Mondays. On other days they generally open from 10am to 2pm and, in some cases, reopen from 4 or 5pm to 8pm. Churches may only be opened for services. In smaller towns it is common for churches, castles and other sights to be kept locked. The

Students enjoy reduced admission fees to many museums and galleries

key *(la clau)*, available to visitors on request, will be with a caretaker, kept at the town hall *(ajuntament)*, or perhaps with the owners of the local bar. Admission is charged for most museums and monuments. On Sundays, museum admission is often free.

FACILITIES FOR THE DISABLED

Catalonia's association for the disabled, the Federació ECOM *(see p133)*, has hotel lists and travel advice for the whole region. Spain's national association, COCEMFE, has a tour company, **Servi-COCEMFE**, that publishes guide books to facilities in Spain and will help plan vacations.

COCEMFE sign for disabled access

Tourist offices and the social services departments of town halls supply information on local facilities. A travel agency, **Viajes 2000**, specializes in vacations for disabled people.

SPANISH TIME

Spain is one hour ahead of Greenwich Mean Time (GMT) in winter *(l'hivern)* and two hours in summer *(l'estiu)*, and uses the 24-hour clock. *La matinada* is the small hours, *el matí* (morning) lasts until about 1pm, while *migdia* (midday) is from 1 to 4pm. *La tarda* is the afternoon, *el vespre* the evening and *la nit* the night.

STUDENT INFORMATION

Holders of the International Student Identity Card (ISIC) are entitled to benefits, such as discounts on travel and reduced entrance charges to museums and galleries. Information is available from all national student organizations and, in Barcelona, from **Viatgeteca**, which sells the international student card and youth hostel cards. **Unlimited Youth Student Travel** specializes in student travel.

ELECTRICAL ADAPTORS

Spain's electricity supply is 220 volts, but the 125-volt system still operates in some old buildings. Plugs for both have two round pins. A three-tier standard travel converter enables you to use appliances from abroad on both supplies. Heating appliances should be used only on 220 volts.

CONVERSION CHART

Imperial to metric
1 inch = 2.54 centimetres
1 foot = 30 centimetres
1 mile = 1.6 kilometres
1 ounce = 28 grams
1 pound = 454 grams
1 pint = 0.6 litre
1 gallon = 4.6 litres

Metric to imperial
1 millimetre = 0.04 inch
1 centimetre = 0.4 inch
1 metre = 3 feet 3 inches
1 kilometre = 0.6 mile
1 gram = 0.04 ounce
1 kilogram = 2.2 pounds
1 litre = 1.8 pints

DIRECTORY

CONSULATES

Australia
Gran Via de Carles III 98, 9°,
08028 Barcelona.
Tel 93 490 90 13.

Canada
Calle Elisenda de Pinós 10,
08034 Barcelona.
Tel 93 204 27 00.

Ireland
Gran Via de Carles III 94, 10°-2nª,
08028 Barcelona.
Tel 93 491 50 21.

United Kingdom
Avinguda Diagonal 477, 13°
08036 Barcelona.
Tel 93 366 62 00.

United States
Passeig de la Reina Elisenda 23,
08034 Barcelona.
Tel 93 280 22 27.

TOURIST OFFICES

Turisme de Barcelona
Plaça de Catalunya 17, subterrani,
08002 Barcelona.
Tel 807 11 72 22.

C/Ciutat 2 (Ajuntament),
08002 Barcelona.
Tel 010.

Estació Sants, Pl Països Catalans,
08014 Barcelona.
Tel 807 11 72 22.

Turisme de Catalunya
Palau Robert, Pg de Gràcia 107,
08008 Barcelona.
Tel 93 238 40 00

DISABLED

Servi-COCEMFE
Calle Eugenio Salazar 2,
28002 Madrid.
Tel 91 413 80 01.

Viajes 2000
Paseo de la Castellana 228-230,
28046 Madrid.
Tel 91 323 25 23.

YOUTH/STUDENT

Unlimited Youth Student Travel & Viatgeteca
Carrer Rocafort 116–122,
08015 Barcelona.
Tel 93 483 83 81.

Personal Security and Health

In Catalonia, as in most parts of western Europe, rural areas are quite safe, while towns and cities warrant more care. Keep cards and money in a belt, don't leave valuables in your car and avoid poorly lit areas at night. If you feel ill, there will always be a local *farmàcia* (pharmacy) open. In Spain, pharmacists prescribe as well as advise. Report lost documents to your consulate *(see p175)* and to the *Policia Nacional* at the local *comissaria* (police station). Emergency numbers are listed opposite.

Front of a high-street *farmàcia* (pharmacy) in Catalonia

IN AN EMERGENCY

The new national telephone number throughout Spain for all emergency services is 112. After dialling, ask for *policia* (police), *bombers* (fire brigade) or *ambulància* (ambulance). Local numbers for the individual emergency services (opposite) still also apply. Outside Barcelona, the largely voluntary *Creu Roja* (Red Cross) often responds to 112 (or other) emergency calls for ambulances.

Ambulances take admissions to hospital *urgències* (accident and emergency) departments.

Red Cross ambulance sign

URGÈNCIES

Accident and Emergency sign

MEDICAL TREATMENT

Any EU national who falls ill in Spain is entitled to social security cover. To claim medical treatment, UK citizens must obtain a European Health Insurance Card (formerly E111) from a post office or GP surgery prior to travelling. Not all treatments are covered by the card, so additional medical insurance is a good idea.

For private medical care in Spain ask at a tourist office, or at your consulate or hotel for the name and number of a doctor. Visitors from the US should make sure their insurance covers medical care abroad. If payment is needed at the time of treatment, ask for an itemized bill. Some insurance companies will ask for an official translation. Extra private

cover may be needed for emergency hospital care.

For non-emergencies, a *farmacèutic* (pharmacist) can advise and, at times, prescribe without a doctor's consultation. The *farmàcia* sign is an illuminated green or red cross. The addresses of those open at night or at weekends are listed in all pharmacy windows.

PERSONAL SECURITY

As in most European cities, pickpocketing in Barcelona is on the rise so it is wise to take sensible precautions when out and about, especially if travelling during peak season. Always be vigilant with handbags, wallets and cameras, especially in crowds, at major tourists attractions, and cafés and bars. In particular, keep an eye on your bag at outdoor cafés, as luggage has been known to disappear. One of the more common tricks is someone distracting your attention by alerting you to a "stain"

on your clothing (this happens a lot in the Metro) or carnation sellers that deftly empty your wallet when you are trying to pay them. Never leave valuables in your car and be aware of people hanging around cash dispenser machines as credit card frauds are also on the increase, especially along the coast. Barcelona is generally safe for walking although it is advisable to avoid the Barri Xinès area at night. It should be remembered, however, that violent crime and muggings in Barcelona are rare.

POLICE IN CATALONIA

In Spain, police services are organized into three forces: the *Guàrdia Civil* (paramilitary Civil Guard), in olive-green,

Policia Nacional   **Mosso d'Esquadra**   **Guàrdia Urbana**

polices mainly borders, airports and rural areas; the *Policia Nacional,* in blue, deals with major crime in larger towns and national security, as well as immigration; and the *Guàrdia Urbana,* also in blue, deals with traffic regulation and the policing of local communities.

But in Barcelona and other major towns the *Guàrdia Civil* and the *Policía Nacional* are being replaced by an autonomous Catalan police force, the *Mossos d'Esquadra.* Most tourists however are likely to be dealing with the *Guàrdia Urbana* who, during peak season, set up a special, multilingual tourist service in a caravan in the Plaça Reial to deal with pickpocketing and petty crime. Most other *Guàrdia Urbana* police stations, at least in the old city, provide the forms you need to fill out when reporting a crime in your own language.

A patrol car of the *Guàrdia Urbana*

A patrol car of the *Policia Nacional*

Fire engine showing the Barcelona fire service emergency number

LEGAL ASSISTANCE

Some holiday insurance policies cover legal costs and provide a help-line you can call for assistance.

If you are arrested, you have the right to telephone your consulate (*see p174*), which should have a list of bilingual lawyers. The *Col.legi d'Advocats* (Lawyers' Association) can guide you on getting legal advice or representation.

If you need an interpreter, ask your consulate or look in the *Pàgines Grogues* (Yellow Pages) telephone directory under *Traductors* (Translators) or *Intèrprets* (Interpreters). *Traductors oficials or jurats* are qualified to translate legal or official documents.

An ambulance displaying the Barcelona 061 emergency number

PERSONAL PROPERTY

Report a loss or theft straight away to the *Guàrdia Urbana,* as many insurance companies give you only 24 hours. You must make a *denúncia* (written statement) to the police and get a copy for your insurers.

Your consulate can replace a missing passport, but cannot provide financial assistance, even in emergencies.

PUBLIC CONVENIENCES

Public conveniences are rare in Catalonia. Most people simply walk into a bar, café, department store or hotel and ask for *els serveis or el lavabo* (in Catalan), or *los servicios* or *los aseos* (in Spanish). On motorways (highways), there are toilets at service stations. Women may have to ask for *la clau* (the key). Always carry toilet tissue with you, as it is often not provided.

OUTDOOR HAZARDS

Catalonia's hot summers, are ideal for forest fires; extinguish cigarettes and take empty bottles away with you.

If climbing or hill-walking go properly equipped and let someone know your route. Do not enter a *vedat de caça* (hunting reserve) or *camí particular* (private driveway).

DIRECTORY

EMERGENCY SERVICES

Police (*Policia*)

Fire Brigade (*Bombers*)

Ambulance (*Ambulància*)
Tel 112 (national number).

Police (local numbers)
Tel 091 – Policia Nacional
092 – Guàrdia Urbana (Barcelona, Lleida, Girona, Tarragona).
Tel 93 344 13 00 – Tourist Guàrdia Urbana office in La Rambla, Barcelona.

Fire Brigade (local numbers)
Tel 080 (Barcelona), 085 (Lleida, Girona, Tarragona).

Ambulance (local numbers)
Tel 061 (Barcelona), use 112, (national number) elsewhere.

Banking and Local Currency

You may enter Spain with an unlimited amount of money, but if you intend to export more than 6,000 euros, you should declare it. Traveller's cheques may be exchanged at banks, bureaux de change (*canvi* in Catalan, *cambio* in Spanish), some hotels and some shops. Banks generally offer the best exchange rates. The cheapest exchange rate may be offered on your credit or direct debit card, which may be used in cash dispensers displaying the appropriate sign.

24-hour Servi Caixa cash dispenser *(see p162)*

BANKING HOURS

As a rule of thumb, banks in Catalonia are open from 8am to 2pm on weekdays. Some open until 1pm on Saturdays, but most are closed on Saturdays from July to September. Branches of some of the larger banks in the centre of Barcelona are beginning to extend their weekday opening hours, but this is not yet a widespread practice.

CHANGING MONEY

Most banks have a foreign exchange desk signed *Canvi/Cambio* or *Moneda estrangera/extranjera*. Always take your passport as ID to effect any transaction.

You can draw up to 450 euros on major credit cards at a bank. Several US and UK banks have branches in Barcelona, including **Citibank**, **Barclays** and **Lloyds TSB**. If you bank with them, you can cash a cheque there.

A bureau de change, indicated by the sign *Canvi/ Cambio*, or the sign "Change", will invariably charge higher rates of commission than a bank, but will often remain open after hours. *Caixes d'estalvi/Cajas de ahorro* (savings banks) also exchange money. They open from 8:30am to 2pm on weekdays, and on Thursdays also from 4:30pm to 7:45pm. They have a highly visible profile, actively supporting the arts and good public works.

CHEQUES AND CARDS

Traveller's cheques can be purchased at **American Express** (AmEx), **Travelex** or your bank. All are accepted in Spain. If you exchange AmEx cheques at an AmEx office, commission is not charged. Cheques in euros can be purchased at any bank. Eurocheques allow you to issue a cheque in euros and can also be exchanged for money at a bank if supported by a Eurocard or Mastercard and a passport. Banks require 24 hours' notice to cash cheques larger than 3,000 euros. If you draw more than 600 euros on traveller's cheques, you may be asked to show the purchase certificate.

The most widely accepted card in Spain is the **VISA** card, although **MasterCard** (Access) /Eurocard and American Express are also useful currency. The major banks will allow cash withdrawals on credit cards. All cash dispensers accept most foreign cards, although commission depends on your own bank. More and more cash machines are now closed at night, particularly in the old city.

When you pay with a card, cashiers will usually pass it through a card reading machine. In shops you will always be asked for additional photo ID. As leaving your passport in the hotel safe is preferable, make sure you have an alternative original document on hand (photocopies will rarely do) such as a driver's license. Cards are not accepted in some smaller bars and restaurants, so check first.

CASH DISPENSERS

If your card is linked to your home bank account, you can use it with your PIN to withdraw money from cash dispensers. Nearly all dispensers take VISA or MasterCard (Access). Cards with a Cirrus or Maestro logo can also be widely used to withdraw money from cash machines.

When you enter your PIN, instructions are displayed in Catalan, Spanish, English, French and German. Many dispensers are inside buildings these days, and to gain access customers must run their cards through a door-entry system.

Servi Caixa cash dispensers can also be used to purchase theatre, concert and cinema tickets, a convenient way to beat the queues for the most popular shows. Credit for mobile phones can also be topped up using one of these dispensers.

DIRECTORY

FOREIGN BANKS

Barclays Bank
Paseo de Gracia 45, 08007 Barcelona. **Tel** *93 481 20 23.*

Citibank
Paseo de Gracia 7, 08007 Barcelona. **Tel** *93 344 17 00.*

Lloyds TSB Bank
Rambla de Catalunya 123, 08008 Barcelona. **Tel** *93 236 33 00.*

LOST CARDS AND TRAVELLER'S CHEQUES

American Express
La Rambla 74, 08001 Barcelona. **Tel** *93 342 73 10.*

Diners Club
Tel *901 10 10 11.*

MasterCard (Access)
Tel *900 97 12 31 (toll free).*

Travelex
Tel *900 94 89 71 (toll free).*

VISA
Tel *900 99 12 16 (toll free).*

THE EURO

Introduction of the single European currency, the euro, has taken place in 12 of the 25 member states of the EU. Austria, Belgium, Finland, France, Germany, Greece, Ireland, Italy, Luxembourg, The Netherlands, Portugal and Spain chose to join the new currency; the UK, Denmark and Sweden stayed out, with an option to review the decision. The euro was introduced on 1 January 1999, but only for banking purposes. Notes and coins came into circulation on 1 January 2002. After a transition period allowing the use of both national currencies and the euro, Spain's own currency, the peseta, was completely phased out by March 2002. All euro notes and coins can be used anywhere within the participating member states.

Bank Notes

Euro bank notes have seven denominations. The 5-euro note (grey in colour) is the smallest, followed by the 10-euro note (pink), 20-euro note (blue), 50-euro note (orange), 100-euro note (green), 200-euro note (yellow) and 500-euro note (purple). All notes show the 12 stars of the European Union.

5 euros

10 euros

20 euros

50 euros

100 euros

200 euros

500 euros

2 euros

1 euro

50 cents

20 cents

10 cents

Coins

The euro has eight coin denominations: 2 euros and 1 euro (silver and gold); 50 cents, 20 cents and 10 cents (gold); and 5 cents, 2 cents and 1 cent (bronze). The reverse (number) side of euros are the same in all Euro-zone countries, but the front is different in each state.

5 cents

2 cents

1 cent

Communications

Standard issue postage stamp

Public telephones, run by the Spanish telecommunications company Telefónica, are easy to find and operate with a card or coins, but international calls have a high charge. The postal service, Correos, is identified by a crown insignia in red or white on a yellow background. Registered mail and telegrams can be sent from all Correos offices. These also sell stamps, but it is more usual, and quicker, to buy them from *estancs* (tobacconists). There are no public phones in Correos offices.

Logo of the Spanish telecom system

USING A COIN AND CARD TELEPHONE

1 Lift the receiver, and wait for the dialling tone and for the display to show *Inserte monedas o tarjeta*.

2 Insert either coins *(monedas)* or a card *(tarjeta)*.

3 Key in the number firmly, but not too fast – Spanish phones prefer you to pause between digits.

4 As you press the digits, the number you are dialling will appear on the display. You will also be able to see how much money or how many units are left and when to insert more coins.

5 When your call is finished, replace the receiver. The phonecard will then re-emerge automatically or any excess coins will be returned.

Spanish phonecard

TELEPHONING

As well as public telephone boxes *(cabines)*, bars often have payphones. Both types take coins. There is a high minimum connection charge, especially for international calls, so it is best to ensure that you have plenty of change ready. Phonecards are a more convenient option and can be bought at *estancs* and newsstands. In addition, some phones are equipped with electronic multilingual instruction displays.

Calls can also be made from *locutoris* (public telephone offices) and paid for afterwards. The cheapest offices are those away from the city centre. Private ones, which are often located in shops, are usually much pricier.

The charges for international calls are divided into four bands: EU countries; non-EU European countries and Northwest Africa; North and South America; and the rest of the world. With the exception of local calls, using the telephone system can be expensive, especially if calling from a hotel, which may add a high surcharge. A call from a *cabina* or a *locutori* costs as much as 35 per cent more

---

USEFUL SPANISH DIALLING CODES

- When calling within a city, within a province, or to call another province, dial the entire number. The province is indicated by the initial digits: Barcelona numbers start with 93, Lleida 973, Girona 972 and Tarragona 977.
- To make an international call, dial 00, followed by the country code, the area code and the number.
- Country codes are: UK 44; Eire 353; France 33; US and Canada 1; Australia 61; New Zealand 64. It may be necessary to omit the initial digit of the destination's area code.
- For directory service, dial 11818.

- For international operator service, dial 1008 for EU countries and 1005 for the rest of the world.
- To make a reversed-charge (collect) call within the EU, dial 900 99 00 followed by the country code; to the US or Canada, dial 900 99 00 followed by 11 or 15 respectively. Numbers for other countries are in the A-K telephone directory under *Comunicaciones Internacionales*.
- To report technical faults, dial 1002.
- The speaking clock is on 093, the weather on 807 17 03 08, wake-up calls on 096.

than a call made from a private telephone.

Reversed-charge (collect) calls made to EU countries may be dialled directly, but most others must be made through the operator.

Spain abolished provincial area codes in 1998, so the full number, including the initial 9, must always be dialled, even from within the area.

POSTAL SERVICE

Correos, Spain's postal service, is rather slow. It is better to send any urgent or important post by *urgente* (express) or *certificado* (registered) mail, or to use a private courier service.

Post can be registered and telegrams sent from all Correos offices. However, it is more convenient to buy stamps for postcards and letters from an *estanc* (tobacconist's).

Postal rates fall into three price bands: Spain, Europe and the rest of the world. Parcels must be weighed and stamped by Correos and must be securely tied with string, or a charge may be made at the counter to have them sealed by a clerk.

Main Correos offices open from 8:30am to 8:30pm from Monday to Friday and from 9am to 7pm on Saturday. Branches in the suburbs and in villages open from 9am to 2pm from Monday to Friday and from 9am to 1pm on Saturday.

ADDRESSES

In Catalan addresses the street name is written first, followed by the building number, the floor number, and the number or letter of the apartment. For example, C/ Mir 7, 5^e-A means apartment A on floor 5 of building number 7 in Carrer Mir. Carrer is often shortened to C/. Floor designations are: *Baixos* (ground floor), *Entresol*, *Principal*, 1^r, 2^n and so on, meaning that 2^n is in fact the 4th level above the ground.

Some of Catalonia's daily papers

Some newer buildings use the less complicated designation of *Baixos* followed 1^r, 2^n and so on upwards. Postcodes (zip codes) have five digits; the first two are the province number.

TELEVISION AND RADIO

Catalans have a choice of watching TV3 in Catalan run by the regional government, or TVE1 and TVE2, Spain's two state television channels. There is a Catalan channel, Canal 33, which has a high cultural content and three Spanish independents: Antena 3, Tele-5 and Canal+ (Canal Plus). A regular foreign language news service is provided by Barcelona Televisio (BTV). Most foreign films on television (and in cinemas) are dubbed. Subtitled films are listed as *V.O. (versión original)*.

Satellite channels such as CNN, Cinemanía and Eurosport and many other European channels can be received in Catalonia.

The main radio stations are Catalunya Ràdio, and COM Ràdio, the Spanish state Radio Nacional de España, and the independent stations Radio 2, broadcasting classical music, and Ser, a Spanish general-interest station.

Catalan magazines

NEWSPAPERS AND MAGAZINES

Some newsagents and kiosks in the city centre stock periodicals in English. Newspapers in English available on the day of publication are the *International Herald Tribune*, the *Guardian International* and the *Financial Times*. Others can be found a day after publication. *The European* newspaper and weekly news magazines such as *Time, Newsweek* and *The Economist* are readily available. *Catalonia Today*, a free daily newspaper in English, is available at kiosks in La Rambla and Plaça Catalunya.

The main Catalan-language newspapers are *Avui* and *El Periódico*. *La Vanguardia*, in Spanish, is published in Barcelona and is widely respected. The other Spanish newspapers are *El País*, *El Mundo* and *ABC*. *El Mundo*, aimed at young people, has a lot of news features; *El País* and *ABC* are strong on international news.

Barcelona's best weekly listings magazine for arts, leisure events and eating out is *Guía del Ocio*, published in Spanish. Lifestyle and sports magazines are also popular.

A newsstand on La Rambla in Barcelona

Catalan mailbox

TRAVEL INFORMATION

Catalonia's three main airports – El Prat, Girona and Reus – receive international flights from all over the globe. While Barcelona's El Prat handles mainly scheduled services, Girona and Reus deal with package holiday flights. Rail networks and toll highways radiate from Barcelona to serve the region's major towns. Barcelona has a well-developed ringroad *(ronda)* system, and a tunnel through the Collserola Hills brings the inland highways right into the city. Both its Metro and suburban train links are excellent but, as much of Catalonia is mountainous, buses or a car are the only way to see many rural sights.

Spain's national airline

Duty-free shopping at Barcelona's El Prat airport

ARRIVING BY AIR

Barcelona is served by many international airlines. The Spanish national carrier, **Iberia**, offers daily scheduled flights to Barcelona from all west European capitals. It also offers connections with, but no direct flights from, eastern Europe. Direct flights from several other east European capitals are, however, offered by other airlines.

British Airways offers daily flights to Barcelona, from Heathrow and Gatwick and four flights a week from Birmingham. **EasyJet** flies from Gatwick, Stansted, Luton, Bristol, Newcastle and Liverpool, while Iberia offers a direct service from Manchester. **Ryanair** flies to Girona and Reus from Stansted, Luton, Bournemouth, East Midlands, Blackpool and Glasgow. **Delta Air Lines** offers direct flights to Barcelona from the US. Iberia operates a comprehensive service from both the US and Canada, offering regular flights from Montreal via Madrid. No airlines operate direct flights between Spain and Australia.

Catalonia's other two international airports handle charter flights: Girona serves the Costa Brava, and Reus, near Tarragona, the Costa Daurada.

For passengers arriving from Madrid or other Spanish cities, Spain's domestic flights are operated by Iberia, its associated airline, **Air Nostrum**, **Air Europa** and **Spanair**.

The most frequent shuttle service between Madrid and Barcelona is Iberia's Pont Aeri (Puente Aéreo). It flies every quarter of an hour at peak times and passengers can buy tickets just 15 minutes in advance using a self-ticketing machine. The flight takes 50 minutes. Other services between Madrid and Barcelona are less frequent but, on the whole, their prices tend to be lower.

The major international car rental companies *(see p187)* have desks at all three terminals of El Prat airport. Girona airport also has some of the main rental companies on site

Pont Aeri
Puente Aéreo

Sign for the shuttle service linking Barcelona and Madrid

DIRECTORY

EL PRAT AIRPORT, BARCELONA

Barcelona's airport is currently being modified and is 12 km (7 miles) from the city centre. Terminal A handles international arrivals and foreign airlines' departures. Terminals B and C are for departures on Spanish airlines and arrivals from European Union countries. Trains to the Plaça de Catalunya in the city centre leave every 30 minutes. A shuttle bus, the Aerobus, departs for the Plaça de Catalunya every 12 minutes. A taxi will take about 15 minutes and cost around €20.

FIRST FLOOR — Terminal C

Terminal B

GROUND FLOOR

Terminal A

Bank

Car rental

KEY

▨	Departures
☐	Arrivals
☐	Public access
▨	Check-in
☐	Customs
▨	Passport control
☐	Passengers only
▨	Restricted access

Car rental

Bank

Meeting point

Bank

Car rental

Bank

---

and cars can be delivered to Reus from nearby Tarragona. There will also be local firms offering tempting deals, but read the small print carefully.

AIR FARES

Air fares to Barcelona and the coastal resorts vary through the year, depending on demand. They are generally highest during the summer months. Special deals, particularly for weekend city breaks in Barcelona, are often available in the winter and may include a number of nights at a hotel. Christmas and Easter flights are almost always booked up well in advance.

Charter flights from the UK to Girona and Reus can be very cheap, but tend to be less reliable, and often fly at unsociable hours.

Flying between Barcelona and other cities in Spain is an expensive way to travel compared with other options.

SEA TRAVEL

In 1998 the **Grimaldi Group** established a new scheduled ferry service between Genoa and Barcelona. US travel company **Atlas Cruises and Tours** offers transatlantic cruises between the US and Barcelona, as well as cruises around the Mediterranean. **Costa Cruises** offers Mediterranean cruises starting in Barcelona, while **Thomson Cruises**, in the UK, has cruises calling at Barcelona, but starting out from Mallorca.

TRAVEL TO THE BALEARIC ISLANDS

Barcelona is the main city on the Spanish mainland from which to reach the Balearic Islands. Flights are run by Iberia, Air Europa and Spanair; a passenger hydrofoil (a kind of catamaran) service, which takes three hours, by **Buquebus**; and car ferry crossings, which take about eight hours, by **Trasmediterránea**. It is wise to book in advance, especially in summer.

Trasmediterránea car ferry to the Balearic Islands in Barcelona harbour

Travelling by Train and Metro

Metro and FGC rail services sign

There are two providers of rail services in Catalonia. The Spanish national **RENFE** *(Red Nacional de Ferrocarriles Españoles)* operates Spain's inter-city services including first-class Talgo and AVE trains and some of Barcelona's commuter services *(rodalies)*. The Catalan government's **FGC** *(Ferrocarrils de la Generalitat de Catalunya)* runs some suburban trains in Barcelona and some special-interest services in Catalonia's provinces. Barcelona also has the Metro, an efficient city-wide network of underground (subway) trains.

Escalator down to a platform *(andana)* at Sants mainline station in Barcelona

ARRIVING BY TRAIN

There are direct international train services to Barcelona from several European cities including Paris, Montpellier, Geneva, Zurich and Milan. Long train journeys can be made more bearable by booking a sleeping compartment on an overnight train. This option is only available on direct services. All trains entering the eastern side of Spain from France go through Port Bou/Cerbère or La Tour de Carol on the Franco-Spanish border. Travelling to Barcelona from departure points not offering a direct service may mean picking up a connection here. International trains arrive at Sants mainline station, located in the centre of Barcelona.

Services to Barcelona from other cities in Spain are fast and frequent. From Madrid, Seville, Málaga, A Coruña or Vigo there is a service called **Auto-Express** which allows you to take your car with you.

EXPLORING CATALONIA BY TRAIN

Catalonia has a network of regional trains *(regionals)* covering the whole of Catalunya and run by RENFE. There are three types – the *Catalunya Exprés* linking the main towns with few stops in between, and the *Regional* and *Delta* trains which take longer and stop frequently. A high-speed Euromed service from Barcelona to Tarragona (continuing south to Castelló, València and Alacant/Alicante) leaves from Sants station.

FGC *(Ferrocarrils de la Generalitat de Catalunya)* is a network of suburban trains run by the Catalan government in and around Barcelona. FGC also runs some other special services, such as Spain's only rack railway (cog railroad) from Ribes de Freser *(see inside back cover)* to Núria in the Pyrenees. It also runs the cable cars and funiculars at the Monastery of Montserrat *(see pp122–3)* and at Vallvidrera, as well as several historic steam trains and an electric train for tourists and enthusiasts. Details are available at the FGC station at Plaça de Catalunya or by calling the FGC number listed above.

RENFE
Logo of the Spanish national rail service

DIRECTORY

PUBLIC TRANSPORT

Information (Barcelona Local Council)
Tel 010.

RENFE Information and Credit Card Bookings
Tel 902 24 02 02 (national).
Tel 902 24 34 02 (international).
www.renfe.es

Secretaria General de Juventud
Young People's Tourist Office,
Carrer de Calàbria, 147.
Tel 93 483 83 83.

FGC Information
Tel 93 205 15 15.

TMB Information
Tel 93 298 70 00 or 012.

BUYING TRAIN TICKETS

Tickets for Talgo, AVE, inter-city and international trains and for other *llarg recorregut* (long-distance) travel by train may be bought at any of the major RENFE railway stations from the *taquilla* (ticket office). They are also sold by travel agents, plus a booking fee. Tickets can be purchased in advance on the RENFE website. During the peak months (July to September), many of the most popular inter-city routes, particularly to the coasts, are booked up weeks in advance, so it's worth planning ahead. You can also reserve tickets by phone. They are held for 48 hours (up to two hours before the train leaves) and can be collected at main

Ticket machine for *regionals* trains

Ticket machine for *rodalies* trains

Automatic ticket barriers at one of Barcelona's Metro stations

indicates a RENFE or FGC connection. Metro trains run from 5am to midnight from Monday to Thursday, from 6am to midnight on Sunday and a weekday public holiday and from 5am to 2am on Friday, Saturday and the day before a public holiday.

BARCELONA TICKETS AND TRAVELCARDS

Visitors to Barcelona will find a range of tickets and money-saving travelcards available to suit their itineraries and length of stay. Some cover train, bus and Metro. Combined tickets allow travellers to hop from Metro to FGC to bus lines without leaving the station to pay again. Tickets are as follows: *T-dia* and *T-mes* are for unlimited daily and monthly travel respectively; the *senzill* ticket, for one single journey, can be used on Metro, bus and FGC; the *T-10*, for ten trips, is for combining journeys on Metro, bus and FGC in one trip (there is a time limit of an hour and a half); the *T-50/ 30* is for 50 journeys in 30 days on Metro, bus and FGC. Details of special tourist travel cards are described on the inside back cover of this guide.

stations. Tickets for local and regional services can be purchased from station booking offices. In some larger stations, they can also be bought from ticket machines. Tickets for *rodalies* (local services) cannot be reserved. A one-way journey is *anada* and a round trip is *anada i tornada*.

TRAIN FARES

Fares for rail travel depend on the speed and quality of the service. Tickets for Talgo and AVE trains are more expensive than local and regional trains. RENFE offers discounts to children and people over 60, groups of ten and through travel cards on local, regional and long-distance trains. Tourists normally resident outside Spain are eligible for a tourist railcard, which allows unlimited travel on RENFE trains.

Interrail tickets for those under 26 and Eurodomino tickets for those over 26 are available to people from EU member states and ten other European countries. They offer discounts on rail travel and can be purchased at Barcelona's Sants and Estació de França stations. Travel cards, available through the **Secretaria General de Juventud**, are for people under 26, of any nationality, and carry a discount of up to 40 per cent on journeys from any point in Spain to Europe. To purchase one of these, you will need proof of your age and identity.

THE BARCELONA METRO

There are six underground Metro lines in Barcelona, identified by number and colour. Platform signs distinguish between trains and their direction by displaying the last station on

Metro interchange sign showing where to change to another line

the line. In the street it is easy to spot a Metro station – look for a sign bearing a red "M" on a white diamond background. The Metro is usually the quickest way to get around the city, especially as some tickets are now valid for the Metro and some FGC lines. A RENFE or FGC sign at a Metro station

A one-way (single) Metro ticket for Barcelona's subway

USING A METRO TICKET MACHINE

Credit cards accepted by the machine are listed here.

3b Insert credit card.

3c Insert banknote(s).

4 Collect your ticket and any change due.

Logo of **Transports Metropolitans Urbans (TMB)**, which integrates all services.

Venda de Bitllets

TMB

1 Select language: Catalan/Spanish, English, French.

2 Select ticket: *senzill* (single trip), *T-10* (10 trips), *T-50/30* (50 trips in 30 days), then quantity required.

3a Insert coins: the coins accepted are listed alongside.

Easy-reach language and ticket-type buttons for wheelchair users.

Travelling by Car and Bus

Barcelona road signs

Driving conditions in Catalonia vary enormously, from the dense road network and heavy traffic in and around Barcelona to almost empty country roads in the provinces, where villages, and in particular petrol (gas) stations, can be far apart. Toll highways *(autopistes)* are fast and free-flowing, but the ordinary main roads along the coast are usually very busy at all times of day. For tourists without private cars, joining an organized bus tour is a good way to visit well-known, but rather more remote, places of interest.

Canvi de sentit **(slip or access road)**
300 m (330 yd) ahead

ARRIVING BY CAR

Many people drive to Spain via the French motorways (highways). The most direct routes across the Pyrenees are the motorways through Hendaye in the west and La Jonquera in the east. Port Bou is on a scenic coastal route, while other routes snake over the top, entering Catalonia via the Vall d'Aran, Andorra, and Puigcerdà in the Cerdanya. From the UK, car ferries run from Plymouth to Santander and from Portsmouth to Bilbao in northern Spain.

**Logo of the National ATESA
car-rental company**

CAR RENTAL

International car rental companies, such as **Hertz**, **Avis** and **Europcar**, as well as some Spanish ones, such as **National ATESA**, operate all over Catalonia. You are likely to get better deals with international companies if you arrange a car from home. A hire car is *un cotxe de lloguer.* Catalonia's three main airports *(see p182)* have car rental desks. However, those at Girona and Reus have irregular opening hours, so if you need a car there, it is best to book in advance and they will meet your requirements. Avis offers deals in chauffeur-driven cars from major cities.

TAKING YOUR OWN CAR

A green card and a bail bond from a motor insurance company are needed to extend your comprehensive cover to Spain. In the UK, the RAC, AA and Europ Assistance have sound rescue and recovery policies with European cover.

Vehicle registration, insurance documents and your driver's licence must be carried at all times. Non-EU citizens should obtain an international driver's licence; in the US, these are available through the AAA. You may also be asked for a passport or national identity card as extra identification.

A country of origin sticker must be displayed on the rear of foreign vehicles. All drivers must carry a red warning triangle, spare light bulbs and a first-aid kit. Failure to do so will incur on-the-spot fines.

**Speed limit 60
km/h (37 mph)**

DRIVING IN CATALONIA

At junctions give way to the right unless directed otherwise. Left turns across the flow of traffic are indicated by a *canvi de sentit* sign. Speed limits for cars without trailers

are now: 120 km/h (75 mph) on *autopistes* and *autovies* (toll and non-toll motorways/highways); 90 km/h (56 mph) on *carreteres nacionals* (main roads) and *carreteres comarcals* (secondary roads); 40 or 50 km/h (30 or 37 mph) in urban areas – look for signs. There are on-the-spot speeding fines of up to 450 euros. The blood alcohol legal limit is 0.5g per litre (0.25 mg per litre in a breath test) – tests are frequently given and drivers over the limit are fined.

Front and rear seat belts must be worn. Ordinary leaded fuel *(benzina),* unleaded fuel *(benzina sense plom)* and diesel *(gas oil)* are all available everywhere and sold by the litre.

AUTOPISTES

On toll motorways *(autopistes)* long-distance tolls are calculated per kilometre. Over some stretches near cities a fixed toll is charged. There are three channels at the *peatge* (toll booths/plaza): *Automàtic* has machines for credit cards or the right coins; in *Manual*

A filling station run by a leading chain with branches throughout Spain

an attendant takes your ticket and money; for *Teletac* you need an electronic chip on your windscreen (windshield). *Autopistes* have emergency telephones every 2 km (1.25 miles) and service stations every 40 km (25 miles).

TAXIS

Barcelona's taxis are yellow and black, and display a green light when they are free. All taxis are metered and show a minimum fee at the start of a journey. Rates increase after 10pm and at weekends, although the minimum fee stays the same. In unmetered taxis, such as those in villages, it is best to negotiate a price for the trip before setting off. Supplements are charged for going to and from the airport and for suitcases. **Radio Taxis** have cars adapted for disabled people, but they need to be booked a day ahead. They also have some cars that will take up to seven people.

One of Barcelona's taxis

PARKING

Central Barcelona has a pay-and-display system, with charges in force from 9am to 2pm and 4pm to 8pm Monday to Friday and all day Saturday. You can park in blue spaces for about 1–2 euros per hour. Tickets are valid for two hours but can be renewed. At underground car parks (parking lots), *lliure* means there is space, *complet* means there is full. Most are attended, but in automatic ones, you pay before returning to your car. Do not park where the pavement edge is yellow or where there is a private exit *(gual)*. Blue and red signs saying "1–15" or "16–30" mean you cannot park on those dates in the month on the side of the street where the sign is placed.

Barcelona bus stop

Granollers bus station in Barcelona province

LONG-DISTANCE BUSES

Spain's largest inter-city bus company, **Autocares Julià**, is an agent for **Eurolines**. This runs regular services from all over Europe to Sants bus station in Barcelona. Buses from towns and cities in Spain arrive at Estació del Nord.

Julià Tours and **Pullmantur** offer tours of Barcelona. A number of companies run day trips or longer tours to places of interest in Catalonia. **Turisme de Catalunya** *(see p175)* in Barcelona has details of trips to all parts of Catalonia; in other towns, local tourist offices will know about tours in their provinces.

BUSES IN BARCELONA

An excellent way to sightsee is by *Bus Turístic*. It runs all year on two routes from Plaça de Catalunya. A ticket, bought on board, is valid for both routes and lets you get on and off or change routes as you please.

The main city buses are white and red. You can buy a single ticket on the bus, or a *T-10* ten-trip ticket at Metro stations, valid for bus, Metro and FGC *(see p185)*. Other combined tickets are described inside the back cover. The *Nitbus* runs nightly from around 10pm to 5am; the *TombBus* covers the big shopping streets from Plaça de Catalunya to Plaça Pius XII; and the *Aerobus* is an excellent service between Plaça de Catalunya and El Prat airport.

DIRECTORY

CAR RENTAL

National ATESA
Tel 93 298 34 33 (Barcelona airport).
Tel 902 100 101.

Avis
Tel 93 298 36 00 (Barcelona airport).

Europcar
Tel 90 210 50 55 (Barcelona airport).
Tel 902 10 50 30.

Hertz
Tel 93 298 36 38 (Barcelona airport).
Tel 902 402 405.

TOUR BUS OPERATORS

Autocares Julià
Tel 90 240 00 80.

Eurolines
Tel 020 7730 8235 in UK.
Tel 90 240 50 40 in Barcelona.

Julià Tours
Tel 93 317 64 54.

Pullmantur
Tel 93 317 12 97.

BUS STATIONS

Estació del Nord
Carrer d'Alí Bei 80.
Tel 90 226 06 06.
www.barcelonanord.com

Estació de Sants
Plaça del Països Catalans.
Tel 90 226 06 06.

TAXIS

Radio Taxis
Tel 93 433 10 20/357 77 55.
Tel 93 300 11 00.
Tel 93 420 80 88 (taxis for the disabled).

BARCELONA STREET FINDER

The map references given with the sights, shops and entertainment venues described in the Barcelona section of the guide refer to the street maps on the following pages. Map references are also given for Barcelona's hotels (see *pp134–41*), restaurants (see *pp146–51*) and cafés and bars (see *pp152–3*). The schematic map below shows the areas of the city covered by the *Street Finder*. The symbols for sights, features and services are listed in the key at the foot of the page.

0 kilometres 2

0 miles 1

KEY TO STREET FINDER

Major sight	Golondrina boarding point	Police station
Place of interest	Cable car	Church
Other building	Funicular station	Post office
Main train station	Tramway stop	Railway line (railroad)
Local (FGC) train station	Taxi rank	Pedestrianized street
Metro station	Parking	
Main bus stop	Tourist information	**SCALE OF MAP PAGES**
Bus station	Hospital with A&E unit	0 metres 250
		0 yards 250

Street Finder Index

General Index

Acknowledgments

Dorling Kindersley would like to thank the following people whose contributions and assistance have made the preparation of this book possible.

Main Contributor

ROGER WILLIAMS contributed to the *Eyewitness Travel Guide to Spain* and has written Barcelona and Catalonia titles for Insight Guides. He was also the main contributor to the *Eyewitness Travel Guide to Provence*. *Lunch with Elizabeth David*, set around the Mediterranean, is his latest novel.

Additional Contributors

Mary Jane Aladren, Pepita Arias, Emma Dent Coad, Rebecca Doulton, Josefina Fernández, Nick Rider, David Stone, Judy Thomson, Clara Villanueva, Suzanne Wales (Word on Spain).

Design and Editorial Assitance

Amaia Allende, Queralt Amella Miró, Gillian Andrews, Imma Espuñes i Amorós, Daniel Campi (Word on Spain), Alrica Green, Jessica Hughes, Elly King, Kathryn Lane, Barbara Minton, Alícia Ribas Sos, Lola Carbonell Zaragoza.

Proofreader

Stewart J Wild.

Indexer

Hilary Bird.

Special Photography

Max Alexander, D. Murray/J. Selmes, Dave King, Ian O'Leary, Alessandra Santarelli, Susannah Sayler, Clive Streeter.

Photography permissions

© Obispado de VIC; © Cabildo de la Catedral de Girona; Teatre Nacional de Catalunya (Barcelona); Institut Mpal. del Paisatge Urba i la Qualitat de Vida, Ajuntament de Barcelona.

Dorling Kindersley would like to thank all the churches, museums, restaurants, hotels, shops, galleries and other sights too numerous to thank individually.

Picture credits

KEY: t=top; tl=top left; tlc=top left centre; tc=top centre; trc=top right centre; tr=top right; cla=centre left above; ca=centre above; cra=centre right above; cl=centre left; c=centre; cr=centre right; clb=centre left below; cb=centre below; crb=centre right below; bl=bottom left; b=bottom; bc=bottom centre; bcl=bottom centre left; br=bottom right; bcr=bottom centre right; d=detail.

Works of art have been reproduced with the permission of the following copyright holders:

Dona i Ocell Joan Miró © ADAGP, Paris & DACS, London 1999; *Morning* George Kolbe © DACS 1999; IOC/Olympic Museum Collections; Tapestry of the Foundation Joan Miró 1975 © ADAGP, Paris & DACS, London; *Rainy Taxi* © Salvador Dalí - Foundation Gala - Salvador Dalí/DACS 1999.

The publisher would like to thank the following individuals, companies and picture libraries for their kind permission to reproduce their photographs:

ACE PHOTO LIBRARY: Mauritius 19t; AISA, Barcelona: 14b, 18b, 23bl, *San Jorge* Jaume Huguet 28c, 40, 41c, 44cb, 46c, 46bl, 176bc; ALAMY IMAGES: Douglas Armand 97cra; Jon Arnold Images 76tr; Andrew Bargery 62br, 76bl; Neil Barks 77tl; Peter Barritt 82tr; Oliver Bee 76clb, 77br; Dalgleish Images 96bl; Iain Davidson Photographic 102tcl, 103tl; Chad Ehlers 97tl; Richard Foot 96tr; B J Gadie 62tc; Stephen Saks Photography 68t; Neil Setchfield 60br. AQUILA PHOTOGRAPHICS: Adrian Hoskins 112bla; 112bl; James Pearce 21b; NATIONAL ATESA: 186cr.

JAUME BALANYA: 81crb; MIKE BUSSELLE: 111b, 112t.

COCEMFE: 154c; CODORNIU: 33t, 33c; BRUCE COLEMAN COLLECTION: Erich Crichton 20tr; José Luis González Grande 21tr; Norbert Schwirtz 21tl; Colin Varwdell 21cra; CORBIS: Peter Aprahamian 62bl, 105br; Carlos Dominguez 11clb; Owen Franken 124tl, 125c; Dave G. Houser 10cla; Andrea Jemolo 82cla; Jose Fuste Raga 11tl; James Sparshatt 82tl; Mark L. Stephenson 83tr; Sandro Vannini 82bc; Vanni Archive 83br.COVER, Madrid: Pepe Franco 154c; Matias Nieto 191b.

EUROPEAN COMMISSION: 179.

FIRO FOTO: 69cl. FRIEIXENET: 32c, 33b; FUNDACION COLLECTION THYSSEN-BORNEMISZA: *Madonna of Humility* Fra Angelico 95t; FUNDACIO JOAN MIRO, Barcelona: *Flama en l'espai i dona nua* Joan Miró 1932 © ADAGP, Paris and DACS, London 1999 88t.

GODO PHOTO: 129t, José Luis Dorada 125t.

ROBERT HARDING PICTURE LIBRARY: 25tr, 59ca, 72ca, 88b, 89b.

THE ILLUSTRATED LONDON NEWS PICTURE LIBRARY: 47t; INDEX, Barcelona: CJJ.19b, 44t, 47c; IMAGE BANK: 24b, 73b; Andrea Pistolesi 92; IMAGES COLOUR LIBRARY: 24c, 183b; AGE Fotostock 76, 113b, 118–119, 155t, 155c, 170cr; NICK INMAN: 20b, 96br.

LIFE FILE PHOTOGRAPHIC: Xabier Catalan 25c; Emma Lee 25cra.

MARKA, Milan: Sergio Pitamitz 62tl; MAS SALVANERA: Ramón Ruscalleda 133t; MARY EVANS PICTURE LIBRARY: 27 (inset); JOHN MILLER: 108; MUSEU NACIONAL D'ART DE CATALUNYA: J. Calveras J. Sagrista 90-91; *La Compañia de Santa Barbara* 1891 Ramon Marti Alsina 45t; MUSEU PICASSO: *Auto Retrato* Pablo Ruiz Picasso © DACS 1999 64bl; ABADIA DE MONTSERRAT (BARCELONA) 122br.

NATURAL SCIENCE PHOTOS: C Dani & I Jeske 170c; NATURPRESS, Madrid: 17b; Oriol Alamany 34c, 37b; Walter Kvaternik 37c, 26–27, 177b; Carlos Vegas 178t, 180tr; Jose A Martinez 109b.

ORONOZ, Madrid: 41b, 42t, 42c, 45bl, 46t.

PHOTOGRAPHERSDIRECT.COM: Michael Dobson/Echo Imagery 107c, 107br; Fran Fernandez Photography 102b, 104b, 105c,

106tl, 107tl; Jan van der Hoeven 101t, 103b, 104cla, 106br. PICTURES COLOUR LIBRARY: 74–75; PRISMA,Barcelona: 4t, *Paralelo Año 1930* Roger Bosch 8–9, 9 (inset), 18t, *Procesión en Santa María del Mar* Carbo Cases 28t, *Jardines de Aranjuez* 1907 Rusiñol y Prats 28b, *Esperando la Sopa* 1899 Isidro Monell y Monturiol 29t, *La Catedral de los Pobres* Mir Trinxet 29c, *Litografía* Tàpiés © ADAGP, Paris & DACS, London 1999 29b, 38–39, 45cb, 46 cra, 131 (inset), 154b, 163c, 173 (inset), 182ca, 187t; Carles Aymerich 22bl, 36c; A. Bofill 19c; Barbara Call 17t; Jordi Cami 34b; Albert Heras 2–3, 36b; Kuwenal 43t, 43c; Mateu 35c.

RAIMAT: 32cb; RED-HEAD: 52; REX FEATURES: 117cb; ELLEN ROONEY:1.

M ANGELES SÁNCHEZ: 35b; SCIENCE PHOTO LIBRARY: Geospace 12; SPECTRUM COLOUR LIBRARY: 24tr; STOCKPHOTOS, Madrid: 170b; Campillo 171t.

JACKET
Front – DK IMAGES: Max Alexander bl; GETTY IMAGES: The Image Bank/Shaun Egan main image. Back – DK IMAGES: Max Alexander clb, bl; Alan Keohane tl; Susannah Sayler cla. Spine – DK IMAGES: Max Alexander b; GETTY IMAGES: The Image Bank/Shaun Egan t.

FRONT END PAPER: clockwise John Miller; Image Bank Andrea Pistolesi; Red-Head; Images Colour Library/ AGE Fotostock.

All other images © DORLING KINDERSLEY. For further information see www.DKimages.com

SPECIAL EDITIONS OF DK TRAVEL GUIDES

DK Travel Guides can be purchased in bulk quantities at discounted prices for use in promotions or as premiums. We are also able to offer special editions and personalized jackets, corporate imprints, and excerpts from all of our books, tailored specifically to meet your own needs.

To find out more, please contact:
(in the United States) **SpecialSales@dk.com**
(in the UK) **Sarah.Burgess@dk.com**
(in Canada) DK Special Sales at **general@tourmaline.ca**
(in Australia) **business.development@pearson.com.au**

English–Catalan Phrase Book

In Emergency

Help!	Auxili!	ow-**gzee**-lee
Stop!	Pareu!	**pah**-reh-oo
Call a doctor!	Telefoneu un metge!	teh-leh-fon-**eh**-oo oon **meh**-djuh
Call an ambulance!	Telefoneu una ambulància!	teh-leh-fon-**eh**-oo oo-nah ahm-boo-**lahn**-see-ah
Call the police!	Telefoneu la policia!	teh-leh-fon-**eh**-oo lah poh-lee-**see**-ah
Call the fire brigade!	Telefoneu els bombers!	teh-leh-fon-**eh**-oo uhlz boom-**behs**
Where is the nearest telephone?	On és el telèfon més proper?	on-ehs uhl tuh-leh-fon **mehs** proo-**peh**
Where is the nearest hospital?	On és l'hospital més proper?	on-ehs looss-pee-**tahl** mehs proo-**peh**

Communication Essentials

Yes	Sí	see
No	No	noh
Please	Si us plau	sees **plah**-oo
Thank you	Gràcies	**grah**-see-uhs
Excuse me	Perdoni	puhr-**thoh**-nee
Hello	Hola	**oh**-lah
Goodbye	Adéu	ah-they-**oo**
Good night	Bona nit	**bo**-nah neet
Morning	El matí	uhl muh-**tee**
Afternoon	La tarda	lah **tahr**-thuh
Evening	El vespre	uhl **vehs**-pruh
Yesterday	Ahir	ah-**ee**
Today	Avui	uh-**voo**-ee
Tomorrow	Demà	duh-**mah**
Here	Aquí	uh-**kee**
There	Allà	uh-**lyah**
What?	Què?	keh
When?	Quan?	kwahn
Why?	Per què?	puhr **keh**
Where?	On?	ohn

Useful Phrases

How are you?	Com està?	kom uhs-**tah**
Very well, thank you.	Molt bé, gràcies.	mol **beh grah**-see-uhs
Pleased to meet you.	Molt de gust.	mol duh **goost**
See you soon.	Fins aviat.	feenz uhv-**yat**
That's fine.	Està bé.	uhs-**tah beh**
Where is/are ...?	On és/són?	ohn ehs/**sohn**
How far is it to ...?	Quants metres/ kilòmetres hi ha d'aquí a ...?	kwahnz meh-truhs/kee-**loh**-muh-truhs yah dah-**kee** uh
Which way to ...?	Per on es va a ...?	puhr **on** uhs **bah** ah
Do you speak English?	Parla anglès?	**par**-luh an-**glehs**
I don't understand	No l'entenc.	noh luhn-**teng**
Could you speak more slowly, please?	Pot parlar més a poc a poc, si us plau?	pot par-**lah** mehs **pok** uh **pok** sees **plah**-oo
I'm sorry.	Ho sento.	oo **sehn**-too

Useful Words

big	gran	gran
small	petit	puh-**teet**
hot	calent	kah-**len**
cold	fred	**fred**
good	bo	**boh**
bad	dolent	doo-**len**
enough	bastant	bahs-**tan**
well	bé	**beh**
open	obert	oo-**behr**
closed	tancat	tan-**kat**
left	esquerra	uhs-**kehr**-ruh
right	dreta	**dreh**-tuh
straight on	recte	**rehk**-tuh
near	a prop	uh **prop**
far	lluny	**lyoon**yuh
up/over	a dalt	uh **dahl**
down/under	a baix	uh **bah**-eeshh
early	aviat	uhv-**yat**
late	tard	**tahrt**
entrance	entrada	uhn-**trah**-thuh
exit	sortida	**soor**-tee-thuh
toilet	lavabos/ serveis	luh-**vah**-boos sehr-**beh**-ees
more	més	mess
less	menys	men**yees**

Shopping

How much does this cost?	Quant costa això?	kwahn kost ehs-**shoh**
I would like ...	M'agradaria ...	muh-grad-uh-**ree**-ah
Do you have?	Tenen?	**tehn**-un
I'm just looking, thank you	Només estic mirant, gràcies.	noo-mess ehs-**teek** mee-**rahn grah**-see-uhs
Do you take credit cards?	Accepten targes de crèdit?	ak-**sehp**-tuhn tahr-**zhuhs** duh **kreh**-deet
What time do you open?	A quina hora obren?	ah **keen**-uh oh-ruh **oh**-bruhn
What time do you close?	A quina hora tanquen?	ah **keen**-uh oh-ruh **tan**-kuhn
This one.	Aquest	ah-**ket**
That one.	Aquell	ah-**kehl**
expensive	car	**kahr**
cheap	bé de preu/ barat	**beh** thuh **preh**-oo/ bah-**rat**
size (clothes)	talla/mida	**tah**-lyah/**mee**-thuh
size (shoes)	número	**noo**-mehr-oo
white	blanc	**blang**
black	negre	**neh**-gruh
red	vermell	vuhr-**mel**
yellow	groc	**grok**
green	verd	**behrt**
blue	blau	**blah**-oo
antique store	antiquari/botiga d'antiguitats	an-tee-**kwah**-ree/ boo-**tee**-gah/dan-**tee**-ghee-**tats**
bakery	el forn	uhl **forn**
bank	el banc	uhl **bang**
book store	la llibreria	lah lyee-bruh-**ree**-ah
butcher's	la carnisseria	lah kahr-nee-suh-**ree**-uh
pastry shop	la pastisseria	lah pahs-tee-suh-**ree**-uh
chemist's	la farmàcia	lah fuhr-**mah**-see-ah
fishmonger's	la peixateria	lah peh-**shuh**-tuh-**ree**-uh
greengrocer's	la fruiteria	lah froo-ee-tuh-**ree**-uh
grocer's	la botiga de queviures	lah boo-**tee**-guh duh keh-vee-**oo**-ruhs
hairdresser's	la perruqueria	lah peh-roo-kuh-**ree**-uh
market	el mercat	uhl muhr-**kat**
newsagent's	el quiosc de premsa	uhl kee-**ohsk** duh **prem**-suh
post office	l'oficina de correus	loo-fee-**see**-nuh duh koo-**reh**-oos
shoe store	la sabateria	lah sah-bah-tuh-**ree**-uh
supermarket	el supermercat	uhl soo-puhr-muhr-**kat**
tobacconist's	l'estanc	luhs-**tang**
travel agency	l'agència de viatges	la-**jen**-see-uh duh vee-**ad**-juhs

Sightseeing

art gallery	la galeria d'art	lah gah-luh-**ree**-yuh **dart**
cathedral	la catedral	lah kuh-tuh-**thrahl**
church	l'església	luhz-**gleh**-zee-uh
	la basílica	lah buh-**zee**-lee-kuh
garden	el jardí	uhl zhahr-**dee**
library	la biblioteca	lah bee-blee-oo-**teh**-kuh
museum	el museu	uhl moo-**seh**-oo
tourist information office	l'oficina de turisme	loo-fee-**see**-nuh thuh too-**reez**-muh
town hall	l'ajuntament	luh-djoon-tuh-**men**
closed for holiday	tancat per vacances	tan-**kat** puhr bah-**kan**-suhs
bus station	l'estació d'autobusos	luhs-tah-see-**oh** dow-toh-**boo**-zoos
railway station	l'estació de tren	luhs-tah-see-**oh** thuh **tren**

Staying in a Hotel

Do you have a vacant room?	¿Tenen una habitació lliure?	teh-nuhn oo-nuh ah-bee-tah-see-**oh lyuh**-ruh

double room with double bed	habitació doble amb llit de matrimoni	ah-bee-tuh-see-**oh** doh-bluh am **lyeet** duh mah-tree-**moh**-nee
twin room	habitació amb dos llits/ amb llits individuals	ah-bee-tuh-see-**oh** am dohs **lyeets**/ am **lyeets** in-thee-vee-thoo-**ahls**
single room	habitació individual	ah-bee-tuh-see-**oh** een-dee-vee-thoo-**ahl**
room with a bath	habitació amb bany	ah-bee-tuh-see-**oh** am **bah**nyuh
shower	dutxa	**doo**-chuh
porter	el grum	uhl **groom**
key	la clau	lah **klah**-oo
I have a reservation	Tinc una habitació reservada	ting oo-nuh ah-bee-tuh-see-oh reh-sehr-**vah**-thah

Eating Out

Have you got a table for...	Tenen taula per...?	**teh**-nuhn **tow**-luh puhr
I would like to reserve a table.	Voldria reservar una taula.	vool-**dree**-uh reh-sehr-**vahr** **oo**-nuh **tow**-luh
The bill please.	El compte, si us plau.	uhl **kohm**-tuh sees **plah**-oo
I am a vegetarian	Sóc vegetarià/ vegetariana	sok buh-zhuh-tuh-ree-**ah** buh-zhuh-tuh-ree-**ah**-nah
waitress	cambrera	kam-**breh**-ruh
waiter	cambrer	kam-**breh**
menu	la carta	lah **kahr**-tuh
fixed-price menu	menú del dia	muh-**noo** thuhl **dee**-uh
wine list	la carta de vins	lah **kahr**-tuh thuh **veens**
glass of water	un got d'aigua	oon **got** dah-ee-gwah
glass of wine	una copa de vi	**oo**-nuh **ko**-puh thuh **vee**
bottle	una ampolla	**oo**-nuh am-**pol**-yuh
knife	un ganivet	oon gun-ee-**veht**
fork	una forquilla	**oo**-nuh foor-**keel**-yuh
spoon	una cullera	**oo**-nuh kool-**yeh**-ruh
breakfast	l'esmorzar	les-moor-**sah**
lunch	el dinar	uhl dee-**nah**
dinner	el sopar	uhl soo-**pah**
main course	el primer plat	uhl pree-**meh** **plat**
starters	els entrants	uhlz ehn-**tranz**
dish of the day	el plat del dia	uhl **plat** duhl **dee**-uh
coffee	el cafè	uhl kah-**feh**
rare	poc fet	pok fet
medium	al punt	ahl **poon**
well done	molt fet	mol **fet**

Menu Decoder *(see also pp30–31 & 144–5)*

l'aigua mineral	lah-ee-gwuh mee-nuh-**rahl**	mineral water
sense gas/amb gas	sen-zuh gas/am gas	still/sparkling
al forn	ahl forn	baked
l'all	**lahl**yuh	garlic
l'arròs	lahr-**roz**	rice
les botifarres	lahs boo-tee-fah-rahs	sausages
la carn	lah **karn**	meat
la ceba	lah **seh**-buh	onion
la cervesa	lah-sehr-**ve**-sah	beer
l'embotit	lum-boo-**teet**	cold meat
el filet	uhl fee-**let**	sirloin
el formatge	uhl for-**mah**-djuh	cheese
fregit	freh-**zheet**	fried
la fruita	lah froo-**ee**-tah	fruit
els fruits secs	uhlz froo-**eets** **seks**	nuts
les gambes	lahs **gam**-bus	prawns
el gelat	uhl djuh-**lat**	ice cream
la llagosta	lah lyah-**gos**-tah	lobster
la llet	lah **lyet**	milk
la llimona	lah lyee-**moh**-nah	lemon
la llimonada	lah lyee-moh-**nah**-thuh	lemonade
la mantega	lah mahn-**teh**-gah	butter
el marisc	uhl muh-**reesk**	seafood
la menestra	lah muh-**nehs**-truh	vegetable stew
l'oli	**loll**-ee	oil
les olives	luhs oo-**lee**-vuhs	olives
l'ou	**loh**-oo	egg

el pa	uhl **pah**	bread
el pastís	uhl pahs-**tees**	pie/cake
les patates	lahs pah-**tah**-tuhs	potatoes
el pebre	uhl **peh**-bruh	pepper
el peix	uhl **pehsh**	fish
el pernil salat serrà	uhl puhr-**neel** suh-**lat** sehr-**rah**	cured ham
el plàtan	uhl **plah**-tun	banana
el pollastre	uhl poo-**lyah**-struh	chicken
la poma	la **poh**-mah	apple
el porc	uhl **pohr**	pork
les postres	lahs **pohs**-truhs	dessert
rostit	rohs-**teet**	roast
la sal	lah **sahl**	salt
la salsa	lah **sahl**-suh	sauce
les salsitxes	lahs sahl-**see**-chuhs	sausages
sec	**sehk**	dry
la sopa	lah **soh**-puh	soup
el sucre	uhl-**soo**-kruh	sugar
la taronja	lah tuh-**rohn**-djuh	orange
el te	uhl teh	tea
les torrades	lahs too-**rah**-thuhs	toast
la vedella	lah veh-**theh**-lyuh	beef
el vi blanc	uhl **bee blang**	white wine
el vi negre	uhl **bee neh**-gruh	red wine
el vi rosat	uhl **bee** roo-**zaht**	rosé wine
el vinagre	uhl bee-**nah**-gruh	vinegar
el xai/el be	uhl **shah**ee/uhl **beh**	lamb
el xerès	uhl shuh-**rehs**	sherry
la xocolata	lah shoo-koo-**lah**-tuh	chocolate
el xoriç	uhl shoo-**rees**	red sausage

Numbers

0	zero	**seh**-roo
1	un (masc)	oon
	una (fem)	**oon**-uh
2	dos (masc)	**dohs**
	dues (fem)	**doo**-uhs
3	tres	trehs
4	quatre	**kwa**-truh
5	cinc	seeng
6	sis	sees
7	set	set
8	vuit	**voo**-eet
9	nou	**noh**-oo
10	deu	**deh**-oo
11	onze	**on**-zuh
12	doce	**doh**-dzuh
13	tretze	**treh**-dzuh
14	catorze	kah-**tohr**-dzuh
15	quinze	**keen**-zuh
16	setze	**set**-zuh
17	disset	dee-**set**
18	divuit	dee-voo-**eet**
19	dinou	dee-**noh**-oo
20	vint	**been**
21	vint-i-un	been-tee-**oon**
22	vint-i-dos	been-tee-**dohs**
30	trenta	**tren**-tah
31	trenta-un	**tren**-tah-oon
40	quaranta	kwuh-**ran**-tuh
50	cinquanta	seen-**kwahn**-tah
60	seixanta	seh-ee-**shan**-tah
70	setanta	seh-**tan**-tah
80	vuitanta	voo-ee-**tan**-tah
90	noranta	noh-**ran**-tah
100	cent	sen
101	cent un	sent oon
102	cent dos	sen dohs
200	dos-cents (masc)	dohs-**sens**
	dues-centes (fem)	**doo**-uhs sen-tuhs
300	tres-cents	trehs-**senz**
400	quatre-cents	kwah-truh-**senz**
500	cinc-cents	seeng-**senz**
600	sis-cents	sees-**senz**
700	set-cents	set-**senz**
800	vuit-cents	voo-eet-**senz**
900	nou-cents	noh-oo-**cenz**
1,000	mil	**meel**
1,001	mil un	**meel oon**

Time

one minute	un minut	oon mee-**noot**
one hour	una hora	**oo**-nuh **oh**-ruh
half an hour	mitja hora	**mee**-juh **oh**-ruh
Monday	dilluns	dee-**lyoonz**
Tuesday	dimarts	dee-**marts**
Wednesday	dimecres	dee-**meh**-kruhs
Thursday	dijous	dee-**zhoh**-oos
Friday	divendres	dee-**ven**-druhs
Saturday	dissabte	dee-**sab**-tuh
Sunday	diumenge	dee-oo-**men**-juh